Survival

GLOBAL POLITICS AND STRATEGY

Volume 67 Number 1 | February–March 2025

'The Russian meat grinder works very slowly but it goes in only one direction – forward – which means a Russian breakthrough is always a salient possibility.'

François Heisbourg, War or Peace in Ukraine: US Moves and European Choices, p. 10.

'The artificial-intelligence-driven targeting system used by the IDF is one proximate cause of the high civilian death toll. It enables the Israelis to claim with superficial validity that they do not deliberately target civilians. But of course, the IDF deliberately chooses the targeting methodology that makes civilian deaths inevitable.'

Steven Simon, After Gaza: American Liberals and Israel, p. 152–3.

'Over the past 40 years, the [Irish] republic has developed into an active, enthusiastic and progressive EU member, politically and culturally liberalising, economically expanding, and in the process casting off the neuralgic Anglophobia produced by centuries of subjugation.'

Jonathan Stevenson, Ireland's Future: United, European and in NATO, p. 204.

Survival

GLOBAL POLITICS AND STRATEGY

Volume 67 Number 1 | February–March 2025

Contents

Cover: Anastasia Potapenko/Suspline Ukraine/JSC "UA:PBC"/Global Images Ukraine via Getty Images

On the cover
Rescue workers examine the rubble of a residential building partially destroyed by a Russian aerial bomb in Zaporizhzhia, Ukraine, on 8 November 2024, in an attack that killed ten people.

On the web
Visit www.iiss.org/ publications/survival for brief notices on new books on Africa, Asia-Pacific, and Russia and Eurasia.

***Survival* editors' blog**
For ideas and commentary from *Survival* editors and contributors, visit https://www.iiss. org/online-analysis/ survival-online.

Survival
GLOBAL POLITICS AND STRATEGY

The International Institute for Strategic Studies

2121 K Street, NW | Suite 600 | Washington DC 20037 | USA
Tel +1 202 659 1490   Fax +1 202 659 1499   E-mail survival@iiss.org   Web www.iiss.org

Arundel House | 6 Temple Place | London | WC2R 2PG | UK
Tel +44 (0)20 7379 7676   Fax +44 (0)20 7836 3108   E-mail iiss@iiss.org

14th Floor, GFH Tower | Bahrain Financial Harbour | Manama | Kingdom of Bahrain
Tel +973 1718 1155   Fax +973 1710 0155   E-mail iiss-middleeast@iiss.org

9 Raffles Place | #49-01 Republic Plaza | Singapore 048619
Tel +65 6499 0055   Fax +65 6499 0059   E-mail iiss-asia@iiss.org

Pariser Platz 6A | 10117 Berlin | Germany
Tel +49 30 311 99 300   E-mail iiss-europe@iiss.org

Survival Online www.tandfonline.com/survival and www.iiss.org/publications/survival

Aims and Scope *Survival* is one of the world's leading forums for analysis and debate of international and strategic affairs. Shaped by its editors to be both timely and forward thinking, the journal encourages writers to challenge conventional wisdom and bring fresh, often controversial, perspectives to bear on the strategic issues of the moment. With a diverse range of authors, *Survival* aims to be scholarly in depth while vivid, well written and policy-relevant in approach. Through commentary, analytical articles, case studies, forums, review essays, reviews and letters to the editor, the journal promotes lively, critical debate on issues of international politics and strategy.

Editor **Dana Allin**
Managing Editor **Jonathan Stevenson**
Associate Editor **Carolyn West**
Editorial Assistant **Anna Gallagher**
Production and Cartography **Alessandra Beluffi, Ravi Gopar, Jade Panganiban, James Parker, Kelly Verity**

Contributing Editors

William Alberque	**Franz-Stefan Gady**	**Nigel Inkster**	**Benjamin Rhode**	**Robert Ward**
Aaron Connelly	**Bastian Giegerich**	**Jeffrey Mazo**	**Ben Schreer**	**Marcus Willett**
James Crabtree	**Nigel Gould-Davies**	**Fenella McGerty**	**Maria Shagina**	**Lanxin Xiang**
Chester A. Crocker	**Melissa K. Griffith**	**Irene Mia**	**Karen Smith**	
Bill Emmott	**Emile Hokayem**	**Meia Nouwens**	**Angela Stent**	

Published for the IISS by
Routledge Journals, an imprint of Taylor & Francis, an Informa business.

Copyright © 2025 The International Institute for Strategic Studies. All rights reserved. No part of this publication may be reproduced, stored, transmitted or disseminated, in any form, or by any means, without prior written permission from Taylor & Francis, to whom all requests to reproduce copyright material should be directed, in writing.

ISBN 978-1-041-07084-9 paperback / 978-1-003-63873-5 ebook

About the IISS The IISS, a registered charity with offices in Washington, London, Manama, Singapore and Berlin, is the world's leading authority on political–military conflict. It is the primary independent source of accurate, objective information on international strategic issues. Publications include *The Military Balance*, an annual reference work on each nation's defence capabilities; *Survival*, a bimonthly journal on international affairs; *Strategic Comments*, an online analysis of topical issues in international affairs; and the *Adelphi* series of books on issues of international security.

Director-General and Chief Executive
Bastian Giegerich

Executive Chairman
John Chipman

Chair of the Trustees
Bill Emmott

Chair of the Council
Chung Min Lee

Trustees
Caroline Atkinson
Neha Aviral
Hakeem Belo-Osagie
John O. Brennan
Chris Jones
Florence Parly
Kasper Rørsted
Mark Sedwill
Grace R. Skaugen
Matt Symonds
Matthew Symonds

IISS Advisory Council
Caroline Atkinson
Linden P. Blue
Garvin Brown
Mark Carleton-Smith
Jong-moon Choi
Alejandro Santo Domingo
Thomas Enders
Yoichi Funabashi
Alia Hatoug-Bouran
Eyal Hulata

Badr Jafar
Bilahari Kausikan
Thomas Lembong
Peter Maurer
Florence Parly
Charles Powell
Mark Sedwill
Debra Soon
Heizo Takenaka
Marcus Wallenberg

SUBMISSIONS

To submit an article, authors are advised to follow these guidelines:

- *Survival* articles are around 4,000–10,000 words long including endnotes. A word count should be included with a draft.
- All text, including endnotes, should be double-spaced with wide margins.
- Any tables or artwork should be supplied in separate files, ideally not embedded in the document or linked to text around it.
- All *Survival* articles are expected to include endnote references. These should be complete and include first and last names of authors, titles of articles (even from newspapers), place of publication, publisher, exact publication dates, volume and issue number (if from a journal) and page numbers. Web sources should include complete URLs and DOIs if available.
- A summary of up to 150 words should be included with the article. The summary should state the main argument clearly and concisely, not simply say what the article is about.

- A short author's biography of one or two lines should also be included. This information will appear at the foot of the first page of the article.

Please note that *Survival* has a strict policy of listing multiple authors in alphabetical order.

Submissions should be made by email, in Microsoft Word format, to survival@iiss.org. Alternatively, hard copies may be sent to *Survival*, IISS–US, 2121 K Street NW, Suite 801, Washington, DC 20037, USA.

The editorial review process can take up to three months. *Survival*'s acceptance rate for unsolicited manuscripts is less than 20%. *Survival* does not normally provide referees' comments in the event of rejection. Authors are permitted to submit simultaneously elsewhere so long as this is consistent with the policy of the other publication and the Editors of *Survival* are informed of the dual submission.

Readers are encouraged to comment on articles from the previous issue. Letters should be concise, no longer than 750 words and relate directly to the argument or points made in the original article.

Survival: Global Politics and Strategy (Print ISSN 0039-6338, Online ISSN 1468-2699) is published bimonthly for a total of 6 issues per year by Taylor & Francis Group, 4 Park Square, Milton Park, Abingdon, Oxon, OX14 4RN, UK. Periodicals postage paid (Permit no. 13095) at Brooklyn, NY 11256.

Airfreight and mailing in the USA by agent named World Container Inc., c/o BBT 150-15, 183rd Street, Jamaica, NY 11413, USA.

US Postmaster: Send address changes to Survival, World Container Inc., c/o BBT 150-15, 183rd Street, Jamaica, NY 11413, USA.

Subscription records are maintained at Taylor & Francis Group, 4 Park Square, Milton Park, Abingdon, OX14 4RN, UK.

Subscription information: For more information and subscription rates, please see tandfonline.com/pricing/journal/TSUR. Taylor & Francis journals are available in a range of different packages, designed to suit every library's needs and budget. This journal is available for institutional subscriptions with online-only or print & online options. This journal may also be available as part of our libraries, subject collections or archives. For more information on our sales packages, please visit librarianresources. taylorandfrancis.com.

For support with any institutional subscription, please visit help.tandfonline.com or email our dedicated team at subscriptions@tandf.co.uk.

Subscriptions purchased at the personal rate are strictly for personal, non-commercial use only. The reselling of personal subscriptions is prohibited. Personal subscriptions must be purchased with a personal cheque, credit card or BAC/wire transfer. Proof of personal status may be requested.

Back issues: Please visit https://taylorandfrancis.com/journals/customer-services/ for more information on how to purchase back issues.

Ordering information: To subscribe to the journal, please contact T&F Customer Services, Informa UK Ltd, Sheepen Place, Colchester, Essex, CO3 3LP, UK. Tel: +44 (0) 20 8052 2030; email subscriptions@tandf.co.uk.

Taylor & Francis journals are priced in USD, GBP and EUR (as well as AUD and CAD for a limited number of journals). All subscriptions are charged depending on where the end customer is based. If you are unsure which rate applies to you, please contact Customer Services. All subscriptions are payable in advance and all rates include postage. We are required to charge applicable VAT/GST on all print and online combination subscriptions, in addition to our online-only journals. Subscriptions are entered on an annual basis, i.e., January to December. Payment may be made by sterling cheque, dollar cheque, euro cheque, international money order, National Giro or credit cards (Amex, Visa and Mastercard).

Disclaimer: The International Institute for Strategic Studies (IISS) and our publisher Informa UK Limited, trading as Taylor & Francis Group ('T&F'), make every effort to ensure the accuracy of all the information (the 'Content') contained in our publications. However, IISS and our publisher T&F, our agents and our licensors make no representations or warranties whatsoever as to the accuracy, completeness or suitability for any purpose of the Content. Any opinions and views expressed in this publication are the opinions and views of the authors, and are not the views of or endorsed by IISS or our publisher T&F. The accuracy of the Content should not be relied upon and should be independently verified with primary sources of information, and any reliance on the Content is at your own risk. IISS and our publisher T&F make no representations, warranties or guarantees, whether express or implied, that the Content is accurate, complete or up to date. IISS and our publisher T&F shall not be liable for any losses, actions, claims, proceedings, demands, costs, expenses, damages and other liabilities whatsoever or howsoever caused arising directly or indirectly in connection with, in relation to or arising out of the use of the Content. Full Terms & Conditions of access and use can be found at http://www.tandfonline.com/page/terms-and-conditions.

Informa UK Limited, trading as Taylor & Francis Group, grants authorisation for individuals to photocopy copyright material for private research use, on the sole basis that requests for such use are referred directly to the requestor's local Reproduction Rights Organization (RRO). The copyright fee is exclusive of any charge or fee levied. In order to contact your local RRO, please contact International Federation of Reproduction Rights Organizations (IFRRO), rue du Prince Royal, 87, B-1050 Brussels, Belgium; email ifrro@skynet.be; Copyright Clearance Center Inc., 222 Rosewood Drive, Danvers, MA 01923, USA; email info@copyright.com; or Copyright Licensing Agency, 90 Tottenham Court Road, London, W1P 0LP, UK; email cla@cla.co.uk. This authorisation does not extend to any other kind of copying, by any means, in any form, for any purpose other than private research use.

Submission information: See https://www.tandfonline.com/journals/tsur20

Advertising: See https://taylorandfrancis.com/contact/advertising/

Permissions: See help.tandfonline.com/Librarian/s/article/Permissions

All Taylor & Francis Group journals are printed on paper from renewable sources by accredited partners.

February–March 2025

THE ADELPHI SERIES

STRATEGY AND GRAND STRATEGY

'Joshua Rovner is one of the most creative
strategic studies scholars of his generation.
Anyone interested in the theory and practice
of strategy and grand strategy should read his
new book.'

HAL BRANDS, Henry A. Kissinger Distinguished Professor
of Global Affairs, Johns Hopkins School of Advanced
International Studies

Joshua Rovner

available at

amazon

OR

R Routledge
Taylor & Francis Group

Adelphi 514–515; published
January 2025; 234x156; 200pp;
Paperback: 978-1-041-02004-2
eBook: 978-1-003-61730-3

Wartime leaders should understand the link between violent means
and political ends. They should also have a sense of how strategic
decisions will affect the post-war peace. Yet they often fail to make these
connections. Mistaking strategy for grand strategy, or misunderstanding
the relationship between them, can frustrate soldiers and statesmen
alike. Sometimes it can lead to national ruin.

In this *Adelphi* book, Joshua Rovner offers a lucid analysis of strategy
(a theory of victory) and grand strategy (a theory of security). He
demonstrates vividly how these concepts interact in case studies from
antiquity to the present, and he describes the implications for war and
peace at a time of extraordinary technological change. Rovner's work
will prove indispensable to policymakers, scholars and anyone seeking
to grasp these essential but often misunderstood concepts.

IISS

THE INTERNATIONAL INSTITUTE
FOR STRATEGIC STUDIES

www.iiss.org/publications/adelphi

War or Peace in Ukraine: US Moves and European Choices

François Heisbourg

Some three years after Russia launched its full-scale invasion of Ukraine, the fate of that beleaguered country remains in the balance. It is difficult to over-state the pivotal consequences that the outcome of the largest armed conflict in Europe since the Second World War will have. The physical future, politi-cal freedom and economic well-being of Ukraine's population is at stake, as is the existence, sovereignty and integrity of the Ukrainian state.[1] At the European level, the outcome will either blunt or sharpen Russia's pursuit of its broader aim to reverse the strategic effects of the break-up of the Soviet Union in 1991 and to recreate a latter-day Russian empire by limiting the sovereignty of the states lying east of the Oder–Neisse line. This was the clear objective in the draft treaties that Russia proffered to the United States and NATO in December 2021, in the run-up to the February 2022 invasion.[2] A Russian victory against Ukraine would entail massive increases in the burden borne by NATO's current members to preclude the fulfilment of the objectives laid out in those treaties. Notwithstanding the costs of the war, Russia's armed forces are larger than they were at its onset, and battle-tested in a way that NATO's armies are not.

At the global level, a territorially diminished Ukraine would likely put an end to successful post-Second World War efforts to counter the unilateral

François Heisbourg is IISS Senior Adviser for Europe.

Survival | vol. 67 no. 1 | February–March 2025 | pp. 7–22   https://doi.org/10.1080/00396338.2025.2459009

annexation of territory in Europe recognised as belonging lawfully to a separate state. Before 2014, Russia had recognised the borders of Ukraine as delineated in their bilateral accords, notably the Russo-Ukrainian treaty of 28 January 2003, in line with the international order established by the victorious powers in the Second World War, including the Soviet Union and the People's Republic of China.[3] Russia's unlawful annexation of Crimea in 2014 laid the groundwork for the order's unravelling, but had gone unrecognised by all but Russia itself and ten outlier states that did not include China.[4] Today, Russia includes in its constitutional territory close to a fifth of Ukraine, including some land it does not control.[5]

Conversely, Russia's inability to bring the war in Ukraine to a conclusion on its terms would likely forestall further adventures against its European neighbours and limit its ability to project its forces and influence further abroad. Moscow's paralysis during the overthrow of its long-standing partners in Syria is at least in part explained by the more pressing needs of its Ukraine operations. More broadly, strategic competition between the United States and China would necessarily be affected. Given the broad-based American consensus on the strategic primacy of the Indo-Pacific theatre and the relationship with China, the fate of Ukraine can hardly be a matter of indifference to whoever is in power in Washington. Whereas a victorious Russia would set a standard of strategic performance that China could be tempted to emulate against Taiwan, Moscow's inability to prevail against Kyiv could lead China to exercise strategic caution. If Russia wins, the strategic challenge posed by China becomes all the greater, even leaving aside the plain fact that Russia and China are closely linked in a strategic partnership.

To these prima facie stakes may be added the imponderables of all great wars, which could include potential knock-on effects such as nuclear proliferation in Iran or South Korea and unknown unknowns such as the fall of the Syrian regime. Such prospects hover over this examination of the current state of the war itself, the uncertain prospects of any deal promoted by US President Donald Trump to end the bloodshed, the no less uncertain future of the United States as a defence guarantor in Europe, and European options in this challenging set of circumstances.[6]

The state of the war: 2025 or bust?

At first blush, the war has not afforded the Kremlin great satisfaction, as it has failed to break Ukraine on the battlefield. Since the war began, Russia has reportedly suffered as many as 700,000 casualties, including up to 200,000 killed in action, and extraordinary losses of materiel, including about 3,000 intercepted cruise missiles and more main battle tanks than the total number fielded by NATO's 32 members.[7] Russian authorities have absorbed these losses without overwhelming difficulty thanks to generous recruitment incentives, foreign mercenaries, abundant legacy materiel in storage and healthy revenue flows for purchasing foreign kit and components. Nevertheless, Russia has precious little to show for the price it has paid. Since December 2022, it has conquered only 3,000 square kilometres of Ukrainian territory, an area similar in size to Luxembourg. Since summer 2023, Russia has lost its ability to prevent the flow of waterborne merchandise, including critical grain exports to much of Africa and the Middle East, to and from Ukraine through the Black Sea and the Danube Delta. Although Russia has dealt harsh blows to Ukraine's infrastructure, its electricity supply remains sufficient to power Ukrainian society and industry.

Ukraine has also eliminated a third of Russia's Black Sea Fleet, with the remaining vessels having to shelter eastward. The large naval base in Sevastopol, Crimea, once a first-class strategic asset, has been turned into a military liability. Ukraine has also managed to bring the war onto Russian soil, hitting with more than symbolic effect air bases, arms plants and oil facilities from Kaliningrad to Murmansk, from the outskirts of Moscow to Tatarstan. In August 2024, its ground forces seized more than 1,300 square kilometres of the Russian region of Kursk, including an important gas-pipeline hub at Sudzha; as of January 2025, Ukrainian forces facing both Russian and North Korean forces still held part of this area.

Ukraine achieved these successes despite belated deliveries of certain platforms such as F-16 fighter aircraft, the United States' ongoing refusal to transfer air-launched deep-strike weapons such as the Joint Air-to-Surface Standoff Missile (JASSM), and, until the last weeks of the Biden administration, the US prohibition against Ukraine's use of US-made weapons beyond the Russian front line.[8] The fact remains that Ukraine has received some

$100 billion in Western military aid, of which $40bn has come from Europe, representing about one-sixth of NATO's military procurement spending.[9]

Yet, since last summer, Ukrainian political and military officials have been stating that the war would end in 2025.[10] Ukrainian President Volodymyr Zelenskyy's 'victory plan', announced in the autumn, ostensibly suggests that Ukraine's intent is to build morale as opposed to imparting 'all is lost' desperation. Private conversations, however, have a distinctly sombre tone. 'We have lost the war' was not the sentence I expected to hear during a late September visit to Kyiv from a very senior official, and it did not express a view unique to that official.

There is substantial concern at the tactical and operational levels. The Russian meat grinder works very slowly, but it goes in only one direction – forward – which means a Russian breakthrough is always a salient possibility. Ukraine has faced grave difficulty in establishing a mobilisation system that provides front-line troops efficiently and, from the standpoint of the prospective recruits and their families, equitably. Desertions are common, demoralisation is widespread, and soldiers in their forties are the rule rather than the exception. Although Ukrainian losses on the battlefield – reportedly about 43,000 killed in action – are considerably lower than Russia's, they are much harder to bear in a country with a population less than a third as large.[11] The United States has urged Ukraine to set the recruitment age at 18 years of age rather than the current 25.[12] The American calculation is understandable, but, especially coming from a country which dropped the draft in 1973, an invitation to shed young blood more liberally is unlikely to win support. Youthful amputees make a grim sight in the streets of Kyiv. To many Ukrainians, the United States' conscription recommendation, coupled with its restrictions on deep strikes against Russian forces, reflected a lack of empathy.

From a strategic perspective, the parlous state of the electricity infrastructure, with only nuclear-power plants escaping direct strikes, is perhaps the most momentous concern. A colder than usual winter and the inadequate kill ratio of anti-ballistic-missile systems against *Iskander*-Ms and North Korean *Hwasong*s could produce economic breakdown and unprecedented hardship for civilians living in Soviet-era high-rises with no central heating, water or sanitation, quelling the 'Blitz Spirit' that has heretofore prevailed. What is clear is that Western aid remains essential, and that to allow Ukraine to stay in the fight it must include increased materiel (notably *Patriot* missile batteries) of greater variety (adding JASSMs, for instance) with less stringent constraints on its use. In spring 2024, Ukraine suffered a crippling ammunition shortage when the Republican-controlled US House of Representatives refused for several months to authorise the funds requested by the Biden administration.

Ukraine is unlikely to be able to cope on the battlefield if the Trump administration similarly cuts off new requests for aid. The same goes for France and Germany. The United States' continuation of looser restrictions on the use of American long-range missiles behind Russian lines will also be critical to maintaining Ukraine's war-fighting viability, as will its allowing allies to lift similar restrictions on Ukraine's use of air-launched cruise missiles such as the French–British *Storm Shadow*/SCALP.[13] Provided Ukraine's Western partners maintain existing arms and munitions flows and keep conditions for their use permissive, the military situation in Ukraine may be more manageable than feared, especially if additional missile defences are provided expeditiously and generously, and perform well during the dreaded energy offensive. What decisions Washington and the European capitals will make on these issues, of course, remains uncertain.

Trump's deal: big, narrow or none at all?

Nearly 18 months before the US presidential election, Trump stated that as president he would settle the Ukrainian war 'within 24 hours'.[14] Although more recently he has ceased to mention that time frame, Trump has continued to voice his ambition of stopping the war, prompting much speculation about what Trump's deal could look like.[15] Although he refused last December to confirm or deny that he had spoken to Russian President Vladimir Putin on the topic since the US presidential election, the issue is very much alive. Trump's advance appointment on 28 November of retired three-star general Keith Kellogg as special envoy for Russia and Ukraine is significant, particularly given his expressed views on what a deal could include or set aside. According to Kellogg, it could involve a ceasefire monitored by an international force, possibly European; the postponement of the issue of Ukraine's NATO membership; and de facto but not *de jure* territorial concessions by Ukraine. Military assistance to Ukraine could be suspended or bolstered depending on the respective attitudes of Ukraine and Russia towards negotiations.

Several basic questions arise. Firstly, will Trump seek a quick deal at the risk of making himself look like a loser? Precedents such as the failed nuclear talks with North Korean leader Kim Jong-un and the successful Abraham Accords between Israel and several Arab states suggest that he tends not to rush things and that, if he considers a gambit to be failing, he will stop talking. This could mean that a deal will not materialise in 2025.

Secondly, will he make this a largely bilateral process with Putin, consulting President Zelenskyy only selectively, since Ukraine would be both the subject and the object of the discussion? And will Trump bring in the European allies given that their interests and military assets would be part of any deal? Precedents, notably involving the wars in the former Yugoslavia, suggest that the US, as prime mover and self-conscious superpower, would prefer to keep interactions bilateral. American diplomat Richard Holbrooke dealt with Serbian president Slobodan Milosevic one on one in the run-up to the Kosovo war in 1999, not always making the European allies happy. Earlier, in Bosnia, even as the US ostensibly worked in a 'quad' format with France, Germany and the United Kingdom to conclude the Dayton Accords in 1995–96, Holbrooke did most of the arm-twisting, bringing in key allies only when he considered it useful. It seems safe to assume that Trump would guard his prerogative at least as jealously.

Thirdly, will Putin be interested in a substantive, good-faith process or will he be playing for the gallery? At the time of writing, he has offered no clear indication that he would be ready to discuss much beyond the colour of the ink in which Ukraine's surrender were signed. Russia's stated demands are still 'denazification' (imposed regime change in Kyiv), demilitarisation (with Russian forces as the ultimate guarantor of an agreement in which Ukraine would retain only residual forces) and neutralisation (the prohibition against membership in military alliances such as NATO or in the European Union's defence arrangements). The risk for Trump would be that he would end up looking like a fool, which he would not relish.

Fourthly, would the alliance-sceptical Trump accept a role for European NATO troops in Ukraine to secure an armistice or otherwise implement a deal? It is unlikely that Europeans would accept the risk of a bigger and more dangerous reprise of their misbegotten missions in Bosnia under a United Nations flag, during which Western blue helmets were seized as hostages along the line of contact. The Bosnia experience ultimately showed that only soldiers operating under a forceful NATO mandate with US support can do the job credibly. Yet such a condition could be a deal breaker for Putin, who might see 'NATO in Ukraine' as tantamount to 'Ukraine in NATO', which he has said he would not accept.[16]

Fifthly, and no less crucially, would the American president and his Russian counterpart focus just on ending the war in Ukraine, termed the 'narrow deal', or succumb to the temptation to go into full Molotov–Ribbentrop mode and attempt to craft a 'big deal' in which the European security order and the strategic role of China would come into play? Putin's pan-European ambitions are well known, the aforementioned 'security treaties' of December 2021 being a recent and detailed template, and he would greatly value securing Trump's support for this agenda. From the US perspective, a key quid pro quo would be the weakening of the China–Russia strategic partnership. But no official signs have emerged that Moscow or Washington is currently contemplating such a course of action. Europeans would likely view it as immensely dangerous. Furthermore, Putin may hope that he can get what he wants in Europe without having to engage in a Europe-for-China trade. An alternative version of a big deal would have Russia drop its arms transfers with Iran and North Korea and limit its dual-technology trade with China while the US lifted some of its sanctions.

Whither Article 5?

Mark Twain would surely opine that the Washington Treaty's Article 5 on mutual allied assistance means much more than it says.[17] The article's language, which leaves the nature of that assistance at the discretion of each member state, is limp in comparison to, say, the EU Lisbon Treaty's Article 42.7.[18] Indeed, Article 5 was watered down to facilitate the Washington Treaty's passage through the US Senate. Historically, however, it has proven to be a muscular deterrent. No adversary – most notably, not the Soviet Union in the throes of the Berlin crises in the early 1960s – has ever seriously attempted to test Article 5. No non-NATO country has deliberately undertaken armed hostilities on NATO territory. Adversaries and allies alike have generally interpreted the provision as fully committing the United States to the defence of Europe. Under this understanding, Ukraine's membership in NATO would ensure its security against Russian attack, which is precisely what motivates the Kremlin's opposition to it. It also explains Finland's dash into NATO, followed by Sweden's, when Russia's invasion of Ukraine raised a salient threat. The dynamic was akin to Otto von Bismarck's *Torschlusspanik*: the fear of being locked out.

In itself, the outcome of the war in Ukraine – whatever it turns out to be – doesn't implicate Article 5's credibility. Ukraine isn't in NATO and the precedent of the forceful annexation of Crimea in 2014 did not lead Russia to test Article 5, even if some analysts had already begun to wonder whether NATO would be able and willing to defend Narva, NATO's outpost 102 km down the road from St Petersburg.[19] But Trump's long-standing rejection of set-piece alliances in general and his animosity towards NATO in particular raise doubts about the actual strength of America's defence guarantee. In February 2024, he stated that the Russians 'could do whatever the hell they want' to a NATO country that hadn't paid its fair share.[20] This Trumpian sally wasn't a frontal assault on Article 5, which remained unnamed, but it shifted the US commitment from treaty obligation to financial deal, if not outright protection racket. Coming on top of America's conceptual revision, the West's inability to secure a satisfactory outcome in Ukraine could change Russia's own assessment of what Article 5 now really means. Trends in European and transatlantic relations are not likely to forestall such a development.

A Russian leader believing that his armed forces would have prevailed in Texas-sized Ukraine may be difficult to deter from going after smaller and less robust targets. For example, seizing Lithuania in order to establish continuity between continental Russia and the Baltic exclave of Kaliningrad would be militarily doable even if a German Bundeswehr brigade were in the process of being deployed in the area. To test the waters, Putin could first go after Moldova, one-fifth of whose territory and population have been under Russian military tutelage and political pressure since the fall of the Soviet Union. Assorted parts could be hived off, with Gagauzia and Transnistria as consolation of sorts for a post-war Ukraine dispensation short of conquest. Then a politically wobbly Romania, a sizeable EU and NATO member, would have to decide whether to choose the path of resistance or go down Prime Minister Viktor Orbán's road for Hungary. Russia could proffer the transfer of a defeated Ukraine's Carpathian district to Hungary, in which case Budapest might not find it convenient to invoke Article 5. The room for mischief is substantial, and much of it could be undertaken through influence and grey-zone operations. It would take only a few ill-advised words from Trump on NATO to set a geopolitical bonfire.

Europe's limitations

Against these constraints and uncertainties, Europe will find it difficult to cope with even the best case, in which Ukraine would continue to hold off Russia's forces and gain a secure peace without subjugation and NATO would endure as a credible transatlantic military alliance with US input at current levels. It would require at the very least Europe's continued transfer of arms, ammunition and other military assistance at existing levels, at a cost of some €20bn a year or about 15% of overall European defence-equipment expenditure.[21] This is now achieved through defence expenditures of 2% of GDP, currently the European NATO average, with 23 out of 31 non-US NATO members meeting or exceeding that target in 2024. Reaching that level, however, has not been easy. Germany, Europe's largest single provider of military assistance to Ukraine but traditionally one of its laggards in terms of overall defence spending, had to pass a €100bn supplemental budget to hit 2%.[22] Furthermore, the current level of effort is insufficient to replenish now-depleted stockpiles, in particular 155-millimetre artillery shells, for which EU funding is proving necessary.[23]

The best-case assumption also does not allow for what NATO views as a prudent hedge against other potential Russian military challenges, falling one-third short of required conventional NATO capabilities in Europe.[24] And, as Ukraine's 'ammunition famine' of early 2024 made brutally clear,

European efforts cannot offset a cut-off of American support to Ukraine in either financial or industrial terms. US military assistance since the full-scale invasion began has totalled some $60bn versus €40bn from Europe. Closing the gap would require 7% of overall European defence spending. This unhappy assessment is not meant as an indictment of Europe's performance. Since Russia's invasion of Ukraine in February 2022, Europe has raised its military spending by substantially more than the US or any other major power during that period. It has provided 40% of the West's military aid to Ukraine, in addition to furnishing most of its non-military funding. There is no burden-sharing scandal here. It is also worth noting that some NATO countries – for instance, Poland at 4.1% and Estonia at 3.4% – devote a similar or larger share of their GDP to their defence efforts than the United States, a superpower with global interests and ambitions that spends 3.4% of GDP on defence.[25]

The best-case cost may increase further if a capable European peace-enforcement force is to be deployed in Ukraine as part of a post-war dispensation. Such a force, supported by US enablers, would comprise multiple battle-ready brigades. NATO forces deployed in much smaller European theatres in Bosnia and Kosovo included, respectively, 50,000 troops and 39,000 troops from NATO countries.[26] In Ukraine, a country many times larger, the line of contact would extend some 1,000 km, necessitating a force strength far bigger than those deployed in the Balkans, even accounting for the contribution of the large battle-hardened Ukrainian army.

In this light, the best case, including the upgrading of NATO's forward-deployed forces, would be difficult to sustain at less than 3% of GDP overall. But this is less than what the main West European countries mustered near the end of the Cold War.[27] It would entail a defence-spending increase of some $125bn from the current aggregate of $380bn. Justifiably, the notion that 3% is the new 2% is firmly part of the conversation in the run-up to NATO's summit in The Hague in June 2025.[28] This no-penalty goal could have the desirable effect of moderating Trump's anti-NATO predispositions, enabling him to claim full credit even though Putin would be the actual agent of change. It may be realisable even if European publics would chafe at the added burden. The citizens of Europe, notably in Germany, continue to recognise the importance of avoiding a defeat at Russia's hands and the resultant tsunami of refugees.[29] One factor that could reverse European public opinion on support for Ukraine, however, is the perception that the bulk of European defence-spending increases was greasing the wheels and lining the pockets of the US defence industry. The European Commission's so-called Draghi Report asserted that two-thirds of new European defence orders went to US firms.[30] Research by the International Institute for Strategic Studies (IISS) debunked this claim, finding that the figure was closer to 30%.[31]

The fact remains that the non-renewal of US aid to Ukraine would more than double the war's bill for the Europeans. Furthermore, the United States' refusal to backstop a European peace-enforcement deployment would make the latter a hard if not impossible sell in both political and practical terms, requiring as it would a number and quality of brigades above and beyond Europe's 'Balkans levels'. If Trump reiterated his invitation to the Russians to do 'whatever the hell they want' elsewhere, devoid of any realistic burden-sharing considerations, he could destroy the transatlantic pact and set the scene for a new Russian neo-imperial adventure. This would be the worst case, and it does not seem out of the question. As with an actual underworld protection racket, here the extorted party has no guarantee that protection will be forthcoming at any price. Initially content with NATO Europe meeting the 2% of GDP target, Trump has moved the bar to 3% and, according to recent accounts, is now aiming for 5%, far above the United States' own defence spending of 3.4% of GDP.[32] The protector insists on more quid than quo, as it were, and his appetite has no apparent limit. Trump has openly threatened Denmark, a close NATO ally, with punitive tariffs and refused to rule out the use of force if that country continues to oppose the United States' annexation of Greenland. Accusations of US extortion and blackmail will henceforth poison the transatlantic debate and inform European policy decisions for better or for worse.[33]

*   *   *

If the US drops out of the picture, the Europeans will have to make up for the henceforth unavailable US capabilities. An IISS study had assessed the extra cost at between $100bn and $350bn – depending on the scenario – before the Russia–Ukraine war demonstrated Russia's war-fighting proclivities and capabilities, and demonstrated the degree to which the arms- and ammunition-consumption rate in modern war had been underestimated.[34] It is entirely unclear that Europe would have the strategic focus and unity of purpose necessary to meet such challenges, which would likely include incurring defence costs far exceeding 3% of GDP. But whatever Europe's specific strategic decisions, it is safe to conclude that the US would face China without the goodwill and cooperation of an EU that remains the world's largest trading bloc, and presumably without the trust of Indo-Pacific partners now also fearing abandonment.

Notes

1   According to the United Nations, Ukraine had 43.5 million inhabitants on the eve of the full-scale invasion, and 6.7m Ukrainians have taken refuge abroad. UN Regional Information Centre for Western Europe, 'Ukraine: Over 6 Million Refugees Spread Across Europe', 11 September 2024, https://unric.org/en/ukraine-over-6-million-refugees-spread-across-europe/.

2   See Steven Pifer, 'Russia's Draft Agreements with NATO and the United States: Intended for Rejection?', Brookings Institution, 21 December 2021, https://www.brookings.edu/articles/russias-draft-agreements-with-nato-and-the-united-states-intended-for-rejection/.

3   'Ukraine and Russian Federation: Treaty Between Ukraine and the Russian Federation on the Ukrainian–Russian State Border (with Annex and Maps), Kiev, 28 January 2003', available from the United Nations Treaty Collection, https://treaties.un.org/doc/Publication/UNTS/Volume%203161/Part/volume-3161-I-54132.pdf.

4   China abstained from the vote on UN General Assembly Resolution 68/262 on 27 March 2014 in response to Russia's annexation of Crimea.

5   The annexed territories include Crimea and the oblasts of Luhansk, Donetsk, Kherson and Zaporizhzhia, totalling 125,000 square kilometres of which 18,000 remain unoccupied. Slivers of Mykolaiv and Kharkiv oblasts are occupied. See 'Russian Annexation of Donetsk, Kherson, Luhansk and Zaporizhzhia Oblasts', Wikipedia, https://en.wikipedia.org/wiki/Russian_annexation_of_Donetsk,_Kherson,_Luhansk_and_Zaporizhzhia_oblasts.

6   See Isaac Arnsdorf, Josh Dawsey and Michael Birnbaum, 'Inside Donald Trump's Secret, Long-shot Plan to End the War in Ukraine', Washington Post, 7 April 2024, https://www.washingtonpost.com/politics/2024/04/05/trump-ukraine-secret-plan/.

7   See US Department of Defense, '"The Common Defence": Remarks by Secretary of Defense Lloyd J. Austin III at the Reagan National Defense Forum (As Delivered)', 7 December 2024, https://www.defense.gov/News/Speeches/Speech/Article/3989588/the-common-defence-remarks-by-secretary-of-defense-lloyd-j-austin-iii-at-the-re/.

8   See Adam Entous, Eric Schmitt and Julian E. Barnes, 'Biden Allows Ukraine to Strike Russia with Long-range U.S. Missiles', *New York Times*, 17 November 2024, https://www.nytimes.com/2024/11/17/us/politics/biden-ukraine-russia-atacms-missiles.html.

9   Derived from Kiel Institute for the World Economy, 'Ukraine Support Tracker: A Database of Military, Financial and Humanitarian Aid to Ukraine', https://www.ifw-kiel.de/topics/war-against-ukraine/ukraine-support-tracker/.

10 See, for example, Max Hunder, 'Zelenskiy Says Ukraine Must Do Everything to End War Next Year', Reuters, 16 November 2024, https://www.reuters.com/world/europe/zelenskiy-says-ukraine-must-try-ensure-war-ends-next-year-through-diplomacy-2024-11-16/.

11 See Alex Binley and Jonathan Beale, '43,000 Troops Killed in War with Russia, Zelensky Says', BBC News, 8 December 2024, https://www.bbc.com/news/articles/c5yv75nydy3o. Other sources suggest that the number may be twice that. See, for example, 'How Many Ukrainian Soldiers Have Died?', *The Economist*, 26 November 2024, https://www.economist.com/graphic-detail/2024/11/26/how-many-ukrainian-soldiers-have-died.

12 See Aamer Madhani, 'White House Pressing Ukraine to Draft 18-year-olds So It Has Enough Troops to Battle Russia', Associated Press, 27 November 2024, https://apnews.com/article/ukraine-war-biden-draft-08e3bad195585b7c3d9662819cc5618f.

13 See Sonya Bandouil, 'UK, France Approve Ukraine's Use of Long-range Missiles for Strikes Inside Russia, *Le Figaro* Reports', Yahoo! News, 17 November 2024, https://www.yahoo.com/news/uk-france-approve-ukraines-long-195839084.html.

14 Max Boot, 'How Trump the Dealmaker Can Broker the Peace in Ukraine', *Washington Post*, 12 November 2024, https://www.washingtonpost.com/opinions/2024/11/12/donald-trump-russia-ukraine-peace-deal/.

15 See, for example, Gram Slattery and Jonathan Landay, 'Trump's Plan for Ukraine Comes into Focus: NATO Off the Table and Concessions on Territory', Reuters, 4 December 2024, https://www.reuters.com/world/trumps-plan-ukraine-comes-into-focus-territorial-concessions-nato-off-table-2024-12-04/.

16 See Samuel Charap, 'A Pathway to Peace in Ukraine', *Foreign Affairs*, 24 December 2024, https://www.foreignaffairs.com/ukraine/pathway-peace-ukraine; and Weiser Center for Europe and Eurasia, University of Michigan, 'A Winning Strategy to End Russia's War Against Ukraine: Policy Recommendations from the University of Michigan Symposium on the Future of Ukraine', 4 December 2024, https://ii.umich.edu/wcee/news-events/news/search-news/a-winning-strategy-to-end-russia-s-war-against-ukraine.html.

17 Article 5, section 1, of the Washington Treaty (also called the North Atlantic Treaty) states that 'the Parties agree that an armed attack against one or more of them in Europe or North America shall be considered as an attack against them all … and each of them will assist the Party or Parties so attacked, by taking forthwith, individually and in concert with the other Parties … such action as it deems necessary, including the use of armed force, to restore and maintain the security of the North Atlantic area'. NATO, 'The North Atlantic Treaty', https://www.nato.int/cps/en/natohq/official_texts_17120.htm.

18 Article 42.7 of the Treaty on European Union states that 'if a Member State is the victim of armed aggression on its territory, the other Member States shall have towards it an obligation of aid and assistance by all the means in their power, in accordance with Article 51 of the United Nations Charter'. European Union, 'Consolidated Version of the Treaty on European Union', 26 October 2012, https://eur-lex.europa.eu/resource.html?uri=cellar:2bf140bf-a3f8-4ab2-b506-fd71826e6da6.0023.02/DOC_1&format=PDF. Member states of the EU that are also NATO members – as of 2024, 23 out of the EU's 27 member states – reaffirm that NATO remains the foundation of their collective defence.

19 See Alexander Motyl, 'Would NATO Defend Narva?', Atlantic Council, 8 September 2008, https://www.atlanticcouncil.org/blogs/new-atlanticist/would-nato-defend-narva/.

20 Quoted in, for example, Kate Sullivan, 'Trump Says He Would Encourage Russia to "Do Whatever the Hell They Want" to Any NATO Country That Doesn't Pay Enough', CNN, 11 February 2024, https://www.cnn.com/2024/02/10/politics/trump-russia-nato/index.html.

21 See NATO, 'Defence Expenditure of NATO Countries (2014–2024)', press release, https://www.nato.int/nato_static_fl2014/assets/pdf/2024/6/pdf/240617-def-exp-2024-en.pdf.

22 See Holger Hansen, 'German Lawmakers Approve 100 Billion Euro Military Revamp', Reuters, 3 June 2022, https://www.reuters.com/world/europe/german-lawmakers-approve-100-bln-euro-military-revamp-2022-06-03/.

23 See 'Making It Happen: How EDA Has Stepped Up in Support of Ukraine', *European Defence Matters*, no. 25, 2024, https://eda.europa.eu/webzine/issue25/focus/eda-steps-in-for-a-two-year-fast-track-project-for-155mm-artillery-shells.

24 Remark under Chatham House Rule, 5 December 2024.

25 NATO, 'Defence Expenditure of NATO Countries (2014–2024)'.

26 IISS, *The Military Balance 1996/97* (Oxford: Oxford University Press for the IISS, 1996); and IISS, *The Military Balance 2000–2001* (Oxford: Oxford University Press for the IISS, 2000).

27 In 1985, the percentages were 3.2% (Germany), 4.1% (France), 5.2% (UK) and 6.7% (US). IISS, *The Military Balance 1987–88* (London: Jane's Information Group, 1987), p. 216.

28 See, for example, Henry Foy et al., 'NATO's Members Discuss 3%

Target for European Spending', *Financial Times*, 11 December 2024, https://www.ft.com/content/c4942166-c61b-46ec-832f-1671aecf1b02.

29   See Ivanna Kostina, 'Total of 57% of Germans Support Providing Military Assistance to Ukraine', *Ukrainska Pravda*, 12 November 2024, https://www.pravda.com.ua/eng/news/2024/11/12/7484037/.

30   See European Commission, 'The Future of European Competitiveness Part B: In-depth Analysis and Recommendations', September 2024, https://commission.europa.eu/document/download/ec1409c1-d4b4-4882-8bdd-3519f86bbb92_en?filename=The%20future%20of%20European%20competitiveness_%20In-depth%20analysis%20and%20recommendations_0.pdf. See also Jacopo Barigazzi, 'Buy Your Guns, Missiles and Tanks at Home, Draghi Tells EU Countries', *Politico*, 9 September 2024, https://www.politico.eu/article/europe-defense-mario-draghi-arms-industry-guns-missiles-tanks-spending/.

31   See IISS, *Building Defence Capacity in Europe: An Assessment* (London: IISS, 2024), https://www.iiss.org/globalassets/media-library---content--migration/files/publications/strategic-dossier-delta/building-defence-capacity-in-european-assessment/pds-dossier-19.11.24.pdf.

32   See Lucy Fisher, Henry Foy and Felicia Schwartz, 'Trump Wants 5% Nato Defence Spending Target, Europe Told', *Financial Times*, 20 December 2024, https://www.ft.com/content/35f490c5-3abb-4ac9-8fa3-65e804dd158f; and Joshua Posaner et al., 'Europe Splits on Trump's Call to Dramatically Boost Defense Spending', *Politico*, 8 January 2025, https://www.politico.eu/article/donald-trump-tells-allies-spend-5-percent-gdp-defense-nato/.

33   See David E. Sanger and Michael D. Shear, 'Trump Floats Using Force to Take Greenland and the Panama Canal', *New York Times*, 7 January 2025, https://www.nytimes.com/2025/01/07/us/politics/trump-panama-canal-greenland.html.

34   See Douglas Barrie et al., 'Defending Europe: Scenario-based Capability Requirements for NATO's European Members', IISS Research Paper, 10 May 2019, https://www.iiss.org/research-paper/2019/05/defending-europe/.

Copyright © 2025 The International Institute for Strategic Studies

American Isolationisms and the Riddle of Trump Redux

John L. Harper

The return of Donald Trump to power, which brings with it the prospect of a reversion to American isolationism, calls for revisiting the history of the phenomenon in America.[1] Many have tried to make sense of the *longue durée* of US foreign relations and an ample literature is the result.[2] The argument here is that the political struggles of the early years of the American republic gave rise to several, at times overlapping, tendencies or 'strands' of thought in the realm of foreign relations: conservative and liberal internationalism; and conservative and liberal isolationism. Imagine a lengthy narrative tapestry where some of the strands periodically disappear below the surface and re-emerge at crucial points.

Did anyone ever call himself or herself an isolationist? In American discourse, the label has been used almost exclusively to compare opponents to ostriches with their heads in the sand.[3] The only major figure who wore the label proudly was probably William E. Borah, a Republican senator from Idaho. 'In matters of trade and commerce', he declared in 1934, 'we have never been isolationist and never will be … But in all matters political, in all commitments of any nature or kind, which encroach in the slightest upon the free and unembarrassed action of our people, or which circumscribe

John L. Harper is Emeritus Professor of American Foreign Policy at The Johns Hopkins University SAIS Europe. He is the author of, among other works, *American Visions of Europe: Franklin D. Roosevelt, George F. Kennan and Dean G. Acheson* (Cambridge University Press, 1994) and *The Cold War* (Oxford University Press, 2011). An earlier version of this essay was presented to a workshop on structural changes to the transatlantic relationship convened on 11 December 2024 in Washington DC by the American Statecraft Program of the Carnegie Endowment for International Peace.

Survival | vol. 67 no. 1 | February–March 2025 | pp. 23–44   https://doi.org/10.1080/00396338.2025.2459010

their discretion and judgement, we have been free, we have been independent, we have been isolationist.'[4] The term will be used here for the sake of convenience, but remembering that few besides Borah have ever used it to describe themselves. Conservative isolationism is synonymous with non-intervention and non-entanglement in the European state system in defence of national sovereignty and autonomy. Liberal isolationism, the more pacific strand, is synonymous with non-intervention and non-entanglement in the European state system in defence of liberal values and in pursuit of progressive reform. The conservative isolationist prizes above all freedom of action, the liberal isolationist, peace.

Strands of thought, 1789–1919

The first decade under the US Constitution witnessed a running conflict between sharply opposed programmes and visions of the country's future. Treasury secretary Alexander Hamilton, the dominant figure in George Washington's first administration, drew inspiration from the former mother country. Great Britain was the infant republic's main trading partner and foreign investor, as well as the most successful of the great powers. Hamilton's programme foresaw a tightly knit union presided over by an executive able to act with a minimum of outside interference in the realm of foreign affairs; a funded debt allowing the state to borrow money in wartime; professional military and naval forces; and state-sponsored development of manufacturing to foster a rudimentary military-industrial complex. Thomas Jefferson, the secretary of state, and his lieutenant James Madison were appalled by the apparent intention of Hamilton and his Federalist supporters to set up a British-style power state. They favoured a looser confederation with ample powers at the state level; an executive subject to congressional supervision in the realm of war-making; a national defence based on civilian militias; free trade and a decentralised banking system, clipping the wings of the investor class and suiting the needs of an agriculture-based economy dependent on foreign markets.[5]

When war erupted between Great Britain and France in 1793, the Federalists saw common cause with the British and their continental allies, while the Democratic Republicans (as Jefferson's party came to be known) supported revolutionary France. The two parties clashed over the definition of American neutrality, the Jay Treaty (settling a series of disputes on allegedly pro-British terms), and whether to go to war with Spain and France in cooperation with Great Britain. But as the dust settled after a tumultuous decade – Jefferson was elected president in 1800 – the foreign-policy implications of the contending programmes were ambiguous rather than straightforward.

Washington's 1796 Farewell Address, written largely by Hamilton, warned against involvement in the 'ordinary vicissitudes' of European politics.[6] This begged the question whether the United States could safely ignore their *extraordinary* vicissitudes, namely, the serious bid for hegemony by a single power. Hamiltonian Federalists saw a long-term interest in helping Britain, insofar as the country's resources permitted, to uphold the European balance, because any country that achieved hegemony on the continent would be strong enough to attack the United States. The US was part and parcel of the broader state system whether it wanted to be or not. If it played its cards correctly, moreover, it was destined to become a leading member. Washington's address spoke of the United States as 'at no distant period a great nation'.[7] Hamilton was a proto-primacist who called the United States 'a Hercules in the cradle'.[8]

This vision of the United States as a great power in the traditional sense gave rise to a persistent strand of thought: conservative internationalism. Hamilton's greatest nineteenth-century disciple was Abraham Lincoln, initially a member of the Whig Party, whose 'American System' of tariffs and government-sponsored internal improvements owed its inspiration to the first secretary of the treasury. As the first Republican Party president, Lincoln led the struggle to preserve Hamilton's tightly knit union. The North's victory in the Civil War set the stage for America's rise to world power. At the turn of the twentieth century, Hamiltonians including Henry Cabot Lodge, Alfred Thayer Mahan and Theodore Roosevelt favoured imperial expansion and entente with Great Britain.

But the expansive, great-power vision was not the only one that emerged from the Federalist camp. In 1798–99, the Federalists split into bitterly divided factions, led respectively by Hamilton and then-president John

Adams. Adams and his followers took as their mottos Washington's advice in the Farewell Address 'to steer clear of permanent alliances', and the passage that would inspire Borah: 'The great rule of conduct … is, in extending our commercial relations to have with them as little *political* connection as possible.'[9] For Hamilton, this was specifically intended as repudiation of the existing alliance with France; for Adams and subsequent 'conservative isolationists', it applied in perpetuity and across the board. In 1798, Hamilton gained command of an army being raised – if Hamilton had his way – to seize New Orleans from Spain, France's ally, in cooperation with Great Britain. Adams proceeded to make peace with France, ending a naval 'quasi-war' and scuppering Hamilton's plan.[10]

Adams was neither a Francophile nor a pacifist, but he feared that Hamilton's war would undermine the country's fiscal solvency and republican stability. Ancient Roman as well as recent French history prompted him to beware of ambitious generals. Adams's outlook also contained a strain of Puritan elitism and ethnocentrism. America was, 'as a City on a Hill', an example for good or ill depending on whether it remained true to its principles. But the city did not intend to impose itself on the outside world, nor did it presume the world would aspire to, or be capable of, following its example. Let the city cultivate its own garden, keeping its hands free and its powder dry.

> History prompted Adams to beware of ambitious generals

Adams's son and political heir John Quincy Adams – secretary of state under James Monroe – championed continental expansion, and the notion that the Old and New Worlds were separate spheres. The 1823 'Monroe Doctrine', composed by Adams, declared US opposition to future colonisation in the Americas and laid down the principle of mutual non-interference between Europe and the United States. In line with Washington's injunction, Adams rejected a British invitation to issue a joint declaration on the future of Latin America. Implicit in the Monroe Doctrine was the principle of *unilateral* American action in its own sphere. It was Adams who famously proclaimed, 'wherever the standard of freedom and Independence, has been or shall be unfurled, there will her

[America's] heart, her benedictions and her prayers be. But she goes not abroad, in search of monsters to destroy.'[11]

During the Civil War, Adams's protégé, secretary of state William Seward, warned the European powers against interference in Mexico, but declined to endorse Poland's 1863 rebellion against Russia. Later in the century, conservatives like former Republican senator Carl Schurz made the case against US expansion into the Pacific. In opposition to conservative internationalists, they advanced a 'continentalist' doctrine according to which the United States was essentially invulnerable unless it foolishly exposed itself to attack. 'Hawaii, or whatever other outlying domain, would be our Achilles Heel.'[12] In 1898, William McKinley's administration annexed Hawaii, and waged the kind of 'splendid little war' Hamilton had hoped for, expelling Spain from Cuba and the Philippines. Conservatives like Schurz, Andrew Carnegie, William Graham Sumner, and John Quincy Adams's grandson Charles Francis Adams, Jr, joined the multipartisan Anti-Imperialist League. To the imperialists' argument that the United States could no longer remain isolated, Sumner replied that it was only by virtue of its ideals that America was isolated, 'isolated in a position which the other nations of the earth have observed in silent envy'.[13] Like John Adams, Sumner feared that in the futile effort to export its ideals, the United States would trample them underfoot at home.

The Anti-Imperialist League's pleadings were for nought. Under Roosevelt, US forces imposed colonial rule on the Philippines, the Monroe Doctrine became a justification for the exercise of police power in the Caribbean, and Washington pursued a 'great rapprochement' with London.[14] The conservative-isolationist strand of thought seemed destined for obscurity. Then came Woodrow Wilson and world war.

A similar pattern emerges on the liberal, Jeffersonian side of the ledger: two distinct strands of thought arise from the same original perspective. What became known as liberal internationalism was (and is) rooted in the conviction that the values enshrined in the 1776 Declaration of Independence are universal – Jefferson's text read 'all men are created equal' – and that America had (and has) a duty and an interest in securing those values abroad. Jefferson was a fervent and optimistic supporter of the French Revolution, writing in 1795 that 'this ball of liberty, I believe most piously, is now so well in motion that it will roll around the globe'.[15] Liberal republics, moreover, were likely to sink or swim together: if the French republic's enemies managed to crush it, the American republic would probably be next. Liberal internationalism became synonymous with anti-imperialism and assisting others trying to follow in America's footsteps: the Latin Americans in the early nineteenth century, the Poles and Czechs after 1918, the 'Third World' after 1945. The classic liberal-internationalist slogan was the one contained in Wilson's 1917 war message: 'The world must be made safe for democracy.' The meaning of the phrase is open to interpretation, but Wilson appears to have believed that history was heading toward the eventual triumph of liberal democracy, and that America was the agent of humanity's deliverance from tyranny and war.

Liberal isolationism, on the other hand, is Jeffersonianism shorn of its messianic impulse, reflecting Jefferson's position during much of his presidency based on bitter experience with both France and Great Britain. Let us focus on consolidating and defending liberty in one country, what Jefferson called an 'Empire of Liberty', through westward expansion and the incorporation of new self-governing states. Let us eschew 'entangling alliances' with the European powers, act as an exemplar rather than a crusader, and above all, let us avoid war.[16]

At the core of liberal isolationism is Madison's warning: 'Of all the enemies to public liberty, war is perhaps the most to be dreaded because it comprises and develops the germ of every other. War is the parent of armies: from these proceed debts and taxes; and armies, and debts, and taxes are the known instruments for bringing the many under the domination of the few.'[17] Standing armies had often been used to suppress dissent, hence the preference for civilian militias. Jefferson sent US frigates to punish the Barbary pirates, but to deal with French and British depredations on American commerce, he preferred peaceable means of coercion.[18] Rather than arm to the teeth to defend a strict definition of neutral rights, Congress, at Jefferson's behest, enacted a ban on imports from Britain in 1806, and an embargo on exports carried in American ships in 1807. When the Madison administration blundered its way into war in 1812, the country was unprepared.

After the early nineteenth century, this strand periodically emerged in the form of liberal and radical opposition to war. Henry David Thoreau was arrested for refusing to pay a poll tax in protest against the Mexican War in 1846. The cream of America's progressive intelligentsia (Felix Adler, John Dewey, William James and Oswald Garrison Villard, to name a few) joined trade-unionist Samuel Gompers, former Democratic president Grover Cleveland and conservatives like Sumner in the Anti-Imperialist League. According to the league's platform:

> The real firing line is not in the suburbs of Manila. The foe is of our own household … If an administration may with impunity ignore the issues upon which it was chosen, deliberately create a condition of war anywhere on the face of the globe, debauch the civil service for spoils to promote the adventure, organize a truth-suppressing censorship, and demand of all citizens a suspension of judgement and their unanimous support while it chooses to continue the fighting, representative government itself is imperiled.[19]

Opposing Wilson, 1915–20

Liberal isolationists spearheaded wartime opposition to Wilson. Their conservative counterparts played a role in sinking his post-war schemes. That said, a handful of progressive Republicans (senators Robert La Follette of Wisconsin, George Norris of Nebraska and Asle Gronna of North Dakota) opposed both entry into war and the Versailles Treaty. Liberal opposition arose from the conviction that Wilson was prepared to tolerate British violations of US neutrality while holding Germany to a stricter standard, a course inevitably leading to war.[20] For William Jennings Bryan, Wilson's secretary of state, avoiding war was worth the sacrifice of neutral rights such as the safe passage of US citizens on vessels belonging to the belligerents. When Wilson insisted otherwise, Bryan resigned.[21] Even after Germany's resumption of unrestricted submarine warfare in 1917, La Follette, Norris and several others – whom Wilson branded 'a little group of willful men' – used the Senate filibuster to block a bill authorising the arming of merchant ships. In opposing the war resolution, Norris levelled a charge that became a fixture of the interwar isolationist narrative: 'We are going into war upon the command of gold.'[22] Indeed, it was no secret that by 1917, J.P. Morgan and other American banks had advanced some $2.3 billion to the Allies.

Although neither La Follette nor Norris was pro-German, and ethnic allegiances were never decisive in driving opposition to Wilson, anti-war sentiment was strongest in areas remote from the Atlantic coast or with significant German populations. Eight of ten members of Wisconsin's congressional delegation voted against the war resolution, and the 50 House members who opposed it were nearly all from the West or Midwest.[23] Once the United States was at war, the administration blanketed the country with pro-Allied propaganda and dealt harshly with dissent. A sweeping 'Espionage Act' – recalling the 1790s Alien and Sedition Acts contested by the Democratic Republicans – quickly went into force.

At the heart of the post-war controversy was Article 10 of the Versailles Treaty, declaring that members of the League of Nations 'undertake to respect and preserve as against external aggression the territorial integrity and existing political independence of all Members of the League'.[24] A conservative-internationalist bloc led by Henry Cabot Lodge supported an Anglo-American security guarantee for France but rejected treaty provisions implying indiscriminate action to preserve peace and gutting congressional war-making powers. The 'Lodge reservations' became the price of Republican support.[25] Fifteen senators including two Democrats and 13 Republicans – the so-called irreconcilables – opposed the treaty with or without reservations. Except for La Follette, Norris and Gronna, the Republicans in this group had supported the war and nearly all were vigorous nationalists, contemptuous of international 'do-goodism' and determined to preserve US freedom of action. Two of the irreconcilables, Borah and Hiram Johnson, Republican of California, became the leading conservative isolationists of the 1930s.[26]

The heyday of isolationisms, 1920–41

Interwar isolationism ran deep and drew on several wellsprings, starting with a collective wish to return to pre-war 'normalcy' and put the world at arm's length. The 1924 Johnson–Reed Act, tightening immigration quotas – and rigging them in favour of Northern Europeans – reflected the post-war mood. In the early 1930s, the view gained traction that the 'war to end all wars' had achieved nothing except to line the pockets of special interests. In the late 1930s, 'the country watched with bitter disillusionment the rise of the dictatorships … On all sides it was felt again that the European system was basically rotten, that war was endemic on that continent, and that the Europeans had only themselves to blame.'[27] Liberal and conservative isolationists shared basic objectives, worked in concert and were frequently lumped together. But, as in the past, they arose from different places on the political spectrum. Among other consequences, this meant that they found it impossible to unite around a more general political programme. The leading historian of 1930s isolationism makes a distinction between the 'timid' and the 'belligerent'.[28]

The *sine qua non* for the timid, or liberal, isolationists was avoiding another war that would kill domestic reform and transfer power to economic elites. Many embraced what the influential historian Charles Beard – himself a member of the camp – called the 'devil theory of war'.[29] The American people, according to the theory, had been duped in 1914–17 by scheming bankers and munitions makers in league with pro-British policymakers.[30] In 1934–36, a committee chaired by Gerald P. Nye, a Republican senator from North Dakota, investigated the activities of the 'merchants of death'. Nye and fellow liberal isolationists supported legislation restricting US trade and financial ties to belligerents. Like Bryan (and Jefferson), they preferred to surrender the right under international law to 'fatten on the follies' of European belligerents, lest the nation embark on the slippery slope to war. At the far end of the liberal spectrum was Louis Ludlow, a Democratic congressman from Indiana, who advanced a constitutional amendment requiring a national referendum before going to war. The measure had broad popular support and was only narrowly defeated in the House.[31]

Conservative, or 'belligerent', isolationists favoured defending traditional neutral rights. Borah and Johnson opposed a provision of the 1937 Neutrality Act allowing strategic raw materials to be purchased by belligerents on a 'cash and carry' basis, meaning carried away in their own ships. 'What sort of government is this, and what sort of men are we', Johnson asked, 'to accept a formula which will enable us to sell goods and then hide?'[32] Conservative isolationists reprised Schurz's notion of America as a kind of continental Switzerland. In general, isolationists showed 'a willingness, even an eagerness, to expand the American military establishment in order to provide an impregnable defense'.[33] Just as liberals and radicals feared war would shift power into the hands of truth-suppressing censors and capitalist oligarchs, the conservative senator Robert Taft, a Republican from Ohio, believed it would lead to socialism. 'Nothing', he argued in September 1939, 'would be so destructive of democratic government as war ... Those who control the present Government apparently believe in a planned economy under Government control.' Entangling the country in European power politics, he warned, would involve it in 'perpetual war'.[34]

In 1940–41, conservative and liberal isolationists joined forces under the banner of the America First Committee (AFC), a last-ditch effort to resist the Franklin Delano Roosevelt administration's adoption of an openly interventionist policy, and to counter organisations like the Committee to Defend America by Aiding the Allies and the Century Group.[35] Membership was predominantly conservative and Midwestern, but the AFC attracted considerable liberal support.[36] It proclaimed a classic set of isolationist principles, among them:

- The United States must build an impregnable defence for America;
- No foreign powers, nor groups of powers, can successfully attack a prepared America;
- American democracy can be preserved only by keeping out of the European war.[37]

Even in the face of German control of the continent, America Firsters clung to the supposedly eternal verities of the Farewell Address and the vision of 'an independent American destiny'.[38] By mid-1941, they were a dwindling minority. The AFC dissolved soon after the Japanese attack on Pearl Harbor on 7 December 1941.

Isolationism's post-1945 demise ... and rise

The Second World War and the challenges of the early post-war period consolidated a synthesis of liberal and conservative internationalism – economic multilateralism combined with the global projection of military power – as the predominant outlook of the US foreign-policy elites. Liberal isolationism disappeared, re-emerging for a time in the form of the anti-Vietnam War movement and a congressional attempt to rein in the 'imperial presidency'. Conservative isolationism persisted in the form of George Kennan's lonely advocacy of European unity and strategic self-reliance as preconditions for the return of the United States to its natural position of detachment once it had helped Europe to recover.[39] A more influential variety of conservative isolationism endured in the form of opposition by a Republican faction to the Truman administration's signature initiatives: the United Nations, the European Recovery Program, the North Atlantic Treaty and the International Trade Organization. Post-1941 conservative isolation-ists resisted their party's conversion to free trade and stood for 'Asia First'. After Pearl Harbor, they deplored a strategy focused on defeating Germany before Japan. After 1945, they opposed a foreign policy that lavished money on Europe and entangled the US in unprecedented commitments there while in their eyes condemning the Nationalist Chinese ally to defeat.

Asia First senators – Taft, Kenneth Wherry of Nebraska, William Knowland of California (also known as 'the senator from Formosa') and Joseph McCarthy of Wisconsin – seized on the 'loss of China' as the perfect tool to lambaste the Truman administration and the Republican internation-alists, who included those internationalists (presidential candidate Thomas Dewey, his adviser John Foster Dulles, and senator Arthur Vandenberg) who had led the party to its fifth-straight defeat in 1948. The Taft-led faction failed to take control of the party, and it remained in the hands of the conservative internationalists Dwight Eisenhower and Dulles. The 1952 election, held during the Korean War, was the first instance in which a majority viewed a Republican, although running against a liberal Democrat, as the candidate more likely to bring peace. In 1964, Barry Goldwater, an Asia Firster widely viewed as a warmonger, went down in resounding defeat. Richard Nixon appeared to put the final nail in the coffin of Asia First isolationism when he broke with the Chinese Nationalist regime and shook hands with Mao Zedong in 1972.

Nixon had promised 'peace with honour' in Vietnam and was said to have a 'secret plan' to end the war when he ran for president in 1968. Shortly

before the 1972 election, his national security advisor Henry Kissinger misleadingly (if not disingenuously) declared that peace was at hand, helping
Nixon to outmanoeuvre and crush Democratic senator George McGovern,
a liberal, anti-war opponent whose slogan was 'Come Home America'.[40] A
degree of retrospective poetic justice was served: Wilson had misleadingly
(if not disingenuously) run on a peace platform in 1916, as had Roosevelt in
1940 and Johnson in 1964. After the 1972 election and the 1973 Vietnam War
armistice, isolationism faded from view.

A vivid strand reappeared in the run-up to the first post-Cold War presidential election in 1992. This was probably to be expected, since to the extent
that conservative Republicans had supported a
policy of global containment, it had been in the name

*The isolationist
revival proved
short-lived*

of anti-communism. The 1992 election featured a
call for a return to pre-1941 'normalcy', foreshadow-
ing 2016. Patrick Buchanan's narrative blamed Wall
Street and immigration for the plight of the American
family and demanded a US withdrawal from Europe,
South Korea and Japan. H. Ross Perot denounced Republican fiscal profli-
gacy and targeted the North American Free Trade Agreement; he garnered
19% of the vote. Bill Clinton, the eventual Democratic victor, took note of
'declinist' arguments pointing to the dangers of 'imperial overstretch' and
focused initially on the domestic economy.[41] The isolationist revival proved
short-lived as the Clinton administration reined in the federal budget deficit
and launched a period of sustained growth, while giving US hegemony
in Europe a new lease on life by intervening in the Balkans and enlarging
NATO. By the end of the 1990s, Clinton, a liberal internationalist at heart,
had embraced what he called 'the inexorable logic of globalization'.[42]

There was nothing inexorable, however, about the choice to lower
barriers to the free movement of goods, capital and labour with a vengeance,
and it was clear even before the 2008–09 financial crisis and recession that
the 25-year cycle of globalisation that preceded it would have devastating
consequences for many. Between 2000 and 2010, employment in the US
manufacturing sector fell by 34%. During the same period, US multinationals
cut domestic employment by 2.9 million while creating 2.4m jobs abroad.

Economists estimate that Chinese imports accounted for nearly 60% of manufacturing-job losses between 2001 and 2019.[43] The first decade of the twenty-first century was the highest for immigration in US history, with the foreign-born population doubling between 1990 and 2010.[44] By 2016, there were an estimated 11m illegal immigrants in the United States. The 'China shock' and immigration surge unfolded simultaneously with the George W. Bush administration's 'global war on terror'. The public's and Congress's initial deference to Bush – one scholar speaks of a 'wholesale legislative abdication'[45] – was striking, but perhaps not surprising in the aftermath of the 11 September 2001 attacks. In time, the evident folly of the Iraq intervention would generate reactions on both ends of the spectrum.

Trump emerged as a figure to be reckoned with by exploiting and encouraging a double revolt whose origins lay in these developments.[46] The revolt targeted the two main pillars of post-1945 foreign policy: economic globalisation and worldwide military interventionism.[47] Francis Fukuyama noted that, given sharply rising inequality and the economic stagnation experienced by much of the population for several decades, the real question was not why populism had exploded in the United States in 2016, but why it had not done so earlier.[48] The answer was probably that igniting the tinder required a demagogic political entrepreneur with the gall, skill and contempt for conventional wisdom that only Trump was able to muster. Ear to the ground, with a preternatural sense that public support for a costly global foreign policy was cracking, Trump incorporated stock isolationist themes into his message: a fixation on national sovereignty and secure borders, an animus toward free trade and multilateral agreements, disdain for the export of democracy and other forms of foreign-policy meliorism, and pointed distrust and scorn toward European allies.[49] The 2016 election also marked the belated return of an appealing version of liberal reformism and non-interventionism in the form of Vermont Senator Bernie Sanders's social-democratic message. But of the two main contenders – Trump and former secretary of state Hillary Clinton – Trump monopolised the anti-war message, allowing him to tap into the anger and feelings of distress afflicting Iraq and Afghanistan war veterans, active military personnel and their families. His pledge to end 'these ridiculous, endless wars' was a key to his success.[50]

Trump 1.0 and Trump redux

Iconic isolationists like Borah, Norris and Taft were staunch defenders of congressional prerogatives who spent most of their careers in opposition to executive power.[51] Trump was the first presidential candidate with an isolationist and protectionist platform to be elected since the 1920s, but in office he proved to be a *sui generis*, hybrid figure. He laid the groundwork for a withdrawal from Afghanistan and made good on his promise to tear up, or suspend compliance with, the Trans-Pacific Partnership, the Paris climate accord, the 1987 Intermediate-Range Nuclear Forces Treaty with Russia, and the Iran nuclear deal. But he acted according to the theory (or the fantasy) that his talents would allow him to impose better bargains rather than opposing international agreements per se. His proudest achievement was the innovative – and as it transpired, deeply flawed – Abraham Accords whereby Israel normalised relations with several Arab states.[52] His rhetoric was often isolationist, but he did not question the goal of maintaining US global primacy and surrounded himself with conventional hardliners such as H.R. McMaster, Mike Pompeo and John Bolton, even if partly for lack of alternatives. He threatened to pull out of NATO, but the world came to see elements of bluff and play-acting in his behaviour. If he had a mentor-model in mind, it was not Taft but Nixon, a quintessential conservative internationalist-primacist. Although lacking Nixon's intellect and vast experience, Trump seems to have been attracted by his hard-fisted realpolitik approach, his supposed mastery of the 'madman theory' of diplomacy, and his predilection for breaking the rules.[53] It may not have escaped Trump that Nixon had won as a 'peace candidate' in 1968 and 1972. Trump probably hoped to pursue a version of triangular diplomacy whereby Russia would be lured away from and used to counterbalance China. For numerous reasons, including resistance by his advisers and his own incompetence, the attempt was stillborn.[54]

The deep significance of the 2024 election, and what it portends for US foreign policy, are obviously matters of conjecture. The contest was not mainly about foreign policy, but a case can be made that Trump's return confirms the US electorate's preference for a foreign policy of greater restraint, what a discerning observer has called its 'inward turn'.[55] Trump's claim that neither the 2022 invasion of Ukraine nor the 7 October 2023 attacks on Israel would have occurred on his watch was hardly credible, especially as to the latter, but polls indicated that voters trusted him more than his Democratic opponent Kamala Harris when it came to restoring peace. Although Harris was undoubtedly 'dealt a bad hand and given little time to play it', she probably used the time she had unwisely by flanking herself with a conservative Republican like Liz Cheney and declining to differentiate herself from Joe Biden's boilerplate and improbable rendition of liberal internationalism and American indispensability. As in 2016, Trump positioned himself as the 'anti-war candidate', and to the extent that the contest was about which side stood for peace, the Democratic candidate gifted the issue to Trump.[56]

A basic question is to what degree Trump's foreign policy will reflect the 'peace preference' and non-interventionist sentiments of a substantial portion of his electorate. Nothing can be ruled out with Trump, but one suspects that his verbal bullying of friendly countries like Canada, Denmark and Panama is a negotiating tactic – or the idle musings of a megalomaniac – rather than a prelude to hostile action. The same was probably true of his statement that there would be 'all hell to pay' without an agreement between Israel and Hamas. It is far from clear what he was threatening to do. Surveying Trump's economic and trade team, one observer foresees a 'gaggle of vying courtiers under an erratic president motivated by instinct and prejudice'.[57] Trump's broader national-security set-up suggests a competition among MAGA true believers (Pete Hegseth, if confirmed as secretary of defense by the Senate) with an uncertain agenda that appears to include purging the Pentagon and deporting Mexicans; opportunistic converts to America First such as Mike Waltz and Marco Rubio, committed to sustaining US primacy across the board; and Asia-first 'prioritisers', including JD Vance, Elbridge Colby and Keith Kellogg, who hope to end the Russia–Ukraine war expeditiously, improve relations with Russia and redirect scarce resources to confronting China.[58]

The implications of a serious American pivot to Asia for transatlantic relations are contradictory to say the least. A fervent Asia Firster like General Douglas MacArthur was ready to leave continental Europe – 'a dying system' – to its own devices even if that meant domination by Russia.[59]

Today's Asia Firsters lack the visceral Europhobia of their predecessors, and are probably sympathetic to Kennan's argument promoting European strategic self-reliance. Let Europe 'pay up' and take on the tasks of protecting and rehabilitating Ukraine is a line that finds favour with the Republican base. The rub is that today's Asia Firsters will also expect the European allies to fall into line when it comes to confronting China, and while haranguing Europe to spend more on defence, they will probably want to maintain limits on European autonomy and preserve the leverage the US derives from its role in protecting Europe. Whatever they may say, it seems unlikely that they would want to renounce Article 5 of the North Atlantic Treaty. Indeed, the second Trump administration's European policy might come to resemble the Nixon administration's aiming to sustain US predominance. Nixon and Kissinger's approach was to support European integration in principle, but prefer bilateral relationships in practice based on distrust of European unity and autonomy. Better a multicentred, subordinate Europe that knew its place in the world than a united, ambitious one that might challenge the US.[60] A hallmark of their approach was deal-making with Moscow and Beijing over the heads of London, Paris and Bonn. In a game of divide and rule, the Trump administration may find willing partners in the current governments of several countries, including Italy, Hungary and Slovakia.

The conclusion of the Russia–Ukraine war on the basis of a ceasefire and armistice – or, less likely, a peace settlement – followed by the United States' shift to East Asia would pose a major challenge to Europe. Even if the US provided some type of security guarantee and continued aid to Ukraine, the Europeans would bear the lion's share of the burden.[61] But such a shift would also pose a basic dilemma for Trump. The Asia Firsters, supported by Rubio and Waltz, may well favour intensifying military pressure on China in the name of deterrence but in all probability feeding Chinese hostility and increasing the chance of war. Trump probably does not believe Taiwan should be defended because it is a vibrant democracy, but the argument that it is a vital piece of geo-economic real estate may have greater appeal. At the same time, Trump will no doubt realise that war over Taiwan would not only leave little of the island intact, but make a mockery of his slogan 'peace through strength' and sink whatever deal-making agenda – for example, a 'phase-two' trade agreement with China – he and his confederate Elon Musk may have in mind.

*　　*　　*

It would be ironic if Trump eventually faced a choice analogous to the one confronting conservative Republicans after the rout of MacArthur's forces in late 1950: escalate the war against China or accept the loss of South Korea and fall back to a straitened defensive line. MacArthur favoured the former course, Taft and former president Herbert Hoover the latter.[62] The Truman administration opted to fight the war to a draw, but if faced with an analogous situation in Taiwan, Trump would probably have no such middle course available. One can hope that he would carefully consider the consequences of trying to defend Taiwan at the risk of undertaking what might become the Punic Wars of the Pacific. The riddle of Trump redux awaiting a solution would seem to be what combination of the belligerent and the pacific in Trump's political programme and personal make-up will find expression in his foreign policy. The only reasonable answer is probably that no one including Trump really knows.

Acknowledgements

The author thanks Dana Allin, Christopher Chivvis, Christopher Hill, Michael Leigh, Marc Trachtenberg and Stephen Wertheim for comments on an earlier version of this essay.

Notes

[1] See, among many other contributions to the recent debate, Charles Kupchan, 'The Deep Roots of Trump's Isolationism', *Foreign Affairs*, 9 September 2024, https://www.foreignaffairs.com/united-states/deep-roots-trump-isolationism-america-first; and Joseph S. Nye, Jr, 'Is America Reverting to Isolationism?', Project Syndicate, 4 September 2023, https://www.project-syndicate.org/commentary/us-republicans-dangerous-isolationism-by-joseph-s-nye-2023-09.

[2] See, for example, Walter A. McDougall, *Promised Land, Crusader State: America's Encounter with the World Since 1776* (Boston, MA: Houghton Mifflin, 1997); and Walter Russell Mead, *Special Providence:*

American Foreign Policy and How It Changed the World (New York: Random House, 2001).

3   For a penetrating discussion, see Stephen Wertheim, 'Internationalism/Isolationism: Concepts of American Global Power', in Daniel Bessner and Michael Brenes (eds), *Rethinking U.S. World Power: Domestic Histories of U.S. Foreign Relations* (London: Palgrave Macmillan, 2024).

4   Quoted in Manfred Jonas, *Isolationism in America, 1935–1941* (Ithaca, NY: Cornell University Press, 1966), p. 5.

5   On the politics of the 1790s, see Stanley Elkins and Eric McKitrick, *The Age of Federalism* (New York: Oxford University Press, 1993); and John Lamberton Harper, *American Machiavelli: Alexander Hamilton and the Origins of US Foreign Policy* (Cambridge: Cambridge University Press, 2004), chs 4 and 7.

6   'Washington's Farewell Address 1796', available from the Avalon Project, Yale Law School, https://avalon.law.yale.edu/18th_century/washing.asp.

7   *Ibid*.

8   'Letter from Alexander Hamilton to George Washington', 14 April 1794, available at Founders Online, https://founders.archives.gov/documents/Hamilton/01-16-02-0208-0002.

9   Quoted in Norman A. Graebner, *Ideas and Diplomacy: Readings in the Intellectual Tradition of American Foreign Policy* (New York: Oxford University Press, 1964), p. 75 (emphasis in original).

10   Among other provisions, the 1800 settlement with France formally terminated the 'perpetual alliance' negotiated in 1778.

11   John Quincy Adams Society, 'JQA's "Monsters to Destroy" Speech, Full Text', speech delivered on 4 July 1821, https://jqas.org/jqas-monsters-to-destroy-speech-full-text/.

12   Schurz (writing in 1893) quoted in Graebner, *Ideas and Diplomacy*, p. 349.

13   Sumner (writing in 1899), quoted in *ibid.*, p. 369.

14   On Anglo-American relations, see Bradford Perkins, *The Great Rapprochement: England and the United States, 1895–1914* (New York: Scribner, 1968).

15   Letter from Thomas Jefferson to Tench Coxe, 1 June 1795, in John Catanzariti (ed.), *The Papers of Thomas Jefferson*, vol. 28 (Princeton, NJ: Princeton University Press, 2000), pp. 373–4. One is reminded of the fatuous optimism generated two centuries later by the fall of the Berlin Wall.

16   The expression 'entangling alliances' is from Jefferson's first inaugural address. See Thomas Jefferson, 'Inaugural Address', 4 March 1801, available from the American Presidency Project, https://www.presidency.ucsb.edu/documents/inaugural-address-19.

17   Quoted in David C. Hendrickson and Robert W. Tucker, 'Thomas Jefferson and Foreign Policy', *Foreign Affairs*, vol. 69, no. 2, Spring 1990, pp. 135–56.

18   The construction of six frigates had been authorised during the Washington administration in 1794.

19   'Platform of the Anti-Imperialist League', 15 June 1898, available from Social History for Every Classroom, https://shec.ashp.cuny.edu/items/show/1125.

20   These included, among many other measures, a unilaterally declared war

zone around Germany enforced with undersea mines, invasive searches and seizures of US ships headed for neutral ports, and the blacklisting of US companies.

21 This followed the sinking by a German submarine of the British liner *Lusitania* in May 1915. Nearly 130 Americans were among the 1,198 passengers who went down with the ship. On Bryan's position, leading to his resignation, see Robert W. Tucker, *Woodrow Wilson and the Great War* (Charlottesville, VA: University of Virginia Press, 2007), ch. 5.

22 Quoted in Graebner, *Ideas and Diplomacy*, p. 452.

23 According to the 1910 census, there were nearly 11 million Americans of recent German origin in a population of 92m.

24 'The Versailles Treaty June 28 1919: Part I', article 10, available from the Avalon Project, Yale Law School, https://avalon.law.yale.edu/imt/parti.asp.

25 The 14 Lodge reservations included the assertion of complete freedom for the US to withdraw from the league if and when it saw fit, no employment of US military forces to preserve peace without congressional authorisation, and total autonomy for the US in interpreting and enforcing the Monroe Doctrine.

26 See John Milton Cooper, Jr, *Breaking the Heart of the World: Woodrow Wilson and the Fight for the League of Nations* (Cambridge: Cambridge University Press, 2001), ch. 6; and Ralph A. Stone, *The Irreconcilables: The Fight Against the League of Nations* (Lexington, KY: University of Kentucky Press, 1970). The treaty, with reservations attached, failed to gain a two-thirds majority in a final vote in March 1920. A coalition of 12 irreconcilable Republicans and 23 Democrats, following Wilson's instructions, voted it down.

27 William L. Langer and S. Everett Gleason, *The Challenge to Isolation, 1937–1940* (New York: Harper Bros., 1952), p. 14.

28 See Jonas, *Isolationism in America, 1935–1941*, chs 2–5.

29 See *ibid.*, ch. 5; and Charles A. Beard, *The Devil Theory of War* (New York: Vanguard Press, 1936).

30 At the core of the latter group were Colonel Edward House, secretary of state Robert Lansing, secretary of war Newton Baker, and US ambassador to Great Britain Walter Hines Page.

31 The 1935 Neutrality Act forbade the sale or shipment of arms to belligerents and allowed the president to warn US citizens that they travelled on belligerent vessels at their own risk. The 1936 act added a ban on loans to belligerents. A 1937 act banned such travel altogether, while adopting a provision allowing belligerents to buy certain strategic raw materials in the United States on a 'cash and carry' basis – that is, carried away in their own ships. The November 1939 act lifted the embargo on arms, which could now be acquired by belligerents on a cash-and-carry basis, but also created extensive 'danger zones' surrounding Great Britain and including the Baltic Sea, where US ships were forbidden to enter. On Ludlow, see Jonas, *Isolationism in America, 1935–1941*, p. 179.

32 Quoted in *ibid.*, p. 196.

33 *Ibid.*, p. 133.

34 Quoted in *ibid.*, p. 266.

35 The Century Group (thus named because it met at the Century Club

in New York) included future secretary of state Dean Acheson. It was
instrumental in devising the 1940
bases-for-destroyers deal with Great
Britain, a milestone in the Roosevelt
administration's move toward intervention in the war.

36 Members or contributors included
liberals like Chester Bowles and
Kingman Brewster, Jr, as well as
future presidents John F. Kennedy
and Gerald Ford.

37 See Justus D. Doenecke (ed.),
*In Danger Undaunted: The Anti-
interventionist Movement of 1940–41
as Revealed in the Papers of the America
First Committee* (Stanford, CA: Hoover
Institution Press, 1990), p. 9.

38 The expression is AFC spokesman
Charles Lindbergh's, quoted in
Graebner, *Ideas and Diplomacy*, p. 607.

39 On Kennan's late-1940s view of
Europe, and of the proper US–
European relationship, see John
Lamberton Harper, *American Visions
of Europe* (Cambridge: Cambridge
University Press, 1994), ch. 5.

40 Nixon won the electoral vote 520–17.

41 Such arguments were popularised by
Paul Kennedy's *The Rise and Fall of
the Great Powers* (New York: Random
House, 1987).

42 See 'Remarks by President Bill Clinton
on Foreign Policy', 26 February 1999,
available from the US Department
of State Archive, https://1997-2001.
state.gov/global/general_foreign_
policy/990226_clinton.html.

43 David Autor, David Dorn and Gordon
Hanson, 'On the Persistence of the
China Shock', National Bureau of
Economic Research, Working Paper
29401, October 2021, https://www.
nber.org/system/files/working_
papers/w29401/w29401.pdf.

44 Stephen Camarota, 'A Record-setting
Decade of Immigration: 2000–2010',
Center for Immigration Studies
Backgrounder, October 2011, https://
cis.org/sites/cis.org/files/articles/2011/
record-setting-decade.pdf.

45 Louis Fisher, *Presidential War Power*
(Lawrence, KS: University of Kansas
Press, 2004), p. 225.

46 Trump's initial venture into politics
was in 1996 when he ran in the prima-
ries choosing a presidential candidate
for the Reform Party founded by Perot.

47 Between 1992 and 2017, the US
conducted some 188 military
interventions abroad. Charles
Kupchan, *Isolationism: A History of
America's Efforts to Shield Itself from the
World* (New York: Oxford University
Press, 2020), p. 325.

48 See Francis Fukuyama, 'American
Political Decay or Renewal? The
Meaning of the 2016 Election',
Foreign Affairs, vol. 95, no. 4, July/
August 2016, pp. 58–68. In explaining
Trump's appeal, some observers
emphasised racial–cultural factors:
the fear, resentment, nostalgia and
outright racism of overlapping blocs of
whites, rural residents and evangelical
Christians who saw their values and
way of life under siege. According to
Robert Kagan, for example, 'the issue
that carried Trump [in 2016] was race,
not economics'. Quoted in Edward
Luce, 'From Dream to Nightmare',
Financial Times, 21–22 September
2024, p. 9. But racial–cultural and
economic factors were interconnected.
Precarious economic conditions, rising
inequality and increasing numbers of

deaths from alcoholism, suicide and drug addiction reinforced political tribalism, conspiracy theories, and the search for scapegoats and champions promising to punish one's enemies and turn back the clock. In 2018, 158,000 US citizens died from so-called deaths of despair, 65,000 in 1995. Anne Case and Angus Deaton, 'American Capitalism Is Failing Trump's Base as "Deaths of Despair" Rise', NBC News, 14 April 2020, https://www. nbcnews.com/think/opinion/american-capitalism-failing-trump-s-base-white-working-class-deaths-ncna1181456.

49 For insights on the parallels between Trump's message and earlier American isolationisms, see Kupchan, *Isolationism*, pp. 340–6.

50 Some 61% of veterans who voted in 2016 supported Trump. See Statista, 'Exit Polls of the 2016 Presidential Elections in the United States on November 9, 2016, Percentage of Votes by Military Service', https://www.statista.com/statistics/631991/voter-turnout-of-the-exit-polls-of-the-2016-elections-by-military-service/. Between 2001 and 2021, about 30,000 veterans of Afghanistan and Iraq died by suicide, a trend visible by 2016. See Alvin Powell, '20 Years Post-invasion, Many Iraq Veterans Haven't Found Peace', *Harvard Gazette*, 17 March 2023, https://news.harvard.edu/gazette/story/2023/03/20-years-post-invasion-many-iraq-veterans-havent-found-peace/.

51 Taft came close to securing the Republican nomination for president in 1952 but failed.

52 The accords did little or nothing to address to plight and legitimate national aspirations of the Palestinians, and the prospect that Saudi Arabia would sign up fed the murderous determination of Hamas to attack Israel and send a message to Riyadh.

53 In Nixon's case, this included the rules of the Bretton Woods financial system, which he partially discarded in 1971.

54 Trump's initial choices of Michael Flynn as national security advisor and Rex Tillerson as secretary of state, both with ties to Russia, presumably aimed to serve this purpose. In an October 2024 interview with Tucker Carlson, Trump was explicit about his hope to 'un-unite' Russia and China. 'Interview: Donald Trump Attends a Town-hall Style Event with Tucker Carlson in Arizona – October 31, 2024', transcript available at CQ Roll Call, https://rollcall.com/factbase/trump/transcript/donald-trump-speech-town-hall-tucker-carlson-glendale-arizona-october-31-2024/.

55 See Dan Caldwell and Reid Smith, 'Trump Must Not Betray "America First"', *Foreign Affairs*, 13 November 2024, https://www.foreignaffairs.com/united-states/trump-must-not-betray-america-first. On the 'inward turn', see polling data from 2018–19 cited in Kupchan, *Isolationism*, pp. 346–50.

56 On Harris's bad hand, see Jeffrey A. Friedman and Andrew Payne, 'Americans Love a Tough Guy: Why Trump Won on Foreign Policy and What the Democrats Can Learn from Him', *Foreign Affairs*, 21 November 2024, https://www.foreignaffairs.com/united-states/americans-love-tough-guy. See also Stephen Wertheim, 'The Cheney-loving Democratic Party Needs a Reckoning About War',

Guardian, 11 November 2024, https://www.theguardian.com/commentisfree/2024/nov/11/the-cheney-loving-democratic-party-needs-a-reckoning-about-war. If ChatGPT had been tasked to generate a stock version of Democratic Party internationalism, it might not have been able to match Harris's February 2024 speech to the Munich Security Conference, replete with sentences such as 'I believe it is in the fundamental interest of the American people for the United States to fulfill our longstanding role of global leadership'. White House, 'Remarks by Vice President Harris at the Munich Security Conference', 16 February 2024, https://www.whitehouse.gov/briefing-room/speeches-remarks/2024/02/16/remarks-by-vice-president-harris-at-the-munich-security-conference-munich-germany/.

57 See Alan Beattie, 'The Contradictions of Trumponomics over Tariffs Lie Exposed', *Financial Times*, 28 November 2024, https://www.ft.com/content/2433eb3d-24a7-4e19-879c-71d0baca1db9.

58 See Majda Ruge and Jeremy Shapiro, 'Polarised Power: The Three Republican "Tribes" that Could Define America's Relationship with the World', European Council on Foreign Relations, 17 November 2022, https://ecfr.eu/article/polarised-power-the-three-republican-tribes-that-could-define-americas-relationship-with-the-world/.

59 MacArthur observed during the war: 'Europe is a dying system. It is worn out and run down, and will become an economic and industrial hegemony [*sic*] of Russia. The lands touching the Pacific with their billions of inhabitants will determine the course of history for the next ten-thousand years.' Douglas MacArthur, *Reminiscences* (New York: McGraw-Hill Books, 1964).

60 As Kissinger put it, 'the United States has global interests and responsibilities. Our European allies have regional interests.' See his 'Year of Europe' address: 'Address given by Henry A. Kissinger (New York, 23 April 1973)', available at https://www.cvce.eu/content/publication/2002/9/30/dec472e3-9dff-4c06-ad8d-d3fab7e13f9f/publishable_en.pdf. That Europe, as Kissinger famously noted, had no phone number to call was a convenient alibi.

61 Trump has ruled out NATO membership for Ukraine, and it is hard to imagine that he would go beyond the June 2024 bilateral security agreement between the US and Ukraine. According to that agreement, the US will provide aid to help Ukraine defend itself, and an attack on either party would be 'a matter of grave concern' to the other, but not a *casus belli*.

62 In a nationwide radio address in December 1950, Hoover spoke of a 'Western Hemisphere Gibraltar of Western Civilization'. Herbert Hoover, 'Our National Policies in This Crisis', in *Addresses Upon the American Road by Herbert Hoover* (Stanford, CA: Stanford University Press, 1955), pp. 3–10, https://hoover.archives.gov/sites/default/files/research/ebooks/b3v7_full.pdf.

Copyright © 2025 The International Institute for Strategic Studies

With the Fall of Assad, Can Syria Rise?

Natasha Hall

On 27 November 2024, Syrian rebels led by Hayat Tahrir al-Sham (HTS) – a former branch of al-Qaeda that renounced its ties to the group and its transnational aims in 2016 – broke out of the isolated northwestern enclave of Syria that it had governed since 2015. As HTS swept eastward and then south to Damascus, other non-state armed groups seized the moment. The Kurdish-dominated, US-supported Syrian Democratic Forces (SDF) took the Albu Kamal border crossing that Syria shares with Iraq. In the south, the Southern Front, an umbrella group of atomised rebel organisations the regime had crushed in 2018, forced state security and military forces to flee. Within 11 days, the rebels had overthrown Syrian President Bashar al-Assad, whose brutal regime had forcibly disappeared, besieged and bombarded – sometimes with chemical weapons – the Syrian people for more than 13 years to stay in power. With his fall, the 54-year Assad dynasty ended abruptly, which altered the balance of power in the region.

Assad himself was not a strong leader. His regime had become a mafia state that was unable or unwilling to provide for loyalists. He held onto power because he had extensive foreign backing from Russia and Iran, while the Syrian opposition had little external support. While the rebels performed remarkably, it was the dramatic disappearance of foreign support that really sealed Assad's fate. Hizbullah and Iran saved him from being ousted in 2012, Russia in 2015. But in 2024, Israel had decapitated

Natasha Hall is a Senior Fellow in the Middle East Program at the Center for Strategic & International Studies.

Survival | vol. 67 no. 1 | February–March 2025 | pp. 45–54   https://doi.org/10.1080/00396338.2025.2459015

Hizbullah's leadership, decimated its rank and file and continuously targeted Hizbullah's and Iran's arms shipments and weapons facilities in Syria, rendering them unable to aid Assad.

Although enlisting Syria as an ally was the first major advance in Russia's march back to international power politics, the Assad regime had upset Moscow by resisting its efforts to push for reconciliation between Syria and Turkiye. Russia was also preoccupied with the conflict in Ukraine and unrest in its near abroad. Lack of Iranian support also may have led the Kremlin to decide that it could not mount another substantial campaign to save a flailing Assad. His fall leaves Iran's 'axis of resistance', already exposed as underpowered in its tepid response to the Gaza war, thoroughly enervated, and Russia's projection of power into the Middle East substantially blunted.

Iran humbled

The loss of Syria as its arms and personnel corridor to Hizbullah could doom Iran's decades-long forward regional-defence strategy.[1] Although HTS, which took control of the government, has appeared pragmatic, offering amnesty to regime soldiers and some former regime officials, it is unlikely to afford Iran a foothold in the country again. The Islamic Revolutionary Guard Corps and numerous Iran-backed militias were Assad's lifeline, helping to besiege and shell opposition-controlled communities throughout the war. HTS's priority is to rebuild the country, which requires the support of Iran's wealthier and more powerful adversaries – in particular, the United States and most Gulf Arab states. To gain it, the group will have to largely freeze out Iran.

Now with no land link to Syria and Hizbullah, Iran may try to leverage its influence and militia proxies in Iraq and the less disciplined Houthis in Yemen. Tehran also appears to be refocusing attention on its nuclear programme. After a period of downplaying major strategic interest in nuclear weapons, Iran is now publicly debating the value of a nuclear deterrent, threatening to pursue nuclear capability and dramatically accelerating its enrichment of uranium to levels close to that needed to produce a weapon.[2] Such a strategy will, however, have limitations, as Iran will be unable to credibly threaten nuclear use to quell internal unrest or subdue hostile neighbours.

In the short term, Iran will likely concentrate on minimising internal unrest, given the potential for the Iranian people to exploit this moment of geopolitical vulnerability to rebel against a repressive government. Iran tolerated Assad's use of chemical weapons against the Syrian population and has reportedly been building up its chemical-weapons arsenal. It could draw on the expertise of 260 Syrian chemical-weapons scientists who find themselves without jobs.

Israel: mowing a bigger lawn

For years, Israel has eschewed diplomacy in favour of temporary military solutions to manage sporadically recurring threats – a practice Israeli officials have called 'mowing the grass'. While this term has primarily been used in relation to Israel's approach to Hamas in Gaza, Israel has extended it regionally, attacking Iran, Lebanon, Syria and Yemen. In the context of Israel's devastation of Hamas and Hizbullah in 2024, taking down Assad appeared to be another part of its regional strategy.

Israel, however, has traditionally preferred to deal with the devil it knows, and toppling Assad probably was not part of its plan. It had long considered the Assad regime unthreatening and easy to penetrate, which in fact facilitated Israel's success in decapitating Hizbullah's leadership and decimating its rank and file. The fall of Assad creates new challenges for Israel. While his ouster completes the disintegration of Iran's forward defence strategy along its borders, it also creates uncertainty. The Assads understood that restraint with its southern neighbour was key to the Syrian regime's survival. Israel is not confident that a new government in Damascus will follow suit.

Israel's discomfort with HTS taking control in Damascus was immediately evident. Within days, Israel launched nearly 500 air attacks on Syrian military facilities and equipment, and invaded the country, taking the strategic Mount Hermon – at 2,800 metres, the highest point in the Eastern Mediterranean. Days later, Israel took control of the Al-Wahda Dam on the border between Jordan and Syria, increasing human insecurity for the two water-impoverished countries. HTS has made a point of publicly communicating to Israel that its fight was not with Israel.[3] The United States has also reportedly encouraged Israel to communicate with the new government.

Since Hamas's 7 October 2023 attack on Israel and the start of the Gaza war, the United States has been reluctant to rein in Israel. In turn, Israel has repeatedly seized risky opportunities to weaken its adversaries. The prevailing assumption in Washington has been that if Israel substantially neutralised its foes and felt secure, it would be more likely to prioritise diplomacy over short-term military solutions. But that has not happened. Given Israel's wariness towards HTS and confidence in its military capabilities, Israel could well choose to continue mowing the lawn in Syria, abjuring diplomacy. By putting HTS on a war footing, this would hinder Syria's ability to become an inclusive democratic country and lead to the militarisation of Syria's transition. The Trump administration may be even less inclined than its predecessor to constrain Israel.

Turkiye: the winner?

As Syrian rebels swept through the country, many saw Turkiye – one of the last refuges for the Syrian opposition and among the few countries in the region not to normalise relations with Assad – as the main beneficiary. Turkiye has long hoped that rebel territorial gains in Syria would enhance its security against the SDF, which has ties to the Turkiye-based Kurdistan Workers' Party (PKK) insurgent group that has violently challenged the Turkish state for decades, and facilitate the repatriation of some of the three million Syrian refugees in Turkiye.[4] But it had also been trying to reconcile with the Syrian government since 2022, with Russia as the arbiter. Accordingly, it seems unlikely that Turkish officials considered Assad's ouster possible or even preferable, or that Turkiye played an active role in the offensive.

It is more probable that Turkish President Recep Tayyip Erdoğan merely gave a green light for what he perceived as a more limited operation that would ease an effort by the opposition Syrian National Army (SNA), which Turkiye supports, to take SDF-controlled territory along the Turkish–Syrian border. With Turkish air support, the SNA cleared SDF elements from Tel Rifaat and Manbij, north of Aleppo city, by mid-December as HTS moved towards Damascus. Despite a US-brokered halt to the offensive, the SDF launched a counter-offensive, taking back several villages and attempting to retake Manbij as the Turks and the SNA pounded Kobani. Kurdish communities are now preparing for the worst.

Both the SNA and Turkiye want to control territory farther east to gain influence in a future Syria and weaken the SDF. However, Turkiye also wants Syria to be hospitable to refugees, which affords the West some leverage. For Syria's transition to become a political success that Turkiye can take credit for and refugees want to return to, Western nations will need to lift sanctions and terrorist designations on rebel groups – especially HTS. Such restraint could not only incentivise the central government to adhere to norms, but also motivate Turkiye to eschew a military solution to its SDF problem. Reinvigorated diplomacy between Turkiye and the PKK, its longtime enemy, holds promise but would likely require US encouragement to bear fruit.

The Kurds: an uncertain future

The US-backed and Kurdish-dominated SDF and the Autonomous Administration of North and East Syria (AANES), the de facto government in the northeast, may have the most to lose in Syria's transition. Should US President Donald Trump resume his 2019 plan to withdraw US troops from Syria, the SDF will face major challenges. The SDF and AANES made enemies among eastern Arab tribes during the counter-ISIS campaign, when, some Syrians believe, these organisations arbitrarily detained innocent people. Many others consider the Kurdish leadership corrupt and have accused it of stealing and selling oil without equitably sharing the revenues with Arab-majority areas such as Deir ez-Zor. Within weeks of Assad falling, the majority Arab communities that the AANES nominally governs staged protests against the administration and demanded a transition to rule by the new Damascus-based government.

The areas the SDF controls contain around 70% of Syria's oil wealth and agricultural land. This will be a prize for other communities and governing authorities, and therefore difficult for the SDF to retain in a politically fluid environment, especially without US support. Within weeks of Assad's ouster, HTS apparently drafted an agreement for the SDF regarding the governance of Syria that included a stipulation that 50% of oil revenues in Kurdish-controlled areas would go to the central state. The draft agreement also reportedly called for all armed groups to be dissolved as the state formed a unitary national military. Perhaps most significantly for regional security, HTS may have determined that the SDF should hand ISIS prisoners over to the new central government.[5] The Kurds would likely push back on these points, understanding that oil revenues and ISIS prisoners were their main sources of leverage. In December, SDF commander Mazloum Abdi had already begun to warn that Turkish-backed incursions were distracting the SDF from combatting ISIS, clearly to prompt external actors – the US in particular – to rein in Turkiye.[6]

In view of Trump's standing disinclination to immerse the United States in Syria – he has said on Truth Social that the US 'should have nothing to do with' Syria and that 'it is not our fight' – the SDF would have to see Washington as an unreliable ally. The previous Trump administration was friendlier with Erdoğan than the Biden administration and allowed the Turkish military to roll back the SDF, and may now tilt even harder towards backing a perceived winner. It is also possible, however, that pro-SDF elements on Trump's foreign-policy team will prevail on him to adopt a more robust stance that continues to value and utilise the SDF.[7] This could mean prioritising diplomacy with an eye to brokering an agreement acceptable to the SDF, Turkiye and the Damascus-based government. But the Trump administration's patience, bandwidth, dexterity and willingness to use available levers – namely, the US troop presence, sanctions and terrorist designations – remain highly uncertain.

Russia: recalibrating

Russia's response to Assad's demise was perhaps its most striking aspect. Aside from minor help with aerial bombardment early on in the rebel offensive, the Kremlin offered only meek public statements of support. This stood in stark contrast to Russia's assertive diplomatic intervention after the Assad regime crossed the United States' red line on chemical weapons in 2013, killing 1,400 Syrians with sarin gas, whereby Moscow struck a deal for Syria to declare and eliminate its chemical-weapon stockpiles and join the Chemical Weapons Convention, preventing a punitive US military strike. In

2015, Russia undertook a brutal military intervention in support of Assad, primarily through aerial bombardment, saving the regime and gaining an open-ended lease on port facilities in Tartous, which the Soviet Union had developed in the 1970s, and the Hmeimim Air Base. These bases allowed Russia to project power across the Mediterranean and into Africa, to Libya and Sudan, where it angled for another warm-water port on the Red Sea.

Russia may simply be recalibrating, calculating that Assad could not be saved, looking to preserve influence in other spheres, and avoiding needless distraction from pressing business in Ukraine. With Trump back in the White House, the Kremlin may assess that the US will cut support for Ukraine and usher in a favourable political resolution of the war, and that most of its attention should be devoted to achieving that result. Suggesting this sort of mindset, Russia was one of the first countries to raise the revolutionary flag over the Syrian Embassy. HTS, for its part, has been discreet, its forces protecting Russian convoys driving to the naval and air bases. But Russia understands that its days as a major player in Syria are over for now. Russian vessels left the port two days before Assad fell and subsequently evacuated most personnel and withdrew equipment.

Meanwhile, Russia is relocating air-defence systems and other advanced weapons from Syria to bases it controls in Libya, and tentatively shifting resources to the Libyan port of Tobruk. But the transition will not be easy. In Syria, Russia had the support of a 54-year dynasty. In Libya, its client, Field Marshal Khalifa Belqasim Omar Haftar, is essentially a warlord who only recently turned politician. And while Haftar controls the eastern half of the country in a relatively frozen conflict, he may be looking at the fate of Assad and wondering if Russia is a dependable backer. The Libyan people also are not keen on expanded Russian influence. In December, Libya's Grand Mufti urged them to expel Russia from the country, and many took to the streets to protest Russian influence.

Russia could try to increase the role of Port Sudan in its foreign-policy strategy, but establishing a permanent base there has been fraught. In December, the *Moscow Times* reported that Sudanese authorities had formally rejected Russia's request for a naval presence in Port Sudan for fear of angering the West, and despite Moscow's offer to provide S-400 missile-defence systems and 50% of Sudan's petrol requirements.[8] Whatever its calculations, Russia remains motivated to sanction-proof its economy, and autocratic leaders are still attracted to a politically kindred sponsor. For this reason, even as Russia's position in the Levant and the Gulf wanes with the ouster of Assad, its status in Africa and elsewhere may increase.

The Gulf states: a future scramble?

The Gulf states could enhance Syria's prospects via aid and investment or they could act as political spoilers. Qatar, the only country to maintain a staunchly critical stance towards the Assad regime, has already promised to increase civil-service employees' salaries by 400% and to work with Turkiye to deploy power ships to provide much-needed electricity to Syria. Qatar has the trust of the current government in Damascus and therefore the upper hand in shaping the country's dynamics.

The roles of Saudi Arabia and the United Arab Emirates (UAE) are less certain. Both normalised ties with Assad in an attempt to increase their own influence and diminish Iran's. That was a fool's errand given how pivotal Iran was to Assad's survival. Going forward, however, some regional power will inevitably fill the vacuum that Iran's marginalisation has left. Bahrain, Oman, Saudi Arabia and the UAE immediately recognised this reality and resumed their diplomatic activities in Damascus just after Assad's fall. Saudi Arabia also urged European officials to lift sanctions on Syria and was reportedly considering sending oil to the country when Iran cut off shipments.

The UAE was at the forefront of normalisation with Assad in 2018 and has a rocky relationship with Qatar and Turkiye – the perceived winners in Syria's transition. Accordingly, Abu Dhabi's prospective relationship with the new leaders in Damascus is likely to be complicated. The UAE may still extend financial assistance to Syria to secure quick influence. Longer-term, though, the UAE and others who judge HTS resistant could choose to back Haftar-like candidates as their preferred leaders and potentially divide the country. Rumours have already circulated that the UAE is considering lending support to certain commanders with this dispensation in mind.

The opportunities for Gulf states to play a positive role in rebuilding Syria and to increase their own influence while diminishing that of their enemies are abundant. The question is whether a scramble for power among them will undermine that potential.

The United States: reluctant gatekeeper

While the United States has publicly lamented its lack of leverage in Syria for 13 years, it has considerable influence over the trajectory of the conflict. For years, the United States has deployed hundreds of troops – as of early 2025, some 2,000 – in resource-rich eastern and northeastern Syria, operating autonomously and in collaboration with the SDF. This small military footprint effectively prevented the former regime from retaking these areas. In addition, the US has been one of the largest donors to the relief effort in Syria and enacted some of the strictest sanctions (including secondary sanctions) on the Assad government and regime officials.

With major partners, the US could use a range of carrots (aid and investment) and sticks (sanctions and terrorism designations) to encourage the next government to fulfil criteria for politically inclusive governance that provides basic services and living wages – a capacity that the Assad regime conspicuously lacked. Furthermore, with Iran now sidelined in Syria, the United States could in theory push for a more stable Middle East in the hope of focusing on other geopolitical priorities in the longer term. It is unclear, however, that a Trump administration that embraces an insular 'America First' mandate will have any taste for the kind of systematic engagement required to facilitate comprehensive stabilisation and transition.

On its policy disposition for Syria, the United States has been listening to Israel, its ally, and to Gulf states such as the UAE and will likely continue to do so. For different reasons, neither country would necessarily welcome a flourishing democracy in the neighbourhood. Even the United States has allowed governments to fall when the elected leadership was not to its liking. Muhammad Morsi's Muslim Brotherhood government in Egypt was a prominent example. Rather than calling General Abdel Fattah al-Sisi's takeover a coup, which would have made it illegal for the United States to continue sending Egypt military aid, the US simply allowed it to proceed unchallenged. One could imagine a similar fate for a new government in Syria that displeased its neighbours and the United States.

* * *

The strategic opportunity presented by Assad's fall is considerable, but so are the challenges to capitalising on it. Syria is left with a leader – Ahmed al-Sharaa – that outside stakeholders are hesitant to embrace or even to refrain from designating a terrorist. Yet time is of the essence. The new Damascus-based government will need to expeditiously secure aid, revenues and investment to pay salaries, provide basic services, rebuild a shattered country and maintain security. At the same time, it will need to mitigate political infighting and divisions. Its ability to do so will depend heavily on outside stakeholders who have not yet decided whether the game is worth the candle.

Notes

1 See Hadi Ajili and Mahsa Rouhi, 'Iran's Military Strategy', *Survival*, vol. 61, no. 6, December 2019–January 2020, pp. 139–52.

2 See Javad Heiran-Nia, 'Iranians Debate Whether It's Time to Develop Nuclear Weapons', Stimson, 8 November 2024, https://www.stimson.org/2024/iranians-debate-whether-its-time-to-develop-nuclear-weapons/; and Jackie Northam, 'The Collapse of the Assad Regime in Syria Has Been a Huge Blow for Iran', NPR, 13 December 2024, https://www.npr.org/2024/12/13/nx-s1-5223675/the-collapse-of-the-assad-regime-in-syria-has-been-a-huge-blow-for-iran.

3 See, for example, Hadeel Al-Shalchi, 'New Leaders in Damascus Call for Cordial Syria Ties with a Resistant Israel', NPR, 27 December 2024, https://www.npr.org/2024/12/27/g-s1-40144/syria-israel-relations-hts-damascus-governor.

4 See Eray Alim, 'The Kurdish Predicament in US–Turkiye Relations', *Survival*, vol. 66, no. 4, August–September 2024, pp. 149–60.

5 See Ariel Oseran (@ariel_oseran), post to X, 12 December 2024, https://x.com/ariel_oseran/status/1867360789650108591.

6 See 'Kurdish Forces Commander Says Islamic State Group Resurging in Syria's East Amid Security Vacuum', Associated Press, 12 December 2024, https://apnews.com/video/syria-war-and-unrest-islamic-state-group-syria-government-bashar-assad-db675ca5b3504e1e8fa42e99d135e9bc.

7 On the SDF's virtues, see Federico Manfredi Firmian, 'Strengthening the US Partnership with the Syrian Democratic Forces', *Survival*, vol. 63, no. 6, December 2021–January 2022, pp. 159–82.

8 See 'Sudan Refuses to Host Russian Naval Base', *Moscow Times*, 18 December 2024, https://www.moscowtimes.ru/2024/12/18/sudan-otkazalsya-razmeschat-bazu-voennogo-flota-rossii-a150862.

Copyright © 2025 The International Institute for Strategic Studies

A Shield for Europe: Reviving the European Defence Community

Federico Fabbrini

At a time when a major conventional inter-state war has returned to the European continent for the first time since the end of the Second World War, the re-election of Donald Trump as president of the United States compounds an acute challenge for European defence. Russia's large-scale aggression against Ukraine has forced the European Union and its member states to face the realities of hard power. EU leaders recognised as much in the Versailles Declaration of March 2022; the war, they stated, 'constitutes a tectonic shift in European history'.[1]

The EU has responded forcefully.[2] Between February 2022 and December 2024, it rolled out 14 rounds of sanctions against Russia; deployed new fiscal tools to support the Ukrainian government and military; invested in the common procurement of weapons and ammunition; and took important steps to reduce its energy dependencies and increase its economic security. The EU's response has also revealed weaknesses, however. The EU failed to meet its target of delivering at least one million rounds of ammunition to Ukraine in a year; it has not yet implemented the plan, outlined in the 2022 Strategic Compass, to establish a rapid-reaction force of just 5,000 troops by 2025; and it has not developed any credible military deterrence against Russia.[3]

Federico Fabbrini is Full Professor of European Law at Dublin City University and the Founding Director of the Dublin European Law Institute. Among other posts, he has been a Fellow in Law, Ethics and Public Policy at Princeton University and a Fernand Braudel Fellow at the European University Institute. He is the author of five monographs with Oxford University Press, including *The EU Constitution in Time of War: Legal Responses to Russia's Aggression Against Ukraine* (Oxford University Press, 2025).

Survival | vol. 67 no. 1 | February–March 2025 | pp. 55–60   https://doi.org/10.1080/00396338.2025.2459016

This EU response is not, of course, the full measure of what Europe writ large has done to support Ukraine. A large share of that support has been supplied through NATO or bilaterally from individual European states. The EU is important, however, because it is the main institution for strictly European cooperation. If Trump's America were to withhold support or block NATO from helping Ukraine – or perhaps even from defending NATO members – the EU would become, by default, the main instrument of European defence solidarity.

Enter the EDC

Yet the EU was never conceived as a wartime organisation. Despite the elaboration of an EU Common Foreign and Security Policy (CFSP) under the 1992 Treaty of Maastricht – a policy which, according to Article 42(2) of the Treaty on European Union, 'shall include the progressive framing of a common Union defence policy' that 'will lead to a common defence'[4] – the requirement that all 27 member states (four of which are neutral) in the European Council unanimously agree on this makes it practically impossible to achieve. As a result, the CFSP has proved to be a paper tiger, producing numerous initiatives with corresponding acronyms, but failing to noticeably improve the security of the continent.[5]

Political developments in the US have made this state of affairs unsustainable. During his first presidency in 2016–20, Trump complained about unfair burden-sharing within NATO, and on the 2024 campaign trail he openly said he would let Russia do 'whatever the hell it wants' to NATO members who do not 'pay [their] bills'.[6] Meanwhile, Trump's vice president, JD Vance, has explicitly proposed ending US military and financial support for Ukraine.[7] This stance is undermining the credibility of NATO as a security umbrella for Europe and is hastening the need for the EU and its member states to take ownership of its defence. At a time when conventional military threats are mounting and the transatlantic relationship is more uncertain than ever, Europe must find a way to achieve defence integration.

One way it might do so is to revive the European Defence Community (EDC). The EDC first emerged in the early 1950s, at the beginning of the European integration process. At that time, the security of Europe was threatened by the Soviet Union, and the Korean War was raging in Asia. In

1951, six countries – Belgium, France, Italy, Luxembourg, the Netherlands and West Germany – founded the European Coal and Steel Community (ECSC) with the 1951 Treaty of Paris, and in 1952 they established the EDC, a new organisation that was explicitly focused on defending Western Europe. (France, which led the way in establishing the EDC, also saw it as a way to deal with the problem of the remilitarisation of Germany.) Given that the Cold War was taking shape by then, the EDC was openly supported by the United Kingdom and the US as well.

The EDC was designed to create a common army, funded by a common budget and governed by supranational institutions. It set up precise operational plans to transfer the command of member states' armed forces to the community. It created a nine-person executive branch, subject to the control of a bicameral legislature comprising a council representing national governments and an assembly that corresponded to the parliament of the ECSC. It also empowered common institutions to order defence industries to produce needed materiel. At the same time, the EDC was integrated into NATO – in fact, in wartime the EDC forces would be subject to the NATO Supreme Allied Commander. Separate mutual-defence pacts were secured between the EDC and NATO, and the EDC and the UK.

On 27 May 1952, the treaty establishing the EDC was signed by the leaders of the six states, including Robert Schuman of France, Konrad Adenauer of West Germany and Alcide De Gasperi of Italy.[8] It was swiftly ratified by Belgium, Luxembourg, the Netherlands and West Germany (where the Federal Constitutional Court rejected a challenge that might have blocked ratification).[9] While Italy was itself preparing to ratify the treaty in August 1954, France's assembly voted to approve a procedural motion that postponed ratification *sine die*. That decision sent European integration down a different track, with West Germany joining NATO in 1955 and the Treaty of Rome establishing the European Economic Community in 1957.

Challenges and opportunities

Even so, the EDC Treaty is not dead. As I have explained in an article published in the *European Law Journal*, once a treaty is signed and ratified, it remains valid for the states that have expressed their consent to be bound by it – even if the treaty has not yet entered into force.[10] Indeed, multilateral treaties usually require a number of ratifications before becoming operational, and significant time may elapse between the signature of a treaty and its entry into force. Since the four states that voted for it never rescinded their ratification, if France and Italy approved the treaty today, the EDC would become operational. It is true that constitutional rules sometimes prohibit parliaments from voting again on a treaty they have rejected. But Italy never voted on the EDC in the 1950s, so it could surely ratify it now. Meanwhile, the vote in France to postpone ratification of the EDC Treaty was taken during the Fourth Republic. This means that the National Assembly of the current Fifth Republic – a new political regime – could very well vote anew on the EDC Treaty, in accordance with Article 53 of France's 1958 constitution.

Of course, while it may be legally feasible to revive the EDC, it may not be politically feasible to do so. The EDC's supranational features could align well with the pro-European sensibilities of France's new Prime Minister François Bayrou, but they would be less welcome to the Gaullist right or the communist left. Moreover, following the snap parliamentary elections called by French President Emmanuel Macron in June 2024, the French National Assembly is now split between three political groups of almost equal size, meaning the president no longer enjoys the parliamentary majority needed to easily implement his agenda. Thus, unlike for most of the Fifth Republic, the approval of bills and the ratification of treaties will require consensus-building and coalition politics. Elsewhere in Europe, it is unclear whether the Meloni government in Italy would support the EDC, and its entry into force could well cause unease even among the four states that ratified it in the 1950s, let alone those outside it, particularly in Eastern Europe. Finally, the entry into force of the EDC would further increase the complexity of European governance by adding another organisation to the EU system of differentiated integration.[11]

Nevertheless, the EDC would have several comparative advantages vis-à-vis other ongoing initiatives to strengthen European defence. Firstly, the EDC would be supranational, affording Europe genuine strategic autonomy while eliminating the risk of national hegemony inside the EU. Secondly, the EDC would, by law, be interconnected with NATO, which should allay any fears of a decoupling from the US and reassure the Americans about European commitments towards the Alliance. Thirdly, the EDC would be open to any EU state that wished to join, but members would have a veto on the accession of uncooperative partners. Finally, the EDC would establish a bridge with the UK, strengthening European security cooperation post-Brexit.

*   *   *

The EDC would strengthen European defence by creating a real European pillar within NATO, thus shielding Europe from the Russian threat and safeguarding the transatlantic partnership. The EDC Treaty has already been negotiated, drafted and signed – and could enter into force with just two more votes. This would be much easier to achieve than the unanimous agreement required to amend the EU treaties or to operationalise their timid defence clauses, or indeed to draft a new intergovernmental treaty among willing member states. President Macron has warned that 'our Europe today is mortal. It could die.'[12] Reviving the EDC would be a creative way of activating existing legal instruments to defend a vulnerable continent.[13]

Notes

1. 'Versailles Declaration', 11 March 2022, para. 6, available at https://www.consilium.europa.eu/media/54773/20220311-versailles-declaration-en.pdf.

2. See Federico Fabbrini, *The EU Constitution in Time of War: Legal Responses to Russia's Aggression Against Ukraine* (Oxford: Oxford University Press, 2025).

3. On the shortfall in shells for Ukraine, see 'EU Will Only Supply Half of Promised Shells to Ukraine to March – Borrell', Reuters, 31 January 2024, https://www.reuters.com/world/europe/eu-will-only-supply-half-promised-shells-ukraine-by-march-borrell-2024-01-31/. On the rapid-reaction force, see Council of the European Union, 'A Strategic Compass for Security and Defence', Doc. 7371/22, 21 March 2022, p. 3, https://data.consilium.europa.eu/doc/document/ST-7371-2022-INIT/en/pdf.

4. 'Consolidated Version of the Treaty on European Union', C 326/15, 26 October 2012, Article 42(2), available at https://eur-lex.europa.eu/

resource.html?uri=cellar:2bf140bf-a3f8-4ab2-b506-fd71826e6da6.0023.02/DOC_1&format=PDF.

5   Among these initiatives are the European Peace Facility (EPF), European Defence Fund (EDF), Permanent Structured Cooperation (PESCO), Act in Support of Ammunition Production (ASAP), European Defence Industry Reinforcement Through Common Procurement Act (EDIRPA) and European Defence Industry Programme (EDIP).

6   See Kate Sullivan, 'Trump Says He Would Encourage Russia to "Do Whatever the Hell They Want" to Any NATO Country that Doesn't Pay Enough', CNN, 11 February 2024, https://edition.cnn.com/2024/02/10/politics/trump-russia-nato/index.html.

7   JD Vance, 'The Math on Ukraine Doesn't Add Up', *New York Times*, 12 April 2024, https://www.nytimes.com/2024/04/12/opinion/jd-vance-ukraine.html.

8   For the purpose of this article, I am using the unofficial English version of the treaty referred to the Committee on Foreign Relations of the US Senate in June 1952 and available at https://aei.pitt.edu/5201/1/5201.pdf.

9   The German challenge is mentioned in Bill Davies, *Resisting the European Court of Justice: West Germany's Confrontation with European Law, 1949–1979* (Cambridge: Cambridge University Press, 2012), p. 53.

10 See Federico Fabbrini, 'European Defense Integration After Trump's Re-election: A Proposal to Revive the European Defense Community Treaty and Its Legal Feasibility', *European Law Journal*, 16 December 2024, https://doi.org/10.1111/eulj.12531.

11 See Frank Schimmelfennig and Thomas Winzen, *Ever Looser Union? Differentiated European Integration* (Oxford: Oxford University Press, 2020).

12 Emmanuel Macron, 'Europe Speech', 24 April 2024, https://www.elysee.fr/en/emmanuel-macron/2024/04/24/europe-speech.

13 For more on the idea of reviving the EDC project, see the Activating the Law Creatively to Integrate Defense in Europe (ALCIDE) project that I lead at https://alcideproject.eu/.

Copyright © 2025 The International Institute for Strategic Studies

Is Indonesia Sleepwalking into Strategic Alignment with China?

Evan A. Laksmana

Over the past two decades, bilateral security cooperation between China and Indonesia has been underwhelming.[1] This state of affairs appeared to change with a joint statement between the two governments released last November following a meeting between Chinese President Xi Jinping and Indonesian President Prabowo Subianto during his official visit to China. The statement indicated that both countries would 'upgrade' their relationship by boosting defence and security cooperation and committed them to holding their first 2+2 defence- and foreign-ministers meeting in 2025.[2]

Indonesia also appeared to implicitly sign on to maximalist Chinese positions on several strategic issues. The statement noted its 'consistent adherence to one-China principle', which verbally departed from Jakarta's long-standing 'one-China policy' characterisation.[3] Indonesia may thereby have lent support to Beijing's campaign to undermine Taiwan's international standing.[4]

The joint statement noted that Indonesia 'considered issues related to Xinjiang and Xizang as internal affairs of China', which it has not indicated in previous joint statements. The document further indicates Indonesia's support for Xi's Global Development Initiative (GDI), Global Security Initiative (GSI) and Global Civilization Initiative (GCI), in contrast with Indonesia's position the previous year, which merely 'took note' of the GSI and GCI.

Evan A. Laksmana is IISS Shangri-La Dialogue Senior Fellow for Southeast Asian Security and Defence, and Editor of the *Asia-Pacific Regional Security Assessment*.

Survival | vol. 67 no. 1 | February–March 2025 | pp. 61–67   https://doi.org/10.1080/00396338.2025.2459017

Perhaps most importantly, the 2024 joint statement effectively acknowledges that China is now Indonesia's maritime neighbour, declaring that both countries will engage in maritime 'joint development in areas of overlapping claims'. Successive Indonesian governments had maintained that under the United Nations Convention on the Law of the Sea (UNCLOS), Indonesia had overlapping claims only with Vietnam and Malaysia in the North Natuna Sea. More broadly, under Indonesian statutory law, the country has maritime and land borders – some still disputed – with ten countries, none of them China. While the implicit revision alone does not in itself legitimise China's 'nine-dash line', expansively delineating its claimed areas in the South China Sea and declared illegal by a 2016 UNCLOS tribunal ruling, it acknowledges that China has overlapping claims with Indonesia sufficient to merit 'joint development' in some parts of the North Natuna Sea even though more than 500 nautical miles separate Indonesia's and China's exclusive economic zones (EEZs) under UNCLOS. A few days after the joint statement was released, Chinese officials added that China was willing to negotiate with Indonesia over the claims. China could be preparing to argue that they are based in part on its 'ownership' of the Spratly Islands, which would undermine the positions of other South China Sea claimants.

The joint statement was a diplomatic victory for China.[5] It gave away practically nothing while bilaterally strengthening its overall strategic position in the South China Sea and beyond. Indonesia appears to be inching towards strategic alignment with China. Reasons could include Prabowo's own impulses, the carelessness of a fledgling foreign minister with a lethargic Foreign Ministry and the business-driven interests of the political elites.

Strategic impulses

Prabowo won office partly because of his foreign-policy credentials. A retired army special-forces general trained by the United States, Prabowo is perhaps Indonesia's most 'internationalist' president since Sukarno, the country's founder. He speaks several foreign languages and grew up in half a dozen countries, and as defence minister under Joko Widodo (Jokowi) travelled abroad extensively. After he was elected in February 2024, he held at least 84 meetings with officials from 38 countries before he was sworn in eight months later.[6] He spent about half of his first month in office on a six-country tour that included stops in China, the United Arab Emirates, the United Kingdom and the United States.

Prabowo's world view seems to coalesce around several themes. The first is that power is the key currency in the international arena; he often quotes Thucydides on how 'the strong do what they can and the weak suffer what they must'.[7] This suggests a kind of geopolitical fatalism. Prabowo noted during the 19th IISS Shangri-La Dialogue in 2022 that 'Southeast Asia, in fact Asia, has been for many centuries the crossroads of imperialism, big-power domination, exploitation, deprivation'.[8]

Secondly, he believes Indonesia's foreign policy needs to be non-aligned by default to show that it 'respects the interests of all our neighbours and of all the big powers in this region'.[9] Non-alignment, as captured by the phrase 'independent and active foreign policy', has been the bedrock strategic position of many Indonesian foreign-policy officials, but Prabowo seems to personally embody and articulate that principle more strongly than most.[10]

Thirdly, he believes Indonesia should always prefer 'collaboration, compromise and cooperation'.[11] During Indonesia's maritime crisis with China in early 2020, a few months into his tenure as defence minister, Prabowo publicly called for restraint, even noting that 'China is a friendly nation'.[12]

Fourthly, he takes the view that Indonesia must be stable domestically before it can be assertive abroad – a familiar theme throughout Indonesian foreign-policy history.[13] He highlighted the point at his inauguration speech and has centred his domestic agenda on social-welfare spending.

Shying away from a competitive posture abroad and enticing major powers with economic engagement to allow Indonesia diplomatic breathing space is consistent with these views. Prabowo's extroverted and somewhat ingratiating personality amplifies them, even if the policy he proposes might ultimately be unworkable.[14] Many officials privately lamented that they did not have Prabowo's ear on foreign affairs. He may well have ignored the advice of Foreign Ministry officials on the joint statement.[15] Prabowo, like Jokowi, could push Indonesia's foreign policy towards modes of cooperation with major powers – including Russia and the United States, as well as

China – that produce domestic political and economic benefits while compromising Indonesia's broader strategic interests.

Ministerial machinery

Prabowo appointed Sugiono, his long-time aide and deputy chair of Gerindra, his political party, as foreign minister. Sugiono has positioned the Foreign Ministry as the mere bureaucratic vehicle for Prabowo's foreign-policy directives rather than a professional agency for formulating and implementing policy. Previously under Jokowi, the ministry had been stagnant if steady, offering no pathbreaking diplomatic ideas or initiatives. Given the ministry's low standing within Prabowo's close circle, Sugiono's deep personal relationship with Prabowo allowed him to assume a dominant role. He has focused on channelling what Prabowo has earlier stated, reflecting little deliberation on Indonesia's increasingly challenging regional and global environment. In his first major speech at the Conference on Indonesian Foreign Policy in late November last year, Sugiono merely reiterated Prabowo's vision for a strong domestic foundation in terms of economic development and welfare without articulating specific policy judgements on, for instance, great-power competition or the role of the Association of Southeast Asian Nations (ASEAN). He then published a similarly cheerleading op-ed in the *Diplomat*. He dismissed criticisms of Prabowo's foreign policy, including the joint statement with China, as not fully grasping his 'forward-thinking' ideas.[16]

In his first annual Foreign Minister's Press Statement on 10 January 2025, Sugiono emphasised that Indonesia was facing a world confronted by multiple crises, with conflicts raging from Europe to the Middle East and in Myanmar. But he voiced the belief that under Prabowo's leadership, Indonesia would 'take its place on the world stage, as befitting its position as a major power, a trusted partner, and a good neighbour'. He added that Indonesia's diplomacy would be 'anticipative, progressive, and visionary … championing humanitarian values, unity and directed to the welfare of the people and justice for all'.[17]

Missing again was anything of substance on US–China strategic competition or ASEAN. Most of the speech focused instead on Prabowo's ideas for the Middle East and Ukraine, and how Indonesian diplomacy could be geared to achieve a 'global role and supremacy' through domestic improvements in energy and food resilience, human-capital development and industrial down-streaming. Lofty talk of 'bridging the Indo-Pacific and developing countries' through the BRICS and pushing for 'ASEAN unity and centrality' was devoid of detail, context or strategy. Indonesian diplomats privately registered consternation.[18] But even if the ministry had pushed back on the imbalance in the joint statement with China, it would have had insufficient bureaucratic capital to engineer substantive changes.

*   *   *

The salience of economic interests in Indonesia's China policy is nothing new. More than a third of roughly 100 bilateral joint documents signed by China and Indonesia between 1999 and 2021 have concerned the economy, trade and investment. Under Jokowi, China became Indonesia's top trading partner and investor. His senior officials have also argued against publicly pushing back on China's aggressive behaviour in the South China Sea for fear of jeopardising economic ties. Prabowo unsurprisingly saw the China trip as largely an economic effort. Indonesian officials stressed the approximately $10 billion-worth of potential commitments that accompanied the joint statement, including deals in the areas of fisheries, oil, the blue economy and 'green minerals'. China, for its part, has played the long game and waited for Indonesia to cave on the areas of overlapping claims in the North Natuna Sea.[19]

The 2024 joint statement could have been drafted by Beijing, but even Chinese diplomats would have expected Jakarta to negotiate and seek to balance out the text. It did not appear to do so. The episode reveals the promises and perils of Prabowo's foreign-policy approach. Expectations have been high that his interest in foreign policy, personal relationships, strategic instincts and international sensibility will end a decade of Jokowi's inward-looking diplomacy. The worry is that the economic benefits that Prabowo seeks to reap will come at the expense of fellow ASEAN members, echoing Jokowi's record. Moving forward, Indonesian foreign policy will likely follow a similar pattern, whereby the president's penchant for international engagement lacks a considered policy foundation in both form and substance.

If Indonesia is sleepwalking into strategic alignment with China, Prabowo's defence and security agenda could also pull the country towards the West. From procurement to training to military exercises, Indonesia's defence capabilities rely heavily on the United States and Europe. Jakarta could seek a kind of strategic compartmentalisation, at once cultivating China's economic largesse and deepening security ties with the West. But should US–China strategic competition intensify, as appears likely, this course may become increasingly untenable.

Notes

1   See Evan A. Laksmana, 'The Underwhelming Defence Ties Between Indonesia and China', IISS Online Analysis, 3 May 2024, https://www.iiss.org/online-analysis/online-analysis/2024/05/the-underwhelming-defence-ties-between-indonesia-and-china/.

2   State Council, People's Republic of China, 'Joint Statement Between the People's Republic of China and the Republic of Indonesia on Advancing the Comprehensive Strategic Partnership and the China–Indonesia Community with a Shared Future', 9 November 2024, https://english.www.gov.cn/news/202411/10/content_WS67301550c6d0868f4e8ecca9.html.

3   See 'Joint Statement on Deepening Comprehensive Strategic Cooperation Between the People's Republic of China and the Republic of Indonesia', China.org.cn, 18 October 2023, http://www.china.org.cn/china/Off_the_Wire/2023-10/18/content_116758121.htm.

4   Beijing's invocation of the 'one-China principle' along with UN General Assembly Resolution 2758 has been widely interpreted as Beijing's attempt to deny Taiwan any independent legal status. See Jacques deLisle and Bonnie S. Glaser, 'Why UN General Assembly Resolution 2758 Does Not Establish Beijing's "One China" Principle: A Legal Perspective', German Marshall Fund, April 2024, https://www.gmfus.org/sites/default/files/2024-04/GMF_UNGA%20Res.%202758_April%202024%20Report.pdf.

5   According to Indonesian sources, the 'consensus document' outlining the framework of the joint development of fisheries and oil and gas in the areas of overlapping claims will remain confidential.

6   See Adhi Priamarizki, 'Prabowo's Post-election Diplomacy: Domestic-driven International Activism', IDSS Paper 24084, 15 October 2024, https://www.rsis.edu.sg/rsis-publication/idss/ip24084-prabowos-post-

election-diplomacy-domestic-driven-international-activism/

7   He invited the pre-eminent realist scholar John Mearsheimer to brief his cabinet during a weekend-long orientation programme.

8   Prabowo Subianto, 'Managing Geopolitical Competition in a Multipolar Region', second plenary session, 19th IISS Shangri-La Dialogue, Singapore, 10 June 2022, https://www.iiss.org/events/shangri-la-dialogue/shangri-la-dialogue-2022/.

9   *Ibid.*

10 See Rushali Saha, 'Indonesian Foreign Policy Is Still Free, More Active', *Interpreter*, 11 December 2024, https://www.lowyinstitute.org/the-interpreter/indonesian-foreign-policy-still-free-more-active.

11 Prabowo Subianto, 'Special Address', speech delivered at the 21st IISS Shangri-La Dialogue, Singapore, 1 June 2024, https://www.iiss.org/events/shangri-la-dialogue/shangri-la-dialogue-2024/plenary-sessions/special-address/.

12 Quoted in Karina M. Tehusijarana, 'Natuna Conflict Pits Prabowo Against Former Allies', *Jakarta Post*, 10 January 2020, https://www.thejakartapost.com/news/2020/01/10/natuna-conflict-pits-prabowo-against-former-allies.html.

13 See, for example, Franklin Weinstein, *Indonesian Foreign Policy and the Dilemma of Dependence: From Sukarno to Soeharto* (Ithaca, NY: Cornell University Press, 1976).

14 See 'Indonesia's Prabowo Is Desperate to Impress Trump and Xi', *The Economist*, 28 November 2024, https://www.economist.com/asia/2024/11/28/indonesias-prabowo-is-desperate-to-impress-trump-and-xi.

15 See 'Confident Prabowo Is "Rowing Between Two Reefs"', Tengarra Strategics, *Jakarta Post*, 25 November 2024, https://www.thejakartapost.com/opinion/2024/11/25/analysis-confident-prabowo-is-rowing-between-two-reefs.html.

16 See Sugiono, 'Bold Diplomacy: Reflections on Indonesian President Prabowo Subianto's Whirlwind Global Tour', *Diplomat*, 16 December 2024, https://thediplomat.com/2024/12/bold-diplomacy-reflections-on-indonesian-president-prabowo-subiantos-whirlwind-global-tour/.

17 See Ministry of Foreign Affairs, Republic of Indonesia, 'Transcript: Annual Press Statement of the Minister for Foreign Affairs of the Republic of Indonesia 2025', 10 January 2025, https://kemlu.go.id/publikasi/pidato/pidato-menteri/transkrip-pernyataan-pers-tahunan-menteri-luar-negeri-ri-tahun-2025?type=publication.

18 Senior and mid-level diplomats expressed worries to the author and other analysts under non-attribution rules.

19 See Evan A. Laksmana, 'Indonesia, China, and the Natuna Linchpin', *Diplomat*, 1 March 2020, https://thediplomat.com/2020/02/indonesia-china-and-the-natuna-linchpin/.

Copyright © 2025 The International Institute for Strategic Studies

Noteworthy

Syria's new day

'Damascus has been liberated, the tyrant Bashar al-Assad has been toppled, and all the unjustly detained persons from the regime's prisons have been released … Long live a free and independent Syria, for all Syrians of all sects.'

A group of Syrian rebels makes a statement on Syrian state television on 8 December 2024.[1]

Korea's crisis

'Honorable citizens, as President, I appeal to you with a feeling of spitting blood.

Since the inauguration of our government, the National Assembly has initiated 22 impeachment motions against government officials, and since the inauguration of the 22nd National Assembly in June, it is pushing for the impeachment of 10 more. This is a situation that is not only unprecedented in any country in the world, but has never been seen since the founding of our country.

It is paralyzing the judiciary by intimidating judges and impeaching a number of prosecutors, and it is paralyzing the executive branch by trying to impeach the Minister of the Interior, the Chairman of the Communications Commission, the Chair of the Board of Audit, and the Defense Minister.

The handling of the national budget also undermined the essential functions of the state and turned Korea into a drug paradise and a public order panic by completely cutting all major budgets for cracking down on drug crimes and maintaining public security.

[…]

The legislative dictatorship of the Democratic Party, which uses even the budget as a means of political struggle, did not hesitate to impeach the budget. The government is paralyzed, and the people's sighs are growing.

This trampling of the constitutional order of the free Republic of Korea and the disruption of legitimate state institutions established by the constitution and laws is an obvious anti-state act that plots insurrection.

[…]

Our National Assembly has become a den of criminals and is attempting to paralyze the nation's judicial administration system through legislative dictatorship and overthrow the liberal democracy system. The National Assembly, which should be the foundation of liberal democracy, has become a monster that collapses the liberal democracy system. Now, Korea is in a precarious situation where it would not be surprising if it collapsed immediately.

Dear citizens, I declare emergency martial law to defend the free Republic of Korea from the threats of North Korean communist forces and to eradicate the shameless pro-North Korean anti-state forces that are plundering the freedom and happiness of our people and to protect the free constitutional order.'

South Korean President Yoon Suk-yeol declares martial law on 3 December 2024.[2]

Survival | vol. 67 no. 1 | February–March 2025 | pp. 68–70   https://doi.org/10.1080/00396338.2025.2459019

Gaza's respite?

'The two belligerents in the Gaza Strip have reached a deal on the prisoner and the hostage swap, and [the mediators] announce a ceasefire in the hopes of reaching a permanent ceasefire between the two sides. Both parties should commit totally to all three phases [of the agreement] to steer away from further bloodshed and steer away escalation in the region. We hope this will be the end of a dark chapter of war.'

Sheikh Mohammed bin Abdulrahman al-Thani, prime minister of Qatar, announces a ceasefire deal between Israel and Hamas on 15 January 2025.[3]

Biden's warning

'I want to warn the country of some things that give me great concern … and that's the dangerous concentration of power in the hands of a very few ultrawealthy people, and the dangerous consequences if their abuse of power is left unchecked. Today, an oligarchy is taking shape in America of extreme wealth, power and influence that literally threatens our entire democracy … We see the consequences all across America. And we've seen it before.
   […]
In his farewell address, President [Dwight] Eisenhower spoke of the dangers of the military-industrial complex. He warned us [then] about, and I quote, "The potential for the disastrous rise of misplaced power." … Six decades later, I'm equally concerned about the potential rise of a tech-industrial complex that could pose real dangers for our country as well.

Americans are being buried under an avalanche of misinformation and disinformation enabling the abuse of power. The free press is crumbling. Editors are disappearing. Social media is giving up on fact-checking. The truth is smothered by lies told for power and for profit. We must hold the social platforms accountable to protect our children, our families and our very democracy from the abuse of power. Meanwhile, artificial intelligence is the most consequential technology of our time, perhaps of all time.

Nothing offers more profound possibilities and risks for our economy, and our security, our society. For humanity. Artificial intelligence even has the potential to help us answer my call to end cancer as we know it. But unless safeguards are in place, A.I. could spawn new threats to our rights, our way of life, to our privacy, how we work, and how we protect our nation. We must make sure A.I. is safe and trustworthy and good for all humankind.'

Joe Biden delivers his farewell speech as US president on 15 January 2025.[4]

Trump's beginning

'Our recent election is a mandate to completely and totally reverse a horrible betrayal, and all of these many betrayals that have taken place, and to give the people back their faith, their wealth, their democracy and indeed their freedom. From this moment on, America's decline is over.
   […]
Never again will the immense power of the state be weaponized to persecute political opponents. Something I know something about. We will not allow that to happen. It will not happen again.

[…]

This week, I will also end the government policy of trying to socially engineer race and gender into every aspect of public and private life. We will forge a society that is colorblind and merit based. As of today, it will henceforth be the official policy of the United States government that there are only two genders: male and female. This week, I will reinstate any service members who were unjustly expelled from our military for objecting to the Covid vaccine mandate with full back pay. And I will sign an order to stop our warriors from being subjected to radical political theories and social experiments while on duty. It's going to end immediately. Our armed forces will be freed to focus on their sole mission – defeating America's enemies.

[…]

A short time from now, we are going to be changing the name of the Gulf of Mexico to the Gulf of America. And we will restore the name of the great president William McKinley to Mount McKinley, where it should be and where it belongs. President McKinley made our country very rich through tariffs and through talent.

He was a natural businessman and gave Teddy Roosevelt the money for many of the great things he did, including the Panama Canal, which has foolishly been given to the country of Panama after the United States – the United States, I mean, think of this, spent more money than ever spent on a project before and lost 38,000 lives in the building of the Panama Canal. We have been treated very badly from this foolish gift that should have never been made. And Panama's promise to us has been broken. The purpose of our deal and the spirit of our treaty has been totally violated. American ships are being severely overcharged and not treated fairly in any way, shape, or form, and that includes the United States Navy. And above all, China is operating the Panama Canal. And we didn't give it to China, we gave it to Panama, and we're taking it back.'

US President Donald Trump delivers his inauguration speech on 20 January 2025.[5]

Sources

1 Assad Arrives in Russia After Fleeing Syria, Russian Media Says', *New York Times*, 8 December 2024, https://www.nytimes.com/live/2024/12/08/world/syria-war-damascus/8b5208d3-a078-5a7d-9f2b-329a675ec952?smid=url-share.

2 'President Yoon's Speech Declaring Martial Law', *New York Times*, 3 December 2024, https://www.nytimes.com/2024/12/03/world/asia/president-yoon-speech-martial-law.html?smid=url-share.

3 Bethan McKernan and Lorenzo Tondo, 'Hamas and Israel Have Agreed Gaza Ceasefire Deal, Qatari PM Says', *Guardian*, 16 January 2025, https://www.theguardian. com/world/2025/jan/15/gaza-ceasefire-deal-agreed-between-hamas-and-israel-qatari-pm-says.

4 'Full Transcript of President Biden's Farewell Address', *New York Times*, 15 January 2025, https://www.nytimes.com/2025/01/15/us/politics/full-transcript-of-president-bidens-farewell-address.html.

5 Melissa Quinn and Caitin Yilek, 'Read the Full Transcript of Trump's Inauguration Speech', CBS News, 20 January 2025, https://www.cbsnews.com/news/transcript-trump-inauguration-speech-2025/.

Copyright © 2025 The International Institute for Strategic Studies

Divisions of Labour: Security Cooperation Between Japan, South Korea and the United States

Takuya Matsuda and Jaehan Park

The alliance system in the western Pacific has customarily been described as 'hub-and-spoke' in character – a collection of bilateral alliances with the United States at the centre. In East Asia especially, troubled history, domestic politics and, most importantly, divergent threat perceptions have hindered US efforts to foster closer security ties between America's two most important regional allies, Japan and South Korea.[1] The return of systemic rivalry in East Asia, however, including expanding security partnerships among authoritarian powers, is bringing those perceptions into closer alignment.[2] At the IISS Shangri-La Dialogue in June 2024, US Secretary of Defense Lloyd J. Austin III noted 'a new convergence' of multilateral defence relationships in the Indo-Pacific.[3]

The US, Japan and South Korea have been developing trilateral security cooperation, notably by way of the Camp David Summit in August 2023.[4] They have made progress mainly at the tactical level, by operationalising a real-time military intelligence-sharing mechanism for missile threats, agreeing to develop a multiyear trilateral military exercise and announcing plans for an institutionalised coordinating body.[5] These are crucial steps for fostering trust, which is vital for effective collective defence. But Japan and South Korea still differ on strategic priorities – especially with respect to the

Takuya Matsuda is an adjunct lecturer at the School of International Politics, Economics and Communication at Aoyama Gakuin University in Tokyo. **Jaehan Park** is an assistant professor of strategic studies and international relations at the S. Rajaratnam School of International Studies (RSIS) at Nanyang Technological University in Singapore and a non-resident fellow with the Asia Program at the Foreign Policy Research Institute.

Survival | vol. 67 no. 1 | February–March 2025 | pp. 71–88   https://doi.org/10.1080/00396338.2025.2459020

Taiwan Strait, which presents one of the most acute strategic challenges in the region.[6] Closer coordination is needed at the strategic and operational levels.[7] To that end, the US, Japan and South Korea should clarify their division of labour.

Taiwan scenarios

American defence analysts have focused on examining what China's subjugation of Taiwan, usually in the form of a full-scale invasion, might portend.[8] But that is only one possibility given China's defensive strategic culture.[9] There are several plausible scenarios for a Chinese effort to establish control of Taiwan.

In a grey-zone provocation, an aggressor seeks to achieve its objectives gradually by way of non-kinetic tools, such as cyber attacks and economic warfare.[10] Beijing has already used various grey-zone tactics to pressure Taipei, perpetrating over 15,000 Chinese cyber attacks in some form on Taiwan in the first half of 2023 alone. In addition, China also severed undersea cables between Taiwan and Lienchiang County – commonly known as Matsu – 20 times in 2023, disconnecting over 14,000 residents from the outside world.[11]

Implicitly threatening military activity is a more advanced option. After Nancy Pelosi, then speaker of the US House of Representatives, visited Taiwan in August 2022, the People's Liberation Army (PLA) conducted air reconnaissance in the Taiwanese Air Defence Identification Zone (ADIZ). In April 2023, PLA combat drones were spotted in the Taiwanese ADIZ for the first time. This past May, the PLA held military exercises following the election of moderate, pro-independence Lai Ching-te as Taiwan's president. In October 2024, the PLA conducted two military drills – one the encirclement of the island, the other a live-fire exercise near Niushan Island – following Lai's defiant speech on Taiwan's national day. In addition, the PLA Navy has begun deploying hydrographic vessels and conducting naval exercises near Taiwan. Finally, the PLA's effective enforcement of no-fly and no-sail zones has often prevented the entry of commercial traffic into Taiwan.[12]

While grey-zone provocations do not necessarily constitute existential threats, military exercises could culminate in the blockade of Taiwan.[13]

Beijing might consider this a viable option for several reasons. Firstly, it would be relatively easy from a logistical standpoint, as Taiwan's major cities, industrial capabilities and port facilities are clustered on the western side of the island, closest to the Chinese mainland.[14] Secondly, it would be an impactful form of coercion, as Taiwan relies on imported energy and food.[15] Thirdly, it is strategically conservative. The United States and its allies still maintain an overall military superiority vis-à-vis the PLA, which makes a full-scale invasion very risky.[16] Russia's poor performance in Ukraine may have reinforced Beijing's restraint.[17] Accordingly, if China does move on Taiwan, a blockade may be its more likely course of action.[18]

Various factors could affect how a blockade would unfold. Initial moves could include lawfare and the low-level use of force. China has already been trying to consolidate its claims that the Taiwan Strait constitutes 'inland waters' and to deny the existence of 'restricted waters' around Kinmen, an island administrated by Taiwan that is only five kilometres from the Chinese city of Xiamen.[19] A logical next step would be to introduce additional legal and policy measures to enforce a one-China policy.[20] Such a move would support China's placing Taiwan under Chinese jurisdiction, expanding its ADIZ to include Taiwanese airspace, asserting control over Taiwanese waters and perhaps backing these measures with cyber attacks. If the US deployed assets to the region, Beijing could dispatch non-military ships, conduct military exercises and install sea mines around Taiwan to demonstrate its willingness to attack US aircraft carriers while conducting political and psychological warfare in Taiwan to sway domestic opinion in favour of Chinese rule.[21]

Should China elect to employ military means directly to deny access, it could draw on the US blockade of Cuba during the Cuban Missile Crisis in 1962 as precedent. Upon hearing that the Soviet Union had deployed nuclear warheads on the Caribbean island, the Kennedy administration imposed a quarantine to prevent the deployment of additional offensive weapons. US carrier strike groups established targets on the island, while aircraft conducted combat reconnaissance near Guantanamo. Other US warships were deployed to a quarantine line 500 miles off the coast of Cuba. Moscow ordered Russian ships headed to Cuba to stop, and eventually withdrew its weapons from the island.[22] China might be able to similarly eject the United States from the Taiwan Strait and achieve its political objectives.

China could tighten a blockade of Taiwan with air and naval assets in ways that would make it difficult for the United States to intervene – for instance, using the coastguard for what it calls 'comprehensive law enforcement operations' and sophisticated cyber and missile capabilities.[23] In 1996, the US was able to dissuade China from escalating military pressure on Taiwan by sending two carrier strike groups to the South China Sea. In the foreseeable future, China could tighten a blockade of Taiwan with air and naval assets, as well as non-conventional tools such as its coastguard, cyber-warfare and missile capabilities, so as to make it difficult for the United States to intervene.[24]

Historically, coercion without the use of direct military force, such as a blockade, has rarely achieved political objectives.[25] China could resort to a full-scale invasion despite the high costs and immense strategic risk. In 2023, CIA director William Burns noted that Chinese President Xi Jinping had ordered the PLA to prepare itself for an invasion by 2027.[26] From Beijing's standpoint, the most effective modality would be a 'fait accompli': unilaterally occupying and annexing a small chunk of land in the expectation that there would be little resistance from the opposing side. The PLA would first destroy Taiwanese and American assets with missiles and conduct cyber attacks to neutralise Taiwan's defences. Should such an operation succeed, China would expect Taiwan's capitulation without much cost to China.[27] Lieutenant-General Wang Hongguang, former deputy commander of the Nanjing Military Region, has argued for sustained bombardment and disruption of communications in the early stage of war, which would open up a two-day window for China to invade the island.[28]

A more dangerous possibility is a protracted war.[29] According to a war game conducted by the Center for Strategic and International Studies (CSIS), the Washington think tank, the PLA Rocket Force is expected to fire missiles while the PLA Navy commences encirclement in the early phase of a conflict. US and allied forces would not be able to approach Taiwan once PLA air and naval assets fully envelop the island, resulting in Taipei's isolation. While the PLA would be able to establish a beachhead in the less densely defended, southern part of the island, its troops would have to fight their way to the north via the mountainous central region to secure the entire island, including Taipei.[30] During this period, as in the Cretan Campaign of 1941, in which German airpower wrested the island away from the British, the success of Chinese landing on Taiwan and, by extension, China's attempt to subjugate it would depend to a large extent on the ability of its air force to establish air supremacy over the island.[31] The United States would suffer significant economic and personnel losses in defending it. Escalation to the nuclear level or horizontal escalation to the opening of a second front would be distinct possibilities.[32]

The alliance's division of labour

The vast geography of the Indo-Pacific and the PLA's growing capabilities have made US military dominance less assured. The division of labour among allies has become correspondingly more critical.[33] The United States needs allied help to ensure active denial and posture resiliency.[34] Alliance division of labour has already been emerging in the Nordic and Baltic regions, accelerated by Finland's and Sweden's accession to NATO.[35] Since the region is continental and fairly confined, it is relatively easy to establish collective security arrangements there. East Asia's maritime geography, however, has made it challenging for US allies and partners to align strategic priorities in that region. South Korea and Japan tend to tailor their efforts to the most salient threats each faces – the former on building up its army to counter North Korean ground forces, the latter on improving its naval capabilities to counter the PLA Navy. Each ally's marginal defence expenditure therefore may not necessarily improve the deterrence posture of the alliance as a whole.[36] A division of labour could enhance deterrence by effectively integrating the respective states' contributions to the overall strategy of denial and cost-imposition.

Japan is the most important front-line maritime ally of the United States, while South Korea sits at the region's geopolitical fault line and is the only ally on the Asian mainland where US ground troops are stationed.[37] Yet Seoul and Tokyo have different stakes in the fate of Taiwan, and diverging roles to play in different scenarios. For instance, many Koreans, including figures in the political opposition, are unconvinced that Seoul would be compelled to get involved in a potential conflict over the island.[38] It faces a belligerent adversary armed with nuclear weapons directly across its border that could take advantage of South Korea's preoccupations during a Taiwan conflict.[39] In contrast, Japan's territorial security is directly affected by the fate of Taiwan, which is only 110 km from Yonaguni, Japan's western-most island. During a PLA military drill in 2022, one of nine missiles it fired landed within 80 km north of the island.[40] In addition, the Senkaku islands, disputed by Japan and China, are only about 120 nautical miles away from Taiwan. Japan accordingly changed its geostrategic focus from the northeast to the southwest in the 2010s.[41] Even so, and even though powerful legal and political constraints inhibiting Japan's use of military force are easing, its active participation in a potential Taiwan conflict is not guaranteed.[42] These qualifying factors reinforce the need for a clear delineation of allied roles and expectations in different scenarios.

In a blockade or some other form of grey-zone coercion, China would not attempt to establish overt political and military control over Taiwan; it would instead attempt to break the Taiwanese people's will to resist, thereby achieving de facto political control without bloodshed. The United States' paramount objective would be to deny China control of Taiwan by main-taining a roughly equivalent balance of military force.[43] To facilitate this goal, it would be reasonable for Washington to ask the two allies to impose additional costs on China for its soft intervention in Taiwan.[44] This would require them to establish a *cordon sanitaire* along the First Island Chain with deployed intelligence, surveillance and reconnaissance (ISR) assets and cyber capabilities, with Taiwan as the focal point. These allied initiatives would bolster Taiwan's will to resist Chinese coercion.

Japan's main task – in line with its putative role of supporting US power projection in the western Pacific[45] – would be to bolster air and sea control over Japanese territorial waters and adjacent areas to deny China's ability to escalate.[46] South Korea, for its part, would need to continue prioritising deterring North Korea, but could also impose prospective costs on Chinese escalation through its 'three-pillar' system's dual-use capabilities, which are designed primarily to pre-emptively destroy some North Korean forces, intercept others, and retaliate against a North Korean attack. Precision-strike capabilities could potentially distract Beijing's attention from the Taiwan Strait to the Korean Peninsula.[47]

More broadly, Seoul and Washington could consider bolstering South Korea's regional defence posture by integrating the three-pillar system into US military capabilities – including ISR and missile defence – which would likely unsettle and better deter Beijing, as well as North Korea.[48] The three-pillar system could also be integrated with Japan's counter-strike capability, enhancing Seoul's defence against Pyongyang's missiles and diverting Beijing's attention away from Taiwan.[49] China would, of course, regard the three allies' joining up defensive capabilities as antagonistic and destabilising, and could well respond with economic punishment, as it did when South Korea agreed to host the United States' Terminal High Altitude Area Defense system. The allies would therefore need to weigh costs and benefits carefully.

The allies should start planning for the worst-case scenario

Some or all of these measures could create uncertainties and distractions for Chinese policymakers, and perhaps dissuade them from resorting to armed conflict.[50] To make them feasible, the US needs to engineer stronger political–military relations between Taipei and Tokyo, and Taipei and Seoul. The three allies should also collaborate more robustly on ISR, both among themselves and with Taiwan, since the value of intelligence is greatest before the actual conflict begins, and on improving cyber capabilities. Seoul might consider establishing a network of ISR and uncrewed capabilities along its western and southern islets, where it has outstanding territorial disagreements with Beijing.

The three allies should also start planning more concretely for the worst-case scenario – China's military invasion of Taiwan. Such an event could culminate in a war between the United States and China with catastrophic consequences not only for East Asia but also globally.[51] For instance, China could pursue diversionary tactics, such as encouraging North Korean missile strikes against Japan, that could discourage Tokyo's active participation in a regional conflict by instilling fear in the Japanese population.[52] Closer strategic coordination among the three countries is crucial for preventing a regional conflagration. Their crucial tasks are to raise China's cost of initiating a military conflict and, in case deterrence fails, to deny Beijing an attractive pathway to vertical or horizontal military escalation.[53] In addition to collaborating on ISR, there are substantial areas for allied cooperation.

The extent to which the US armed forces based in Japan could operate freely in the region would depend heavily on political decisions made by the Japanese government.[54] Japan's key role is to facilitate the seamless deployment of Japan-based American forces to defend Taiwan. Japan will need to make steady progress in discussions with the United States on revamping the alliance command-and-control structure, which would make US intervention in a Taiwan scenario more credible.[55] Japanese civilian facilities close to Taiwan will play a vital role in enabling effective US intervention in a war, which means prioritising the optimisation of rear-echelon support for the US military and arranging for its access to civilian ports and airports, especially in islands adjacent to Taiwan. These steps will also be critical to the dispersal of US forces to reduce their vulnerability to PLA missile strikes.[56]

Japan's newly installed Ground Self-Defense Force (JGSDF) bases in Yonaguni, Ishigaki and Miyako, though primarily for its defence of its remote islands in conjunction with sea and air control, could help establish an anti-access/area-denial (A2/AD) bubble against China.[57] In particular, the long-range *Patriot* PAC-3 radars and the JGSDF Type-12 surface-to-ship missile systems that have been installed on some of these bases could complicate China's strategic calculations by restricting its freedom to manoeuvre in areas adjacent to Taiwan even if Tokyo's political and legal constraints precluded it from directly defending Taiwan.

With a full-scale Chinese invasion of Taiwan, South Korea would face an alliance-management dilemma. It may be predisposed to minimising its involvement for fear that any diversion of resources would leave it vulnerable to North Korea, yet such a stance would likely undermine Washington's confidence in Seoul. Hence, it would most likely hedge between partial neutrality and involvement.[58] Under partial neutrality, Seoul would acquiesce to the United States' redeployment of some of its assets in South Korea to the Taiwan Strait.[59] CSIS posits that the US would have to release two out of four squadrons, while the Institute for National Security Strategy, a South Korean government think tank, estimates that approximately 5,000 American personnel would be needed.[60]

Under partial involvement, South Korea could also provide rear-area support, cooperating with the United States on logistics (for instance, transport of troops and materiel via commercial vessels), intelligence (say, by way of its own unmanned assets) and non-combatant evacuation operations. These measures might not elicit major Chinese backlash, but could still satisfy alliance regional-security requirements.[61] This form of support would compromise South Korea's deterrent vis-à-vis North Korea to some degree, but probably not critically. Given that South Korea could be compelled to allow a partial redeployment of US troops and to provide some form of rear-area support in an actual contingency, Washington should consider increasing the number of ground troops stationed on Korean soil and planning for the redeployment of US air and naval assets to other theatres – including Taiwan.

*   *   *

A better coordinated trilateral defence relationship is a crucial component of an allied strategy of denial and cost imposition. An effective alliance division of labour would block Beijing's path to expanding a war geographically or adopting diversionary tactics. In addition, greater strategic cohesion between Seoul and Tokyo would reduce their vulnerability to attempts by adversaries to drive a wedge between them, which will become more important as authoritarian powers in the region such as China, Russia and North Korea increase their cooperation.[62] Despite recent strategic convergence between Seoul and Tokyo, long-standing political differences have not been completely resolved. Changes in political leadership could derail trilateral security cooperation. Nevertheless, clarifying the division of labour among the three states would further institutionalise security collaboration and thereby discourage future backsliding.

An effective division of labour between the United States, Japan and South Korea could also provide useful precedent and proof of concept for other defence frameworks in the region. One candidate would be that of Australia, Japan and the United States, which likewise calls for operational coordination between a front-line state (Japan), a security provider (the US) and a source of strategic depth (Australia) that enhances force survivability.[63] Another would be the US–Japan–Philippines trilateral defence relationship, for which tighter joint planning could improve regional security and stability, in particular by checking Chinese efforts to drive a wedge between the Philippines – another front-line state in maritime territorial disputes with China – and the United States.[64] Most importantly, optimised and formalised alliance divisions of labour can strengthen deterrence by increasing denial capabilities, preventing horizontal escalation and enhancing posture resilience, which in turn could dissuade China from using force.

Acknowledgements

The authors wish to thank Zack Cooper, Ju-Hyung Kim and Kevin Kim for their helpful suggestions.

Notes

[1] For various explanations of this dynamic, see Kent Calder, 'Securing Security Through Prosperity: The San Francisco System in Comparative Perspective', *Pacific Review*, vol. 17, no. 1, April 2004, pp. 135–57; Victor D. Cha, 'Powerplay: Origins of the U.S. Alliance System in Asia', *International Security*, vol. 34, no. 3, Winter 2009/2010, pp. 158–96; Christopher Hemmer and Peter J. Katzenstein, 'Why Is There No NATO in Asia? Collective Identity, Regionalism, and the Origins of Multilateralism', *International Organization*, vol. 56, no. 3, Summer 2002, pp. 575–607; and Yasuhiro Izumikawa, 'Network Connections and the Emergence of the Hub-and-spokes Alliance System in East Asia', *International Security*, vol. 45, no. 2, Fall 2020, pp. 7–50.

[2] See Michael Beckley, 'Delusions of Détente: Why America and China Will Be Enduring Rivals', *Foreign Affairs*, vol. 102, no. 5, September/October 2023, pp. 8–25; Andrea Kendall-Taylor and Richard Fontaine, 'The Axis of Upheaval: How America's Adversaries Are Uniting to Overturn the Global Order', *Foreign Affairs*, vol. 103, no. 3, May/June 2024, pp. 50–63; Tomohiko Satake, 'Explaining the Difference Between Australia–Japan and Japan–ROK Security Cooperation', *Pacific Review*, September 2024; and Robert Ward, 'A Fragile Convergence: The US–Japan–South Korea Camp David Summit',

Survival, vol. 65, no. 5, October–November 2023, pp. 25–36.

3 US Department of Defense, '"The New Convergence in the Indo-Pacific": Remarks by Secretary of Defense Lloyd J. Austin III at the 2024 Shangri-La Dialogue', 1 June 2024, https://www.defense.gov/News/Speeches/Speech/Article/3793580/the-new-convergence-in-the-indo-pacific-remarks-by-secretary-of-defense-lloyd-j/.

4 See White House, 'Commitment to Consult', 18 August 2023, https://www.whitehouse.gov/briefing-room/statements-releases/2023/08/18/commitment-to-consult/; and Tongfi Kim, 'By Any Other Name? The Camp David Summit, US–Japan–South Korea Trilateral Security Cooperation and Military Alliances', CSDS Policy Brief, 22 January 2024, https://csds.vub.be/publication/by-any-other-name-the-camp-david-summit-us-japan-south-korea-trilateral-security-cooperation-and-military-alliances/.

5 See US Department of State, 'US–Japan–Republic of Korea Trilateral Meeting', 31 May 2024, https://www.state.gov/briefings-foreign-press-centers/trilateral-press-briefing.

6 See Adam P. Liff, 'Beyond Territorial Defense …? The US–Japan and US–ROK Alliances and a "Taiwan Strait Contingency"', *Pacific Review*, September 2022, pp. 1– 30.

7 See Stacie L. Pettyjohn and Becca Wasser, 'No I in Team: Integrated Deterrence with Allies and Partners', Center for a New American Security, 14 December 2022, https://s3.us-east-1.amazonaws.com/files.cnas.org/documents/IntegratedDeterrence_Final-1.pdf.

8 See, for instance, Brendan Rittenhouse Green and Caitlin Talmadge, 'Then What? Assessing the Military Implications of Chinese Control of Taiwan', *International Security*, vol. 47, no. 1, Summer 2022, pp. 7–45.

9 See Burgess Laird, 'War Control: Chinese Writings on the Control of Escalation in Crisis and Conflict', Center for New American Security, 30 March 2017, https://s3.us-east-1.amazonaws.com/files.cnas.org/documents/CNASReport-ChineseDescalation-Final_2023-06-13-155721.pdf; and Andrew Scobell, *China's Use of Military Force: Beyond the Great Wall and the Long March* (Cambridge: Cambridge University Press, 2003).

10 Such options have gained traction in recent years due to the rising costs of full-scale military operations and technological advances in the quasi-military capabilities of non-kinetic tools. See Michael J. Mazarr, *Mastering the Gray Zone: Understanding a Changing Era of Conflict* (Carlisle, PA: US Army War College Press, 2015).

11 See Aaron Bateman, 'Undersea Cables and the Vulnerability of American Power', *Engelsberg Ideas*, 7 May 2024, https://engelsbergideas.com/essays/undersea-cables-and-the-vulnerability-of-american-power/; and Jonathan Chin, 'Taiwan Must Harden Undersea Cables, NSB Says', *Taipei Times*, 2 May 2024, https://www.taipeitimes.com/News/taiwan/archives/2024/05/02/2003817262.

12 See Bonny Lin et al., 'Tracking China's April 2023 Military Exercises

Around Taiwan', *ChinaPower*, 15 September 2024, https://chinapower. csis.org/tracking-chinas-april-2023-military-exercises-around-taiwan/; Jacob Stokes, 'Resisting China's Gray Zone Military Pressure on Taiwan', Center for a New American Security, December 2022, https://s3.us-east-1. amazonaws.com/files.cnas.org/ documents/GreyZone_Final.pdf; and 'US Releases Video of Encounter with Chinese Warship Near Taiwan', Voice of America, 5 June 2023, https://www. voanews.com/a/us-releases-video-of-encounter-with-chinese-warship-near-taiwan/7123398.html.

13 During the Cuban Missile Crisis, the Kennedy administration used the term 'quarantine' instead of blockade to neutralise military connotations. In practice, a 'blockade' and 'quarantine' have essentially identical objectives: the imposition of political will by way of access denial short of full-scale invasion.

14 See Chris Buckley et al., 'How China Could Choke Taiwan', *New York Times*, 25 August 2022, https://www.nytimes. com/interactive/2022/08/25/world/asia/ china-taiwan-conflict-blockade.html.

15 Imported crude oil, coal and coal products, and liquefied natural gas, all transported by sea, accounted for 44%, 30% and 19% respectively of Taiwan's total energy demands in 2022. Joseph Webster, 'Does Taiwan's Massive Reliance on Energy Imports Put Its Security at Risk?', Atlantic Council, 7 July 2023, https://www.atlanticcouncil. org/blogs/new-atlanticist/does-taiwans-massive-reliance-on-energy-imports-put-its-security-at-risk/.

16 See Eric Heginbotham et al., *The US–China Military Scorecard: Forces, Geography, and the Evolving Balance of Power 1996–2017* (Santa Monica, CA: RAND Corporation, 2015).

17 See Yasuhiro Kawami, 'Analysis of the Air and Maritime Blockade Operations Against Taiwan by the People's Liberation Army – What Can Be Inferred from Military Exercises, etc.', Sasakawa Peace Foundation, 7 June 2023, https://www.spf.org/ japan-us-taiwan-research/en/article/ kawakami_01.html. Beijing has closely monitored the situation in Ukraine and is increasingly worried about the possibility of a 'proxy' conflict over Taiwan. See Bonny Lin and Brian Hart, 'Accelerating Profound Changes Unseen in a Century: Chinese Assessments of and Responses to Russia's Invasion of Ukraine', in Hal Brands (ed.), *War in Ukraine: Conflict, Strategy, and the Return of a Fractured World* (Baltimore, MD: Johns Hopkins University Press, 2024), pp. 239–57.

18 See Jude Blanchette and Hal Brands, 'Not Just Boots on the Beach: How China Can Use Deception, Confusion, and Incrementalism to Change the Status Quo on Taiwan', *Marshall Papers*, Center for Strategic and International Studies, 25 July 2024, https:// csis-website-prod.s3.amazonaws. com/s3fs-public/2024-07/240725_ Blanchette_Boots_Beach_0. pdf?VersionId=8NIi72JHcsPUkM4qo_ scVRLVCx.jrl8z.

19 See Cheng-fung Lu, 'China's Claim of the Taiwan Strait as "Inland Waters" and the Kinmen Incident', *Prospects & Perspectives*, no. 14, Prospect Foundation, 6 March 2024, https:// www.pf.org.tw/en/pfen/33-10594.html.

20 Such a possibility is discussed in Lefteris Kafatos, 'Minemura Kenji: How China Might Force Taiwan to Unify in 2025', *Japan Lens*, 4 February 2024, https://thejapanlens.com/2024/02/04/minemura-kenji-how-china-might-force-reunification-with-taiwan-in-2025/. For more on how China might use lawfare, especially the Anti-Secession Law, see Bonny Lin and I-Chung Lai, 'Employing "Non-peaceful" Means Against Taiwan: The Implications of China's Anti-Secession Law', Center for Strategic and International Studies, 15 October 2024, https://www.csis.org/analysis/employing-non-peaceful-means-against-taiwan.

21 See Kafatos, 'Minemura Kenji'.

22 See Jeffrey G. Barlow, 'The Cuban Missile Crisis', in Bruce A. Elleman and S.C.M. Paine (eds), *Naval Blockades and Seapower: Strategies and Counter-strategies, 1805–2005* (Abingdon: Routledge, 2006), pp. 157–67.

23 See John Dotson, 'The PLA's Joint Sword 2024B Exercise: Continuing Political Warfare and Creeping Territorial Encroachment', Global Taiwan Institute, 30 October 2024, https://globaltaiwan.org/2024/10/the-joint-sword-2024b-exercise/; Amrita Jash, 'China's Military Exercises Around Taiwan: Trends and Patterns', Global Taiwan Institute, 2 October 2024, https://globaltaiwan.org/2024/10/chinas-military-exercises-around-taiwan-trends-and-patterns/; S. Philip Hsu, 'Domestic Power Reshuffles in 2022 and U.S.–Taiwan–China Relations', Brookings Policy Brief, May 2023, https://www.brookings.edu/wp-content/uploads/2023/05/FP_20230515_taiwan_hsu.pdf; and Bonny Lin and Brian Hart, 'How Is China Responding to the Inauguration of Taiwan's President William Lai?', *ChinaPower*, 5 November 2024, https://chinapower.csis.org/china-respond-inauguration-taiwan-william-lai-joint-sword-2024a-military-exercise/.

24 See Kristen Gunness and Phillip C. Saunders, *Averting Escalation and Avoiding War: Lessons from the 1995–1996 Taiwan Strait Crisis* (Washington DC: National Defense University Press, 2022).

25 See John J. Mearsheimer, *The Tragedy of Great Power Politics* (New York: W. W. Norton & Co., 2014).

26 See Michael Martina and David Brunnstrom, 'CIA Chief Warns Against Underestimating Xi's Ambitions Toward Taiwan', Reuters, 2 February 2023, https://www.reuters.com/world/cia-chief-says-chinas-xi-little-sobered-by-ukraine-war-2023-02-02/. See also Katsuji Nakazawa, 'Analysis: Xi Floats 2027 as a New Milestone Year', Nikkei Asia, 10 December 2020, https://asia.nikkei.com/Editor-s-Picks/China-up-close/Analysis-Xi-floats-2027-as-new-milestone-year.

27 See Andrew F. Krepinevich, 'The Big One: Preparing for a Long War with China', *Foreign Affairs*, vol. 103, no. 1, January/February 2024, pp. 104–18.

28 See 'America and China Are Preparing for a War over Taiwan', *The Economist*, 9 May 2023, https://www.economist.com/briefing/2023/03/09/america-and-china-are-preparing-for-a-war-over-taiwan.

29 See Iskander Rehman, *Planning for Protraction: A Historically Informed*

Approach to Great-power War and Sino-US Competition (Abingdon: Routledge, 2023).

30   On the difficulties the United States might face, see Mark F. Cancian, Matthew Cancian and Eric Heginbotham, 'The First Battle of the Next War: Wargaming a Chinese Invasion of Taiwan', Center for Strategic and International Studies, January 2023, https://csis-website-prod.s3.amazonaws.com/s3fs-public/publication/230109_Cancian_FirstBattle_NextWar.pdf?VersionId=XlDrfCUHet8OZSOYW_9PWx3xtcoScGHn.

31   See Iskander Rehman, 'Britain's Strange Defeat: The 1941 Fall and Its Lessons for Taiwan', *War on the Rocks*, 28 May 2024, https://warontherocks.com/2024/05/britains-strange-defeat-the-1941-fall-of-crete-and-its-lessons-for-taiwan/.

32   See Joshua Rovner, 'Two Kinds of Catastrophe: Nuclear Escalation and Protracted War in Asia', *Journal of Strategic Studies*, vol. 40, no. 5, February 2017, pp. 696–730.

33   See Kelly A. Grieco and Jennifer Kavanagh, 'The Elusive Indo-Pacific Coalition: Why Geography Matters', *Washington Quarterly*, vol. 47, no. 1, Spring 2024, pp. 103–21.

34   See Hal Brands and Zack Cooper, 'Dilemmas of Deterrence: The United States' Smart New Strategy Has Six Daunting Trade-offs', *Marshall Papers*, Center for Strategic and International Studies, March 2024, https://csis-website-prod.s3.amazonaws.com/s3fs-public/2024-03/240312_Brands_Dilemmas_Deterrence.pdf.

35   See Matti Pesu, 'NATO in the North: The Emerging Division of Labour in Northern European Security', *FIIA Briefing Paper*, no. 370, September 2023, https://www.fiia.fi/wp-content/uploads/2023/09/bp370_nato-in-the-north.pdf; and J. Andrés Gannon, 'What Can Finland and Sweden Learn from the Baltic States' Defence Specialisation?', NDC Policy Brief, no. 15, NATO Defence College, 27 September 2022 (updated 22 March 2024), https://www.ndc.nato.int/news/news.php?icode=1741.

36   On target balancing, see Steven E. Lobell, 'A Granular Theory of Balancing', *International Studies Quarterly*, vol. 62, no. 3, September 2018, pp. 593–605.

37   On Japan, see Ju Hyung Kim, 'What Would Be Japan's Role in a New Korean War?', *War on the Rocks*, 3 October 2024, https://warontherocks.com/2024/10/what-would-be-japans-role-in-a-new-korean-war/; and Takuya Matsuda, 'Explaining Japan's Post-Cold War Security Policy Trajectory: Maritime Realism', *Australian Journal of International Affairs*, vol. 74, no. 6, June 2020, pp. 687–703. On Korea, see Jaehan Park, 'The Korean Peninsula: The Geopolitical Pivot of Northeast Asia', *Orbis*, vol. 65, no. 2, April 2021, pp. 322–41.

38   See 'DP Chief Lee's "Xie Xie" Comment Sparks Controversy', KBS, 28 March 2024, https://world.kbs.co.kr/service/news_view.htm?lang=e&Seq_Code=184519.

39   See Sungmin Cho, 'The Crisis in East Asia', *War on the Rocks*, 4 April 2024, https://warontherocks.com/2024/04/the-crisis-in-east-asia-korea-or-taiwan/; and Hanbyeol Sohn, 'How the Next Taiwan Crisis Connects

to Korea', *PacNet*, 19 March 2024, https://pacforum.org/publications/pacnet-17-how-the-next-taiwan-crisis-connects-to-korea/.

40 See 'Chinese-fired Ballistic Missiles Fall into Japan's EEZ', Kyodo News, 5 August 2022, https://english.kyodonews.net/news/2022/08/a901e23a7695-urgent-chinese-fired-ballistic-missiles-fall-into-japans-eez-govt.html.

41 See Lionel P. Fatton, 'Sailing Close to the Wind: Japan's Forward Deterrence Posture Toward the Taiwan Strait', *Asian Security*, vol. 20, no. 1, January 2024, pp. 1–19; and Alessio Patalano, 'Seapower and Sino-Japanese Relations in the East China Sea', *Asian Affairs*, vol. 45, no. 1, February 2014, pp. 34–54.

42 On this point, see Jeffrey W. Hornung et al., *Fighting Abroad from an Ally's Land: Challenges and Opportunities for US Forces in the Indo-Pacific* (Santa Monica, CA: RAND Corporation, 2024), https://www.rand.org/pubs/research_reports/RRA1985-1.html; Adam P. Liff, 'The US–Japan Alliance and Taiwan', *Asia Policy*, vol. 17, no. 3, July 2022, pp. 125–60; and Mike Mochizuki, 'Tokyo's Taiwan Conundrum: What Can Japan Do to Prevent War?', *Washington Quarterly*, vol. 45, no. 3, Fall 2022, pp. 81–107.

43 See Elbridge Colby, *The Strategy of Denial: American Defense in an Age of Great Power Conflict* (New Haven, CT: Yale University Press, 2021); and Grieco and Kavanagh, 'The Elusive Indo-Pacific Coalition'.

44 See Bradford A. Lee, 'Strategic Interaction: Theory and History for Practitioners', in Thomas G. Mahnken (ed.), *Competitive Strategies for the 21st Century: Theory, History, and Practice*

(Stanford, CA: Stanford University Press, 2012), pp. 28–46.

45 See Alessio Patalano, *Japan as a Sea Power: Imperial Legacy, Wartime Experience, and the Making of the Post-war Navy* (London: Bloomsbury, 2015), p. 152.

46 See Jeffrey W. Hornung, *Japan's Potential Contributions in an East China Sea Contingency* (Santa Monica, CA: RAND Corporation, 2020), https://www.rand.org/pubs/research_reports/RRA314-1.html; and Tomohisa Takei, 'Kaiyō Shinjidai ni Okeru Kaijyōjieitai' [JMSDF in the new maritime era], *Hatou*, vol. 11, 2008, pp. 2–29.

47 For a general description of the three-pillar system, see Manseok Lee and Hyeongpil Ham, 'South Korea's Conventional Forces Buildup: The Search for Strategic Stability', *War on the Rocks*, 16 April 2021, https://warontherocks.com/2021/04/south-koreas-conventional-forces-buildup-the-search-for-strategic-stability/; and Republic of Korea, Ministry of National Defense, '2022 Defense White Paper', February 2023, pp. 57–62, https://www.mnd.go.kr/user/mndEN/upload/pblictn/PBLICTNEBOOK_20230728040601910.pdf.

48 See Cha Du Hyeogn and Yang Uk, 'Sam-chook Chegye-ui Baljeon Bangyang: Dokjajeonryuk-eso Dongmaeng Jeonryuk-uroeui Balsang Junhwan' [Paths for three-pillar system: from autonomous force to an allied force], Issue Brief, Asan Institute, 14 August 2023, https://www.asaninst.org/contents/3; and Sohn, 'How the Next Taiwan Crisis Connects to Korea'.

49 See Ju Hyung Kim, 'Matching Japan's Counterstrike Capability with South

Korea's Three Axis System', *Diplomat*, 3 October 2024, https://thediplomat-com. proxy1.library.jhu.edu/2024/10/match ing-japans-counterstrike-capability-with-south-koreas-three-axis-system/.

50 See Thomas G. Mahnken, 'A Maritime Strategy to Deal with China', *Proceedings*, vol. 148, no. 2, February 2022, p. 1,428, https://www.usni.org/magazines/proceedings/2022/february/maritime-strategy-deal-china.

51 See, for example, Rachel Metz and Erik Sand, 'Defending Taiwan: But … What Are the Costs?', *Washington Quarterly*, vol. 46, no. 4, Winter 2023, pp. 65–81.

52 See Jaganath Sankaran, *Bombing to Provoke: Rockets, Missiles, and Drones as Instruments of Fear and Coercion* (Oxford: Oxford University Press, 2023).

53 See Markus Garlauskas, 'The United States and Its Allies Must Be Ready to Deter a Two-front War and Nuclear Attacks in East Asia', Atlantic Council, 16 August 2023, https://www.atlantic council.org/in-depth-research-reports/report/the-united-states-and-its-allies-must-be-ready-to-deter-a-two-front-war-and-nuclear-attacks-in-east-asia/.

54 See Hornung et al., *Fighting Abroad from an Ally's Land*.

55 Jeffrey Hornung and Zack Cooper, 'Shifting the US–Japan Alliance from Coordination to Integration', *War on the Rocks*, 2 August 2024, https://warontherocks.com/2024/08/shifting-the-u-s-japan-alliance-from-coordination-to-integration/; and Christopher B. Johnstone and Jim Schoff, 'A Vital Next Step for the US–Japan Alliance: Command and Control Modernization', Center for Strategic and International Studies, 1 February 2024, https://www.csis.org/analysis/vital-next-step-us-japan-alliance-command-and-control-modernization.

56 See Stacie L. Pettyjohn, Andrew Metrick and Becca Wasser, 'The Kadena Conundrum: Developing a Resilient Indo-Pacific Posture', *War on the Rocks*, 1 December 2022, https://warontherocks.com/2022/12/the-kadena-conundrum-developing-a-resilient-indo-pacific-posture/.

57 See Michael Beckley, 'The Emerging Military Balance in East Asia: How China's Neighbors Can Check Chinese Naval Expansion', *International Security*, vol. 42, no. 2, Fall 2017, pp. 78–119; and Hornung, *Japan's Potential Contributions in an East China Sea Contingency*.

58 Peter K. Lee, 'South Korea's Entanglement in a Taiwan Contingency', *Asia Policy*, vol. 19, no. 2, April 2024, pp. 20–8.

59 Although the details have not been worked out, the legal basis for such a possibility was presented in the putative 'strategic flexibility' agree-ment of 2006 whereby Seoul would 'understand' the deployment of US assets in South Korea to other theatres. See Sean McCormack, 'United States and the Republic of Korea Launch Strategic Consultation for Allied Partnership', US Department of State, 19 January 2006, https://2001-2009.state.gov/r/pa/prs/ps/2006/59447.htm.

60 See Cancian, Cancian and Heginbotham, 'The First Battle of the Next War', pp. 60–1; and Kim Sang-jin and Jang Yoon-seo, 'Nuga Jibgwon-haedo Han Gunsa Yeokhal Hwakdae Yogu, "Big Card" Joonbi Hara', [Korea's increased military role expected whoever wins the election,

'big card' is needed], *JoongAng*, 5 August 2024, https://www.joongang. co.kr/article/25268426.

61 See Oriana Skylar Mastro and Sungmin Cho, 'How South Korea Can Contribute to the Defense of Taiwan', *Washington Quarterly*, vol. 45, no. 3, Fall 2022, pp. 109–29.

62 See Thomas J. Christensen, *Worse Than a Monolith: Alliance Politics and Problems of Coercive Diplomacy in Asia* (Princeton, NJ: Princeton University Press, 2011); and Maximilian Ernst and Tongfi Kim, 'Smart Balancers Kill Many Birds with Few Stones – Sino-Russian Security Cooperation in the Maritime Domain', *Naval War College Review*, vol. 76, no. 2, Spring 2023, pp. 39–65. On wedge strategies, see Yasuhiro Izumikawa, 'To Coerce or Reward? Theorizing Wedge Strategies in Alliance Politics', *Security Studies*, vol. 22, no. 3, July 2013, pp. 498–531.

63 See Andrew Carr, 'Australia's Archipelagic Deterrence', *Survival*, vol. 65, no. 4, August–September 2023, pp. 79–100; and Thomas Wilkins, 'U.S.–Japan–Australia Trilateralism: The Inner Core of Regional Order Building and Deterrence in the Indo-Pacific', *Asia Policy*, vol. 19, no. 2, April 2024, pp. 159–85.

64 See Gregory B. Poling and Japhet Quitzon, 'Sustaining the US–Philippines–Japan Triad', *CSIS Briefs*, February 2024, https:// csis-website-prod.s3.amazonaws. com/s3fs-public/2024-02/240212_Poling_Sustaining_Triad.pdf; and Andrew Taffer, 'The Puzzle of Chinese Escalation vs Restraint in the South China Sea', *War on the Rocks*, 26 July 2024, https:// warontherocks.com/2024/07/ the-puzzle-of-chinese-escalation-vs-restraint-in-the-south-china-sea/.

Copyright © 2025 The International Institute for Strategic Studies

NATO's New Members and the Baltic Strategic Balance

Victor Duenow

The strategic balance in the Baltic Sea changed dramatically with the end of the Cold War and the accession of the three Baltic states as NATO members. Still, NATO would have struggled to establish control in the Baltic and, after Russia's annexation of Crimea in 2014, the Alliance was challenged to fully reassure its exposed and vulnerable new members. While Finland and particularly Sweden inched towards more cooperative relations with their NATO neighbours, their traditionally staunch neutrality complicated both regional strategic calculations and Alliance military planning. Although Russian revanchism was increasingly straining that status, it appeared unlikely to budge.[1]

Furthermore, Russia's comprehensively modernised anti-access/area-denial (A2/AD) capabilities in the Baltic Sea were considered a highly sophisticated threat whose penetration would incur prohibitive costs for enemy forces. Russia made a credible case that its advanced A2/AD systems formed a nearly insurmountable bulwark and that any attempt to penetrate its defensive network would be costly and futile.[2] Kaliningrad, which Moscow fortified, became a Russian bastion that extended Russia's A2/AD capabilities into the Baltic Sea, enabling Russian forces to impede NATO access to the sea and hold NATO member states at risk of long-range strikes.[3] Seasoned

Victor Duenow is a commander in the US Navy and a PhD candidate at the US Naval Postgraduate School.

Survival | vol. 67 no. 1 | February–March 2025 | pp. 89–98   https://doi.org/10.1080/00396338.2025.2459021

and highly reputable analysts did suggest that these capabilities were not as formidable as the Russians advertised.[4] But without actual combat to test them, NATO was compelled to err on the side of caution.

The accession of Finland and Sweden to the Alliance, ending their neutrality, and the lacklustre performance of Russia's A2/AD assets in the Black Sea, exposing significant gaps in its A2/AD architecture, have afforded NATO an advantageous position in the Baltic Sea and allowed it to assume supposedly the most capable posture in the Baltic.

Russian maritime capabilities

Russia's presumed ability to execute effective maritime operations and keep NATO from defending its member nations became a real concern – especially for the Baltic states – in light of Russia's overtly hostile actions in Ukraine before it invaded in February 2022. Ukraine, however, has been able to roll back Russian ground-based A2/AD systems by destroying several of its components, including S-400, S-300 and *Pantsir* air-defence systems.[5] Robert Dalsjö and his team, leading Swedish analysts, correctly anticipated that Russia's most sophisticated A2/AD systems would fall short due to ranges restricted to the radar horizon at sea level, a limited ability to track sufficient targets, ammunition shortages and difficulty detecting low-flying targets.[6] In fact, Russia's assets have been unable to provide adequate cover for Russia's Black Sea Fleet against Ukraine's unconventional and missile attacks both at sea and in port, forcing Russia to withdraw vessels from Crimea and the western Black Sea to safeguard its fleet.

Ukraine also dealt a stunning blow to the Russian Navy when it sank the *Moskva*, its Black Sea flagship and supposedly its most capable naval A2/AD asset in the region. A string of other naval losses ensued, as Russia lost a third of its naval assets in the Black Sea, including a submarine.[7] Russia's inability to maintain maritime supremacy there allowed Ukraine to continue grain exports without having to renew its original grain deal with Russia.

Likewise, Russian air power has failed to live up to its pre-war hype. Although its missile systems have successfully struck targets, Russia has been unable to produce them in quantities sufficient to achieve a decisive advantage. Crewed aircraft have been even more problematic, unable to destroy Ukraine's A2/AD assets and generally limited to front-line attacks as opposed to deep penetration into Ukraine.[8] The relegation of Russian crewed aircraft to marginal roles has been key to Ukraine's ability to prolong the war and hold off Russia.

Asymmetric maritime-warfare tools remain potentially useful to Russia. It possesses one of the largest sea-mine inventories in the world, estimated at over 250,000 munitions.[9] Combining these mines with irregular deployment platforms such as merchant or fishing vessels could allow Russia to gain a momentary advantage in terms of sea denial, mitigating deficiencies in its A2/AD capabilities. Russia's capacity to damage undersea infrastructure such as cables and pipelines by means of special-purpose vessels including both submarines and surface craft, in which it has invested significant resources, affords it the most formidable asymmetric means of disruption.[10] Cables and pipelines are particularly consequential targets because they have lengthy repair or replacement times, attacks on them are presumptively if not inexorably covert, and they are difficult to deter. They would be especially devastating to the Baltic states and Finland, which designed and built their infrastructure precisely to reduce their dependency on Russia.[11] And any interference with undersea infrastructure connecting the Baltic states to the rest of NATO would reduce its ability to counter other Russian moves.

In the last two years, NATO has substantially improved its monitoring and patrolling to address such threats. Capping a series of recent incidents during a period of grey-zone tensions, Finnish authorities in late 2024 detained a Russian shadow-fleet tanker, the *Eagle S*, on suspicion of sabotaging undersea cabling by deliberately dragging its anchor.[12] A key issue is the extent to which Russia could sustain an asymmetric strategy beyond the grey zone in a period of full-on confrontation.

A NATO lake?

The vulnerability of the Baltic states to Russia's incursions out of its Baltic Fleet base in Kaliningrad and Russia's use of Kaliningrad to deny rapid maritime reinforcement have long been NATO concerns.[13] The addition of Finland and Sweden to NATO has undoubtedly shifted the strategic balance in the Baltic in NATO's favour, and the underperformance of the Russian military in Ukraine and the Black Sea are added factors. But the confined and complex character of the Baltic still means that both NATO and Russia will, in effect, be shooting fish in a barrel, so both will continue to face significant challenges. Dubbing the Baltic Sea a 'NATO lake' remains unwarranted, even hubristic.[14] As John Deni has noted, 'the members of the Alliance on the Baltic Sea … and the United States confront a dynamic regional security picture that will require further refinement of capabilities and increased capacity as well as more considered efforts in collective cooperation through both NATO and the European Union', and the amount and versatility of allied naval power available for the region remains limited.[15] That said, there are a number of ways in which the Alliance could exploit its new-found advantage.

The expanded access that Sweden and Finland provide diminishes Russia's capacity to deny NATO use of the Baltic Sea. By accessing the Baltic through Sweden and Finland, NATO can bypass the Kaliningrad *oblast* and reinforce the Baltic states more directly and rapidly. While the Baltic states are still the most vulnerable members of NATO, they have more strategic depth. Sweden and Finland can now provide ports for resupply, staging areas for ground forces and additional basing for aircraft. The corresponding ability to procure resources – gear, munitions and provisions – locally shortens the length of supply chains, diversifies resource bases, increases sustainability and resilience, and makes it more difficult for Russia to sever NATO supply lines. Finland and Sweden also have specific naval capabilities – such as Sweden's submarine fleet – tailored to the Baltic's unique characteristics.[16]

The Kaliningrad *oblast* no longer looms as an insurmountable obstacle. The area still hosts Russian A2/AD capabilities that can hold NATO maritime assets at risk, but their effective range is significantly shorter than once believed. Because Kaliningrad lies on the southern shore of the Baltic, NATO forces can avoid serious threats by skirting the northern shore and gain additional distance by transiting Swedish territorial waters.[17] To further counter Kaliningrad's A2/AD and air-reconnaissance capabilities, NATO could garrison the Swedish island of Gotland.[18] By preventing Russian aircraft from operating freely and identifying NATO vessels, NATO forces can limit Russian anti-ship missiles to line-of-sight targets.[19] A2/AD assets in Kaliningrad would also be priority NATO targets in any conflict with Russia, which limits their effectiveness over time.

An expanded NATO enlarges its scope for blockade and sea denial vis-à-vis Russia. The Danish Strait is now well within NATO territory, allowing the Alliance to establish a low-risk blockade of any Russian maritime traffic entering or exiting the Baltic Sea. The region remains a vital energy corridor for the transportation of Russian crude oil and petroleum, accounting for over 70% of Russia's oil and petroleum exports and over 50% of its energy revenues.[20] Denying Russia its use could prove devastating to its economy. Beyond that, NATO could in theory hold the Russian navy in port in Kaliningrad and prevent its use of St Petersburg by way of naval mines and more advanced munitions, readily deployable by virtue of NATO's air and naval superiority, whose effectiveness Russia's short Baltic coastline would only amplify.[21] In the unlikely event that Russia were willing to allow its vessels to risk transiting minefields, they would have to contend with formidable NATO air and naval power.

NATO could in theory hold the Russian navy in port

If Russian A2/AD assets have been unable to prevent Ukraine – which lacks a conventional navy – from sending unarmed vessels carrying grain across the Black Sea, it is unlikely that Russia would be able to prevent a robustly equipped NATO maritime force from doing so. NATO's increased conventional superiority will likely prompt Moscow to adopt a more asymmetric strategy. Asymmetric measures, though potentially effective, are not a panacea. While mining could theoretically impede NATO maritime operations, the Baltic is heavily trafficked and monitored, and NATO and the Baltic states have invested heavily in deploying countermeasures and practising their application. Countering mines is not a simple or quick mission, but Moscow's ability to interfere with it will likely be considerably reduced.[22] Although Russia would have the advantage of surprise in executing maritime manoeuvres at the onset of hostilities, it would diminish with time and repetition.[23] Its use of cyber attacks to enhance surprise has been less consequential than predicted.[24]

Russia could also mount an insurgent campaign in the Baltic similar to the one Ukraine marshalled against Russia in the Black Sea. But NATO warships have proven more capable than Russian ones of destroying incoming missiles, most recently in the Red Sea against the Yemen-based Houthi rebel group.[25] These same vessels have also demonstrated the ability to offensively strike targets with reliability and precision, and key NATO members have developed weapons and procedures for effectively resisting small-boat swarm attacks.[26] This has required the deployment of the most capable NATO vessels, equipped with high-end systems. In the Baltic Sea, deploying any conventional naval forces will involve risk, especially at the onset of any confrontation. That is one reason Alliance navies themselves are increasingly exploring the deployment of uncrewed platforms in confined waters. At the same time, although Russian uncrewed drones could threaten NATO assets, the Alliance's sophisticated defences and countermeasures make Russian success on a par with Ukraine's in the Black Sea improbable.

*   *   *

NATO has some way to go before it can realise these potential advantages. Increased funding and procurement at the national level are required.[27] The fact that, in response to the *Eagle S* incident, NATO launched yet another new surveillance and patrolling mission, *Baltic Sentry*, highlighted that more needs to be done. The scale of the challenge of defending the Baltic states remains formidable, and involves more than the Baltic Sea, as their exposure to direct land attack remains acute.

Moreover, while the Russo-Ukrainian war has transformed the Alliance's maritime posture, its maritime strategy is still a work in progress. NATO has produced a new strategic framework, the Concept for Deterrence and Defence of the Euro-Atlantic Area, that is purpose-built for 'a new era of confrontation with Russia'.[28] New regional-defence plans for the Northwest, Centre and Southeast quadrants have also emerged. Regarding the Northeast Quadrant, however, which NATO regional commands are responsible for what specific parts of the Baltic remains unsettled, reflecting the divergence among the Baltic and Nordic states on where their priorities should lie, as well as burden-sharing issues.[29] Germany has just inaugurated a new maritime headquarters for the Baltic, but exactly how it will work in relation to other NATO commands has yet to be determined.[30]

Indeed, the effective regionalisation of NATO that expansion has brought has introduced new and considerable planning challenges.[31] These hurdles indicate that NATO, though it now appears to have the upper hand, is not going to have a cakewalk in the Baltic. Notwithstanding the underperformance of Russia's A2/AD capabilities, its Black Sea experience has shown that confined waters are a tough environment for any surface naval forces and the Ukrainians have shown that it doesn't take exquisite technology to stiffly challenge them.

Notes

1 See Kevin A. Chaney, *NATO or Neutrality: Decisions by Denmark, Finland, Norway, and Sweden* (Monterey, CA: Naval Postgraduate School, 2017); Leo G. Michel, 'Finland, Sweden, and NATO from "Virtual" to Formal Allies?', *Strategic Forum*, no. 265, February 2011, https://ndupress.ndu.edu/Portals/68/ Documents/stratforum/SF-265.pdf; and Dov S. Zakheim, 'The United States and the Nordic Countries During the Cold War', *Cooperation and Conflict*, vol. 33, no. 2, June 1998, pp. 115–29.

2 See Keir Giles and Mathieu Boulegue, 'Russia's A2/AD Capabilities: Real and Imagined', *Parameters*, vol. 49, nos 1–2, Spring/Summer 2019, pp. 21–36.

3 See Sergey Sukhankin, 'David vs. Goliath: Kaliningrad Oblast as Russia's A2/AD "Bubble"', *Scandinavian Journal of Military Studies*, vol. 2, no. 1, August 2019, pp. 95–110.

4 See Robert Dalsjö, Christofer Berglund and Michael Jonsson, 'Bursting the Bubble – Russian A2/AD in the Baltic Sea Region: Capabilities, Countermeasures, and Implications',
Swedish Defense Research Agency (FOI), March 2019, p. 26; and Robert Dalsjö and Michael Jonsson, 'More than Decorative, Less than Decisive: Russian A2/AD Capabilities and NATO', *Survival*, vol. 63, no. 5, October–November 2021, pp. 169–90.

5 See Isabel Brugen, 'Three Russian S-400 Reportedly Destroyed as Moscow Says ATACMS "Thwarted"', *Newsweek*, 27 October 2023, https://www.newsweek. com/russian-s-400-destroyed-attack-ukraine-atacms-1838477; and Sakshi Tiwari, 'Russian S-400 "Falls Apart" in Ukraine War; Moscow Forced to Pull Its SAMs from Kaliningrad to Frontlines – UK', *EurAsian Times*, 27 November 2023, https://www.eurasiantimes.com/ left-borders-with-nato-nations-s400/.

6 See Dalsjö, Berglund and Jonsson, 'Bursting the Bubble'.

7 See Nick Childs, 'The Black Sea in the Shadow of War', *Survival*, vol. 65, no. 3, June–July 2023, pp. 25–36; and Paul Kirby, 'Russian Landing Ship *Caesar Kunikov* Sunk off Crimea, Says Ukraine', BBC News, 14 February

2024, https://www.bbc.com/news/world-europe-68292602.

8   See Matthew S. Galamison and Michael B. Petersen, 'Airpower Lessons for NATO from Ukraine: Failures of the Russian Aerospace Forces in Ukraine', *Air & Space Operations Review*, vol. 2, no. 3, Fall 2023, pp. 4–19.

9   See Sydney Freedberg, 'Minefields at Sea: From the Tsars to Putin', *Breaking Defense*, 23 March 2015, https://breakingdefense.com/2015/03/shutting-down-the-sea-russia-china-iran-and-the-hidden-danger-of-sea-mines/.

10 See Thomas Nilsen, 'From This Secret Base, Russian Spy Ships Increase Activity Around Global Data Cables', *Barents Observer*, 12 January 2018, https://www.thebarentsobserver.com/news/from-this-secret-base-russian-spy-ships-increase-activity-around-global-data-cables/226047.

11 See Heather Conley et al., 'Protecting Undersea Infrastructure in the North American Arctic: Lessons from Incidents in the Baltic Sea and High North', German Marshall Fund, May 2024, https://www.gmfus.org/sites/default/files/2024-10/Protecting%20Undersea%20Infrastructure%20in%20the%20North%20American%20Arctic.pdf.

12 See 'Swedish Navy Recovers Eagle S Anchor Linked to Cable Damage', *Helsinki Times*, 7 January 2025, https://www.helsinkitimes.fi/finland/finland-news/domestic/25941-swedish-navy-recovers-eagle-s-anchor-linked-to-cable-damage.html.

13 See Mark Seip, 'Nordic–Baltic Security and the US Role', Issue Brief, Atlantic Council, 25 September 2015, https://www.atlanticcouncil.org/wp-content/uploads/2015/09/Nordic_Baltic_Security_web_0925.pdf.

14 See, for example, John R. Deni, 'Is the Baltic Sea a NATO Lake?', Carnegie Endowment for International Peace, 23 December 2023, https://carnegieendowment.org/research/2023/12/is-the-baltic-sea-a-nato-lake?; Marion Messner, 'The Baltic Sea Is Far from a "NATO Lake"' – The Alliance Must Strengthen Its Defences', Chatham House, 22 April 2024, https://www.chathamhouse.org/2024/04/baltic-sea-far-nato-lake-Alliance-must-strengthen-its-defences; and Julian Pawlak, 'No, Don't Call the Baltic a "NATO Lake"', RUSI, 5 September 2022, https://rusi.org/explore-our-research/publications/commentary/no-dont-call-baltic-nato-lake.

15 Deni, 'Is the Baltic Sea a NATO Lake?'.

16 See, for example, Stuart Rumble, 'Sweden's Silent *Gotland* Class Submarines Tailor-made for Protecting Baltic Sea', *Forces News*, 18 October 2023, https://www.forcesnews.com/technology/weapons-and-kit/swedens-silent-gotland-class-submarines-tailor-made-protecting-baltic.

17 See Giles and Boulegue, 'Russia's A2/AD Capabilities: Real and Imagined', p. 25.

18 See Tim Marshall, 'Is the Baltic Sea a "NATO Lake"? Only if Gotland Is a NATO Island', Geographical, 30 July 2024, https://geographical.co.uk/geopolitics/is-the-baltic-sea-a-nato-lake-only-if-gotland-is-a-nato-island.

19 See Dalsjö, Berglund and Jonsson, 'Bursting the Bubble', p. 34.

20 Monitoring Group of the Black Sea Institute of Strategic Studies and the Black Sea News, 'Crude Oil and Oil

Products Exports from the Russian Baltic and Black Sea Ports in April–August 2024', Black Sea News, 9 October 2024, https://www.blackseanews.net/en/read/221802; and U.S. Energy Information Administration, 'Country Analysis Brief: Russia', 29 April 2024, pp. 12–14, https://www.eia.gov/international/content/analysis/countries_long/Russia/pdf/russia.pdf.

21 See Sabine Siebold, 'Germany, Eight Other Baltic Sea Nations Seek to Jointly Buy Naval Mines', Reuters, 9 July 2024, https://www.reuters.com/world/europe/germany-eight-other-baltic-sea-nations-seek-jointly-buy-naval-mines-2024-07-09/.

22 See Norwegian Armed Forces, 'Standing NATO Mine Countermeasures Group One', 18 April 2024, https://www.forsvaret.no/en/exercises-and-operations/international-operations/SNMCMG1. Mine removal is a slow and tedious process, but NATO countries possess the most advanced mine-countermeasures equipment available and regularly practise mine-removal techniques in joint-warfare settings.

23 See Koichiro Takagi, 'How the US Conquered Information Warfare in Ukraine with Open-source Intelligence', Commentary, Hudson Institute, 1 March 2024, https://www.hudson.org/information-technology/how-us-conquered-information-warfare-ukraine-open-source-intelligence-koichiro-takagi.

24 See Robert Dalsjö, Michael Jonsson and Johan Norberg, 'A Brutal Examination: Russian Military Capability in Light of the Ukraine War', Survival, vol. 64, no. 3, June–July 2022, pp. 7–28.

25 See 'Royal Navy Destroyer HMS Diamond Shoots Down Houthi Missile', Naval News, 25 April 2024, https://www.navalnews.com/naval-news/2024/04/royal-navy-destroyer-hms-diamond-shoots-down-houthi-missile/.

26 See Eugene Gholz, 'Strait of Hormuz – Small Boats', Strauss Center for International Security and Law, 1 August 2008, https://www.strausscenter.org/strait-of-hormuz-small-boats/; and Kris Osborn, 'Navy Refines Small Boat Attack Defenses', Warrior Maven, 5 September 2019, https://warriormaven.com/sea/navy-refines-small-boat-attack-defenses.

27 See Deni, 'Is the Baltic Sea a NATO Lake?'.

28 Katherine E. Dahlstrand, Sean Monaghan and Sara Bjerg Moller, 'Understanding NATO's Concept for Deterrence and Defense of the Euro-Atlantic Area', Research Brief, Center for Strategic and Budgetary Assessments, 20 May 2024, https://csbaonline.org/uploads/documents/NATOs_DDA_Concept.pdf.

29 See Katherine E. Dahlstrand, 'Achieving the Promise of NATO's New Northeast Quadrant', Carnegie Middle East Center, 11 December 2024, https://carnegieendowment.org/research/2024/12/achieving-the-promise-of-natos-new-northeast-quadrant?lang=en&center=middle-east.

30 See 'Germany Inaugurates New Naval HQ on the Baltic Sea', DW, 21 October 2024, https://www.dw.com/en/germany-inaugurates-new-naval-hq-on-the-baltic-sea/a-70553331.

31 See Dahlstrand, 'Achieving the Promise of NATO's New Northeast Quadrant'.

Copyright © 2025 The International Institute for Strategic Studies

Finance, Strategy and European Autonomy

Elmar Hellendoorn

Financial trends are closely linked to questions of national security and geo-politics. They are implicated in the erosion of the Atlantic order and the fragility of Western societies, and in the strategic challenges being faced by Europe in particular. Three key trends stand out: financialisation, European dollar-dependence and Western public indebtedness. These continue to make European societies more vulnerable to hybrid challenges, such as financial pressure and digital attacks. These may come not just from adversaries, but from allies too: financial developments are increasing American influence in Europe while diminishing European influence in the United States. To strengthen Europe's economic security and to rebalance transatlantic relations, policymakers across Europe must learn to think in terms of geofinance – to look at finance from a perspective of strategy and realpolitik.

The Atlantic order has relied on the alignment of American values, inter-ests and capabilities with European security.[1] In the aftermath of the Second World War, US political and financial elites subscribed to the Western – or Atlantic – values enshrined in the North Atlantic Treaty, which was drawn up 'to safeguard the freedom, common heritage and civilisation of [Atlantic] peoples, founded on the principles of democracy, individual liberty and the rule of law'.[2] Yet notions of a 'Western civilisation' or an 'Atlantic order'

Elmar Hellendoorn is a senior fellow at the Atlantic Council's GeoEconomics Center and an adviser in the public and private sector. He can be contacted at elmar.hellendoorn@gmail.com.

Survival | vol. 67 no. 1 | February–March 2025 | pp. 99–122   https://doi.org/10.1080/00396338.2025.2459014

led by the United States appear to carry significantly less weight among moneyed elites in the US today.[3]

The 2008 global financial crisis and the ensuing eurozone crisis made clear that the geostrategic centre of the world order was shifting toward Asia and away from the Atlantic. Financially and industrially, Europe no longer seemed to hold the balance as it had after the Second World War, when an American military commitment to Western Europe was deemed necessary to prevent Soviet domination. In 2012 the Obama administration announced its 'pivot to Asia'.[4]

This reorientation was determined in part by financial considerations. Starting with the First World War, the US was in a position to finance its military, diplomatic and economic involvement in Europe, which has underpinned the Atlantic order. Under current conditions, however, the United States may no longer be willing or indeed able to pay for its involvement in Europe. At the same time, several financial developments appear to be increasing American influence in and leverage over Europe even as the United States' commitment to Europe wanes. From the European perspective, the control wielded by the US over the global financial and telecommunications infrastructure – sometimes referred to as the United States' 'underground empire' – may even be seen to increasingly present a challenge, if not a threat, to the continent's desire for greater strategic autonomy and economic security.[5]

Financialisation and its consequences

Since early 2024, Rob Bauer, the chair of NATO's military committee, has been calling for a change in emphasis from efficiency to effectiveness in the way Western economies and countries are organised. He has argued that greater societal resilience is needed in the face of not only conventional military threats, but also a wide range of hybrid threats.[6] Left unmentioned has been the role of financial trends, especially financialisation, in continuing to drive the dominant 'efficiency' approach, which has contributed to Europe's strategic fragility and dependence on the United States.

Financialisation is commonly understood as the growing importance of financial motives, markets, institutions and players. Processes of financialisation have not only economic effects, but also a strategic impact, affecting the national security and diplomacy of Western countries.[7] A trend toward financialisation has been increasingly in evidence as the 1944 Bretton Woods financial order has gradually declined alongside the erosion of Great Depression- and New Deal-era financial regulations in the United States. Those regulations governed the behaviour of American banks by, for example, placing strict limits on the interest they could charge (under 'Regulation Q') and separating commercial from investment banking (Glass–Steagall Act). The Bretton Woods system was an effort to create a stable monetary system by subjecting the world's currencies to a multilateral order of strictly managed exchange rates. This order limited competitive behaviour among central banks, as well as preventing the disruptive impact of private international financial markets or speculative 'hot money'. In a sense, Bretton Woods could be seen as the international extension of the New Deal.[8] The late Mathieu Segers described it as 'banking without banks'.[9]

Over time, however, financial markets began to regain authority over their own functioning, and international capital controls were liberalised.[10] Both states and businesses sought more liquidity, and capital owners sought higher returns. In the mid-1950s, the self-regulating 'Eurodollar' offshore market emerged in the City of London. There, banks could trade among themselves, as well as on behalf of their (vetted) international clients, unrestricted by domestic, onshore regulations.[11] In 1971, having faced a decade-long outflow of gold as a consequence of its overseas military commitments in Europe and Asia, the Nixon administration decided it could no longer maintain the Bretton Woods system of pegging the US dollar to the price of gold.[12] From then on, the dollar would 'float freely' against other currencies, giving markets a much greater role in determining currency prices. After the 1973 OPEC oil embargo and the surge in oil prices, oil exporters accumulated vast dollar surpluses. These 'petrodollars' had to be reinvested, giving higher yields.[13] Similarly, countries that were net exporters of manufactured goods, starting with Japan (which was later joined by China), accumulated dollar surpluses that also had to be recycled. Lastly, the rise of pension funds added trillions of dollars to markets in search of yields.[14]

Driven by a quest for higher returns and more liquidity, market actors innovated and financial regulations evolved. By the 1980s, the contours of financialisation had become more visible. Foreign-exchange futures allowed for much greater currency speculation, revolutionising the functioning of international money markets. Other kinds of derivatives also took off. The creation of short-term, high-interest 'junk bonds' spurred the emergence of private-equity hostile takeovers.[15] The rise of securitisation, especially of mortgages, was also crucial in the creation of an ever more complex market for 'sophisticated', high-yielding financial instruments, providing liquidity. This led to several boom–bust cycles, including the 2008 global financial crisis and the subsequent eurozone crisis.[16]

The essential point is that financialisation's cumulative effect has been to make relatively short-term financial speculation more profitable in the aggregate than longer-term capital investments in low-yielding industrial assets. Proponents of financial liberalisation and innovation argue that this allows for a more efficient allocation of capital, stimulating less-productive assets to become productive, thus fostering economic growth. Critics will point out that short-term speculation leads to bubbles and instability, as well as greater social-economic inequality.[17] Both may hold true. However, in the context of today's geopolitical turbulence, it seems urgent and necessary to think more deeply about how financialisation has affected the national and economic security of Europe and the United States.[18]

In his 2024 report on European competitiveness, Mario Draghi, former president of the European Central Bank, pointed out that the European Union would need additional investments of around €800 billion per year to restore Europe's techno-industrial and strategic position. To do so, he suggested creating additional and common European debt and finalising the EU Capital Markets, in addition to developing a stronger pension-fund system and reviving securitisation to mobilise and efficiently distribute the required capital.[19] While reforms are necessary, some elements of Draghi's proposals may actually accelerate the financial dynamics that have already strategically weakened Europe.[20] As the merchant banker Daniel Pinto argued in his 2014 book *Capital Wars*, the ascendance of the self-serving logic of finance and debt-fuelled governments over the spirit of industry and entrepreneurship has made Europe's strategic position more fragile.[21]

Put differently, financialisation is a key driver of deindustrialisation.[22] Other drivers include globalisation, which is intertwined with financialisation. Shareholder value has become central to many boardroom decisions. Financial-market dynamics, such as the prices of stocks, bonds and futures, have often become more important in shaping corporate decisions than the dynamics of supply and demand. Since the 1980s, there has also been a rise in mergers and acquisitions, including leveraged buyouts, and in foreign direct investment. Under these conditions, current or projected market valuations have become a chief benchmark for an increasing number of Western companies and industries. Short-term profitability, cost-cutting and efficiency gains became the central theme, if not the dogma, of business management.[23] This trend also boosted the reach of American accountancy firms, corporate culture and business-consultancy practices in Europe, furthering America's 'Irresistible Empire' and displacing Europe's traditional bourgeois civilisation.[24] Following the American example, European industries were liquidated, their machinery sold to China and their real estate sold to property developers and global speculators. Syndicated labour was laid off and subsequent generations of workers moved into the 'gig economy' and what David Graeber has called 'bullshit jobs' in the services sector.[25]

> *A consequence of financialisation has been the privileging of efficiency*

A direct consequence of financialisation has been the privileging of economic efficiency over robustness and effectiveness.[26] At the firm level, the increased focus on efficiency has led to offshoring supply chains, outsourcing non-vital operations such as research and development (R&D), and increasing automation and digitisation, as well as to growth in US-style management consultancies – which help companies to become more efficient.[27]

The offshoring of supply chains by American and European industries has led to a greater dependence on overseas production facilities and local suppliers in China and beyond. While this shift helped to cut costs, it hollowed out Europe's industrial-manufacturing base, while strengthening China's. As a result, both Europe and the US have become relatively vulnerable to economic coercion and other forms of economic statecraft, and to hybrid strategies. The offshoring of supply chains has also made Europe's economy more dependent on US military strategy and the US Navy, because the sea lines of communication that connect Europe's ports to Asia's run through multiple naval choke points such as the Red Sea and the Malacca Strait. Recent Houthi attacks on shipping vessels near Yemen demonstrate the relative vulnerability of Europe's maritime trade.

A key consequence of outsourcing has been the emergence of start-ups and venture capital.[28] Industrial conglomerates used to maintain in-house R&D departments and laboratories.[29] These still exist, but the development of new technologies has been increasingly outsourced to capital markets, where start-ups seek investments from venture capitalists – which can operate in partnership with or as autonomous arms of larger conglomerates.[30] However, because Europe's capital markets are less well developed than those of the United States, European innovators tend to leave the continent to access capital. This 'scale-up gap' is one of the major concerns of the Draghi report.[31]

In another bid to enhance efficiency, European companies, like American ones, have sought to automate and digitalise their processes. Barring a few exceptions, doing so has increased Europe's dependence on American technology companies providing software, cloud services and other 'data solutions'. For reasons including the absence of deep capital markets in Europe, there has been a lack of European alternatives to US Big Tech. To the extent that there are significant European technology companies, such as the Netherlands-based chip-machine producer ASML, the US government goes to great lengths to control their activities.[32] The EU has acknowledged a need for more 'digital sovereignty'.[33]

The pervasive use of digital information and communications technology by governments, companies and private individuals has made Europe and its economy highly vulnerable. The Echelon and Snowden affairs indicate that US Big Tech and American intelligence agencies cooperate, and that the resulting position of 'information dominance' has led to the surveillance of European governments and companies.[34] Some have argued that Europe's businesses are in an unfair competition with their American counterparts, which indirectly benefit from US intelligence advantages.[35] The summer 2024 failure of millions of Windows systems worldwide owing to a faulty software update by security vendor CrowdStrike further underscored how dependent Europe's economy and infrastructure are on US technology.[36] This was an unintended failure, but during the initial phase of the Russia–Ukraine war, Washington ordered Microsoft to switch off the operating system of a Russian-funded bank based in Europe.[37]

Lastly, the financialisation of the European economy has enhanced the role of different kinds of American financial players in Europe. US investment banks, asset managers and private equity dominate their counterparts in Europe.[38] As a consequence, large parts of the European economy are now under the strong influence, if not the direct control, of Wall Street firms, which are ultimately subject to US laws and Washington's financial statecraft. Moreover, the dominance of US asset managers leads to outflows of mobilised capital from Europe into the American economy.[39] This state of affairs recently led former Italian prime minister Enrico Letta to call Europe a 'financial colony' of the US.[40]

Dollar-dependence or de-dollarisation?

In the wake of Russia's 2022 invasion of Ukraine and the subsequent, unprecedented Western use of financial sanctions, there was much speculation about the future role of the US dollar. Some believed that de-dollarisation was imminent, as China, Russia and their partners in the Global South launched initiatives toward that objective. At the same time, sceptics argued that the dollar would remain dominant despite recurring doubts about its future.

A more nuanced view is that 'de-dollarisation' occurs not overtly, but stealthily, and that states are learning to work around the US financial system to limit the effects of sanctions. Moreover, while the traditional view holds that the dollar's dominance will endure because it is so deeply 'networked', multicurrency orders have existed in the past. Historical evidence also indicates that changing international currency patterns are closely related to political, diplomatic and strategic goals, which have shaped the 'active portfolio management' of central-bank reserve managers.[41]

Paradoxically, while several powers across Asia and the Global South are actively working to diminish their dollar-dependence, Europe seems to have become *more* dependent upon the US dollar, reinforcing American leverage over European foreign policy. Just before the 2008 global financial crisis, the euro seemed on track to fulfil the decades-old desire of Europe's leaders to end their dependence on American dollar politics; to make Europe's financial sector more independent; and to be able to trade with third countries using the European currency instead of US dollars. Instead, the role of the dollar in Europe's financial system seems to have been reinforced by the crisis, while the euro's international role has largely stagnated.[42]

The euro's international role has largely stagnated

During the 2008 financial crisis and the subsequent eurozone crisis, Wall Street and the US Federal Reserve (Fed) once again set the rhythm for European banks.[43] Unable to sell the large number of dollar-denominated financial assets on their balance sheets, European banks faced an acute shortage of dollars, and the European financial system faced collapse. The Fed quickly set up a number of swap lines to European central banks, through which dollars were made available – that is, loaned – to European banks. This happened again during the subsequent eurozone crisis, and during the March 2020 COVID-19 crisis.[44] Access to the Fed's swap lines comes at the cost of significant interest over the life of the loans, and there is always the risk that during future financial crises, dollar liquidity may once again dry up.

According to the financial historian Adam Tooze, the Fed consciously 'stray[ed] into geopolitical terrain' when it rolled out the system of central-bank swap lines during the 2008 global financial crisis and the ensuing eurozone crisis. In doing so, it created a US-centred hierarchy among central banks. This financial hierarchy was aligned with the geopolitical pattern of America's alliances and partnerships. While close allies like the EU and Japan received access to the Fed's unlimited swap lines, smaller allies and emerging economies could only access more limited swap lines. Countries like China, India and Russia did not have access to the Fed's swap-line system.[45]

While it is not exactly clear how American diplomatic and strategic considerations affected the Fed's swap-line arrangements, the correlation is clear.[46] If a future financial crisis in Europe were to coincide with a transatlantic diplomatic crisis, Europe's central banks and financial markets may not have guaranteed access to the necessary dollar liquidity through the Fed's swap lines and emergency lending facilities. Taking into account that Europe and the United States have experienced severe diplomatic crises in the past, bankers might be advised to consider that a diplomatic crisis may aggravate key financial risks.

In 2018, the United States and Europe clashed over the Trump administration's decision to withdraw from the Joint Comprehensive Plan of Action (JCPOA) – or Iranian nuclear agreement – forcing European companies to cease doing business with Iran. European banks faced the risk of being cut off from the American financial system and thus from US-dollar funding. The European effort to create a mechanism – Instrument in Support of Trade Exchanges (INSTEX) – to continue trading with Iran was a disappointment. By that time, American authorities had been targeting European banks' international, dollar-based financial operations for over a decade, leading to tremendous fines, most notably in 2015, when a fine of $8.9bn was imposed on BNP Paribas for financing Cuba, Iran and Sudan.[47] While BNP Paribas had done nothing wrong according to European law or the policies of European capitals, the United States had placed the three countries on a sanctions list.

Europe's INSTEX failure revealed that the US can also sanction individual European politicians and business professionals if they are deemed to have acted against American interests: the Trump administration threatened to sanction people involved in the roll-out of INSTEX, for example.[48] At any time, the US government can impose financial sanctions against individuals by blacklisting them, which makes normal life near impossible. Since European banks, including those in Switzerland, are effectively under American control, European individuals may be left with no place to safely store their wealth. This could easily become problematic for individual European politicians or businesspeople who disagree with American policies in the Middle East or on trade relations with China, for example.

While the dollar remains dominant in Europe, the hegemonic position of the dollar in other parts of the world appears less secure. The price of gold has risen enormously in recent years, which can be seen as a hedge against the dollar either depreciating or being weaponised.[49] Similarly, Bitcoin and other digital assets continue to emerge as increasingly significant stores of value. A longer-term downward trend in central-bank US-dollar reserves can be seen as other, non-traditional reserve currencies are increasingly used, including not just the Chinese renminbi as expected, but also the Australian dollar, the Canadian dollar, the South Korean won, the Singaporean dollar and the Nordic currencies. Relative holdings of US dollars in central-bank foreign-exchange reserves declined by 12% between 2000 and 2020, from 71% to 59%.[50]

Apart from the emergence of market-driven dollar alternatives, several countries, led by China, are pursuing policies to decrease dollar dominance.[51] A key element is the creation of the Cross-Border Interbank Payment System (CIPS) as an alternative to the US-controlled Society for Worldwide Interbank Financial Telecommunication (SWIFT) interbank payments system. China's commercial state banks already play a primary role in private lending across the Global South.[52] China's central bank has also established a network of swap lines with trading partners across the world to allow them easy access to renminbi for trade finance, reducing the need for dollars in China's bilateral trade.[53]

As an important corollary to building an alternative financial infrastructure, China has become increasingly successful in persuading natural-resource exporters to consider pricing their exports in renminbi, and not just in dollars. Facing US sanctions, Iran, Russia and Venezuela are the most high-profile cases of countries that have switched to renminbi for their oil exports.[54] Other hydrocarbon exporters appear to be in discussions with Beijing about renminbi-denominated oil contracts.[55] While large-scale oil pricing using Chinese currency remains hypothetical for now, there is a risk that countries will build up much smaller dollar reserves, which will leave fewer dollars to be recycled into US government debt, adding to emerging US debt-funding problems.

American and European indebtedness

In April 2024, the historian Niall Ferguson observed that the US was now spending more on its debt servicing than on its defence budget. According to Ferguson, 'any great power that spends more on debt service (interest payments on the national debt) than on defense will not stay great for very long. True of Hapsburg Spain, true of *ancien régime* France, true of the Ottoman Empire, true of the British Empire, this law is about to be put to the test by the US.'[56] In 2024, the United States spent $826bn on defence and $950bn on debt servicing.[57]

Worse, at least since the March 2020 debt crisis, US Treasuries – the official form taken by US debt – have become more difficult to sell, and markets for US debt have become much less predictable, spurring growing concern about US debt-funding.[58] In the absence of structural fiscal reforms and the introduction of adequate taxation, US debt levels may become unsustainable. Official projections estimate that US public debt will rise from 99% of GDP in 2024 to 122% in 2034, with budget deficits between 5.5% and 7%, far above the average of 3.7% seen over the last 50 years. In the coming decade, these levels will require markets to absorb another $22 trillion of US Treasuries, from $26trn in 2024 to $48trn in 2034.[59] If the markets are not able to absorb that amount of US debt, the strategic consequence for Europe may be that the US becomes unable or unwilling to finance a military that can simultaneously shore up NATO and sustain a strategic competition with China.

Of course, while the US may have spent relatively more on defence during the Cold War, perceptions of market developments and an emphasis on fiscal prudence continuously shaped the American commitment to Europe even then. As early as the mid-1950s, president Dwight Eisenhower was suggesting that the US might 'sit back [from Europe] and relax somewhat'.[60] In subsequent decades, US military strategy was deeply intertwined with the position of the dollar and US debt, right up to the 'peace dividend' reflected in Bill Clinton's balanced budget.[61]

Today, rating agencies have downgraded US debt because of the country's domestic politics and debt ceilings.[62] Meanwhile, the structure of US debt markets is relatively centralised around a number of primary dealers, which can add to liquidity problems, as witnessed in March 2020.[63] In October 2014 and February 2021, there were two short 'flash crashes' or heavy swings in the market for US Treasuries, the causes of which remain unclear.[64] Furthermore, in 2023, one primary dealer bank was hit by a ransomware attack, disrupting US Treasuries markets.[65] It remains to be seen whether the market reforms that are currently being implemented will improve or worsen the situation.[66]

Further problems for US debt include the breakdown of US military hegemony. In exchange for a US military presence during the Cold War, both West Germany and Saudi Arabia agreed to 'offset' or 'recycle' the income from their dollar-denominated industrial and hydrocarbon exports into US government debt, providing steady demand for US Treasuries.[67] Other major exporters and key holders of US debt, like China, may consider it advantageous to diversify their asset holdings away from US debt. In fact, as early as 2009, considerable American diplomatic effort was apparently required to persuade China to continue buying US Treasuries.[68]

Unfortunately, many EU member states already face significant constraints in their desire to sustain increased levels of military spending to meet the NATO target of at least 2% of GDP. Because of their already high debt levels and budget deficits, several key European states will likely face tough choices if they want to build up their militaries. The choice is between greater indebtedness, higher inflation and thus more political turmoil, which also risk weakening the euro; or cutting back on social expenditure and costly decarbonisation plans to divert funds to defence budgets.[69] Higher taxation on big tech, capital gains and the top 1% (or 0.1%) of wealthy citizens might also offer much-needed additional income to pay for European defence. Ultimately, to become more strategically autonomous, the EU will need higher real growth, which will likely require reforms to 'definancialise' member-state economies, establishing a more balanced relationship between finance and the real economy.

The competing logics of finance and strategy

In the June–July 2024 issue of *Survival*, François Heisbourg urged that planning begin for a 'post-American Europe'.[70] From a strategic standpoint, a post-American Europe seems indeed to lie ahead as the nuclear deterrent the US has extended across Europe comes into question. From a financial standpoint, however, Europe is becoming *more* American. Jean-Jacques Servan-Schreiber warned in the 1960s that American corporations were colonising Europe, and a financialised version of this conquest appears to have succeeded in recent decades.[71]

Since the earliest origins of European integration, Europeans have in fact made plans for a post-American Europe.[72] Visions of Atlantic unity were often put to the test by discord across the Atlantic, spurring European integration. In 1956, as the Suez Crisis came to a head with the Franco-British intervention, the United States used its currency power to separate Britain from its continental ally.[73] And while Moscow was threatening to rain nuclear hellfire on London and Paris, Eisenhower left his European allies in the cold. These events forced a breakthrough in the relaunch of European integration: the Rome Treaties were signed a few months after Suez, and a joint European nuclear-weapons project briefly emerged.[74] As the continent faces a fresh round of nuclear threats from Moscow and financial pressures from Washington, it may be experiencing a strong sense of déjà vu.

Renè Aninao, an astute analyst of political risk, regularly quips that 'financial markets are more powerful than nuclear weapons'.[75] Regardless of whether this is strictly correct, it does encourage us to think about finance as a force in geopolitics that may be capable of structuring international order and diplomatic relations in ways similar to nuclear weapons. However, academics and policymakers have only recently started to recover from the long, artificial separation of economics and security, and many are still searching for the intellectual and conceptual tools to gauge the power of finance.[76] This search was underscored by Daleep Singh, who served as deputy national security advisor in the Biden White House and devised the US sanctions against Russia, when he called for a 'doctrine for economic statecraft'.[77] Singh's call is not dissimilar to the American and allied quest for nuclear doctrine in the 1950s and 1960s, when strategists and policymakers were striving to align foreign and nuclear policies.[78]

The noted historian Frank Gavin has persuasively argued that when thinking about nuclear weapons, an understanding of history helps to show that US nuclear statecraft did not follow clear theoretical patterns or official doctrines. In reality, nuclear policymaking was subject to much more complex, multifaceted processes and interconnected with, among others, fiscal and monetary policy.[79] Similarly, to plan responses to the broader implications of financialisation, partial de-dollarisation and Western indebtedness, a nuanced perspective that is rooted in historical insights and strategic thought is needed. This would be more helpful than any neat, theoretical economic framework.

It has already become much more common to note the impact of geopolitical dynamics and national-security considerations on the international economy.[80] 'Geo-economic' analysis accepts that geopolitics shapes and even drives economic choices, overturning the liberal-internationalist idea that welfare optimisation and economic relationships drive diplomatic and security dynamics. Geo-economically inspired states or alliances seek to maximise their economic security, meaning their access to and control over the strategic economic resources they believe will be necessary to achieve key objectives such as national security, social-economic stability, national grandeur, or even upholding civilisational values such as those enshrined in the preamble of the North Atlantic Treaty. The imperative of 'economic security' and the logic of geo-economic policymaking are today being used to justify the renaissance of industrial and technological initiatives across the Atlantic.

As noted, the Draghi report concluded that Europe will need an estimated €800bn per year to shore up its economic security. However, the United States' 'financial colonisation' of the continent could mean that, ultimately, European economic security depends on American financial players. To move away from that scenario, Europe would not only have to further develop its capital markets, but also control them. Doing so may be consistent with the European institutionalist tradition of 'functionalist', sectoral integration, but Draghi's financing proposals would likely require a greater role for financial motives, markets, institutions and players in Europe's economy, thus driving further financialisation.

Ultimately, the current transatlantic financial relationship appears consistent with the longer historical record, which reveals a complex interplay of finance and geopolitics.[81] As Fernand Braudel has observed, since the emergence of finance in the Middle Ages, the relationship between 'the banker' and 'the prince' has been crucial in shaping the historical evolution of capitalism and world order.[82] But this relationship has never been stable for long, oscillating between intimate alliances, neutral partnerships and explicit rivalries.[83] Moreover, bankers and princes have their own respective hierarchies, adding another layer of rivalries, alliances, compromises and complexities.[84]

Contemporary thinking on the hierarchies present in today's financialised world economy often places the US dollar on top and European financial actors in subservient roles.[85] But the shape and structure of world order is much in flux, and power relations appear uncertain. Is the Atlantic relationship one side of an EU–US–China 'power triangle', or is the world better described as bipolar, with the US and China each managing networks of allies, partners and clients – not least the Middle Eastern princes, many of whom control vast financial resources? IMF officials today speak of the geopolitical fragmentation of the world economy.[86]

European policymakers may find that the concept of 'geofinance' can help to make better sense of the trends that have been shaping the continent's fortunes and choices.[87] This term describes the partial domination of financial dynamics by geopolitics, national security and diplomacy. It points to the fact that many financial developments have geopolitical and strategic implications. Conceptually, geofinance is the opposite of financialisation, which implies the domination of geopolitics by financial motives, markets, institutions and players.[88] These two currents follow different logics, both when used analytically and as a guide to action. The logic of finance, per Perry Mehrling, reduces everything it touches to a matter of cash flow and the settlement of accounts – which is subject to the hierarchical dynamics of the international financial system.[89] Geofinance follows the logic of strategy, which, per Edward Luttwak, is paradoxical: in situations of war and conflict, one always has to take into account the will, capabilities and actions of the adversary. In that context, it can be the longer, slower, less efficient route which leads to survival and victory.[90] Yet Europe and the West more broadly may still be in thrall to the logic of finance.

As international conflict becomes more pronounced, the logic of strategy is increasingly steering financial decisions and dynamics. It is more likely, however, that the decision-making of, for example, Chinese sovereign-wealth funds will be in line with the Chinese Communist Party's foreign-policy objectives than the decision-making of American investment banks or private-equity firms will follow US national-security policy. Nonetheless, the activities of both 'state capitalist' and 'liberal capitalist' actors can change the strategic map: outcomes matter as much as intentions.

Financial, economic and geopolitical dynamics are in constant interaction, pushing and pulling, reinforcing and weakening each other. The relationship between them can be described as triangular, but there is no clear mathematical or predetermined pattern to precisely describe how and when this interaction will play out. Instead of theory, historical insights can give us a better sensibility of the complexities we face. As Isaiah Berlin forcefully argued, by believing in some form of historical inevitability, we deprive ourselves of our individual responsibility to act.[91] In other words, relying on the financial markets to raise capital is not enough: strategy and leadership are required to strengthen Europe's position.

Notes

1   See Mathieu Segers, *The Origins of European Integration: The Pre-history of Today's European Union, 1937–1951* (Cambridge: Cambridge University Press, 2023).

2   NATO, 'The North Atlantic Treaty', 4 April 1949, https://www.nato.int/cps/en/natohq/official_texts_17120.htm.

3   See, for example, Robert Strausz-Hupé, *The Estrangement of Western Man* (London: Victor Gollancz, 1953); and Kenneth Weisbrode, *The Atlantic Century: Four Generations of Extraordinary Diplomats Who Forged America's Vital Alliance with Europe* (Cambridge, MA: Da Capo Press, 2009).

4   See, for example, Nina Silove, 'The Pivot Before the Pivot: U.S. Strategy to Preserve the Power Balance in Asia', *International Security*, vol. 40, no. 4, Spring 2016, pp. 45–88.

5   On the United States' 'underground empire', see Henry Farrell and Abraham Newman, *Underground Empire: How America Weaponized the World Economy* (New York: Henry Holt, 2023).

6   NATO, 'Opening Remarks by the Chair of the NATO Military Committee, Admiral Rob Bauer and NATO Deputy Secretary General Mircea Geoană at the Meeting of the Military Committee in Chiefs of Defence', 17 January 2024, https://www.nato.int/cps/en/natohq/opinions_221752.htm; and NATO, 'Speech by the Chair of the NATO Military Committee, Admiral Rob Bauer', 24 October 2024, https://www.nato.int/cps/en/natohq/opinions_230079.htm.

7   See Gerald Epstein (ed.), *Financialization and the World Economy* (Cheltenham: Edward Elgar, 2005), p. 3.

8   See Jeffry Frieden, 'The Political Economy of the Bretton Woods

Agreements', in Naomi Lamoreaux and Ian Shapiro (eds), *The Bretton Woods Agreements: Together with Scholarly Commentaries and Essential Historical Documents* (New Haven, CT: Yale University Press, 2019), pp. 21–37; and Benn Steil, *The Battle of Bretton Woods: John Maynard Keynes, Harry Dexter White, and the Making of a New World Order* (Princeton, NJ: Princeton University Press, 2013).

9   Segers, *The Origins of European Integration*, pp. 119–25.

10   On the evolution of the governance of global capital flows, see Rawi Abdelal, *Capital Rules: The Construction of Global Finance* (Cambridge, MA: Harvard University Press, 2007).

11   See Catherine Schenk, 'The Origins of the Eurodollar Market in London: 1955–1963', *Explorations in Economic History*, vol. 35, no. 2, 1998, pp. 221–38.

12   See Francis Gavin, *Gold, Dollars, and Power: The Politics of International Monetary Relations, 1958–1971* (Chapel Hill, NC: University of North Carolina Press, 2004).

13   See Duccio Basosi, 'Oil, Dollars, and US Power in the 1970s: Re-viewing the Connections', *Journal of Energy History*, no. 3, May 2020, pp. 1–10, https://energyhistory.eu/en/node/192.

14   Natascha van der Zwan, 'Financialisation and the Pension System', *Journal of Modern European History*, vol. 15, no. 4, 2017, pp. 554–78.

15   See Bryan Burrough and John Helyar, *Barbarians at the Gate: The Fall of RJR Nabisco* (New York: Random House, 2004 [1990]).

16   See John Kay, *Other People's Money: The Real Business of Finance* (New York: PublicAffairs, 2015).

17   On bubbles and instability, see Robert Aliber and Charles Kindleberger, *Manias, Panics, and Crashes: A History of Financial Crises*, 7th ed. (New York: Palgrave Macmillan, 2015). On inequality, see Thomas Piketty, *Capital in the Twenty-first Century* (Cambridge, MA: Belknap Press of Harvard University Press, 2014).

18   See Adam Tooze, *Crashed: How a Decade of Financial Crisis Changed the World* (New York: Viking, 2018).

19   Mario Draghi, 'The Future of European Competitiveness: A Competitiveness Strategy for Europe', EU Commission, September 2024, ch. 5 ('Financing Investments'), pp. 59–62.

20   For an overall more positive assessment of this aspect of Draghi's report, see Stefano Battiston et al., 'Financialization in the EU and Its Consequences', *European Policy Brief*, no. 2, 2018, pp. 1–13; Hung Tran, 'Financialization Has Increased Economic Fragility', Atlantic Council, 1 December 2023, https://www.atlanticcouncil.org/blogs/econographics/financialization-has-increased-economic-fragility/; and Erik Jones and Matthias Matthijs, 'The Biggest Threat to Europe. It's Not Trump – It's the EU's Weak Defense Policy and Stagnant Single Market', *Foreign Affairs*, 13 January 2025, https://www.foreignaffairs.com/europe/biggest-threat-europe.

21   Pinto is the chairman of the board, chief executive and founding partner of Stanhope Capital. Daniel Pinto, *Capital Wars: The New East–West Challenge for Entrepreneurial Leadership and Economic Success* (London: Bloomsbury, 2014). John Kenneth

Galbraith was warning as early as 1967 that industries and entrepreneurs risked losing their autonomy by becoming dependent on outside sources of capital. John Kenneth Galbraith, *The New Industrial Society* (Boston, MA: Houghton Mifflin Company, 1967), pp. 80–5.

22 Of course, other factors can also contribute to deindustrialisation, such as high energy prices and the regulatory burden.

23 See William Lazonick, 'Profits Without Prosperity', *Harvard Business Review*, September 2014, https://hbr.org/2014/09/profits-without-prosperity. For a journalistic critique, see Rana Faroohar, *Makers and Takers: How Wall Street Destroyed Main Street* (New York: Crown Business, 2016).

24 See Victoria de Grazia, *Irresistible Empire: America's Advance Through Twentieth-century Europe* (Cambridge, MA: Harvard University Press, 2005).

25 David Graeber, *Bullshit Jobs: A Theory* (New York: Simon & Schuster, 2018).

26 This paragraph partially overlaps with Elmar Hellendoorn, 'Crucial Connections: Finance and Hybrid Conflict', *Atlantisch Perspectief*, no. 4, December 2024, pp. 28–32.

27 For more on the influence of American-style management thinking on Europe's political and corporate leadership, see Henry Mance, 'Mariana Mazzucato: "The McKinseys and the Deloittes Have No Expertise in the Areas that They're Advising In"', *Financial Times*, 13 February 2023, https://www.ft.com/content/fb1254dd-a011-44cc-bde9-a434e5a09fb4; and Chris Hurl and Leah Werner, *The Consulting Trap: How Professional Service Firms Hook Governments and Undermine Democracy* (Halifax: Fernwood Publishing, 2024).

28 See Tom Nicholas, *VC: An American History* (Cambridge, MA: Harvard University Press, 2019), pp. 233–320.

29 See William Lazonick, 'Innovative Business Models and Varieties of Capitalism: Financialization of the U.S. Corporation', *Business History Review*, vol. 84, no. 4, Winter 2010, pp. 675–702.

30 For a critique of financialisation's effects on innovation, see Clayton M. Christensen, Stephen P. Kaufman and Willy Shih, *Innovation Killers: How Financial Tools Destroy Your Capacity to Do New Things* (Boston, MA: Harvard Business Review Press, 2010). See also Pete Engardio and Bruce Einhorn, 'Outsourcing Innovation', in David Mayle (ed.), *Managing Innovation and Change* (London: SAGE, 2005), pp. 36–43.

31 Draghi, 'The Future of European Competitiveness'. See also Chiara Fratto et al., 'The Scale-up Gap: Financial Market Constraints Holding Back Innovative Firms in the European Union', European Investment Bank, June 2024.

32 See John Krige, 'Building a U.S. Regulatory Empire in the Chip War with China', *Technology and Culture*, vol. 65, no. 4, October 2024, pp. 1,081–108.

33 See Julia Carver, 'More Bark than Bite? European Digital Sovereignty Discourse and Changes to the European Union's External Relations Policy', *Journal of European Public Policy*, vol. 31, no. 8, 2024, pp. 2,250–86.

34 See Duncan Campbell, 'Interception Capabilities 2000', in European Parliament, 'Report on the Existence of a Global System for the Interception

of Private and Commercial Communications (ECHELON Interception System)', Report A5-0264/2001, 11 July 2001, https://www.europarl.europa.eu/doceo/document/A-5-2001-0264_EN.html; Glenn Greenwald, *No Place to Hide: Edward Snowden, the NSA, and the U.S. Surveillance State* (New York: Metropolitan Books, 2014); Shane Harris, *@War: The Rise of the Military—Internet Complex* (Boston, MA: Houghton Mifflin Harcourt, 2014); and Laura Poitras, 'NSA Spied on European Union Offices', *Der Spiegel*, 29 June 2013, https://www.spiegel.de/international/europe/nsa-spied-on-european-union-offices-a-908590.html.

35 See Éric Denécé and Claude Revel, *L'autre guerre des États-Unis* (Paris: Robert Laffont, 2005); and Ali Laïdi, *Le droit: Nouvelle arme de guerre économique* (Arles: Actes Sud, 2019).

36 See Barath Raghavan and Bruce Schneier, 'The CrowdStrike Outage and Market-driven Brittleness', Lawfare.com, 25 July 2024, https://www.lawfaremedia.org/article/the-crowdstrike-outage-and-market-driven-brittleness; and John Thornhill, 'Digital Paralysis Shows the Dangers of E-globalisation', *Financial Times*, 19 July 2024, https://www.ft.com/content/076847c7-1505-415e-9c8e-2b030d8731ee.

37 See Jacob Atkins, 'Solvent but Bankrupt: How Sanctions Felled Amsterdam Trade Bank', Global Trade Review, 31 May 2022, https://www.gtreview.com/news/europe/solvent-but-bankrupt-how-sanctions-felled-amsterdam-trade-bank/.

38 See Claudia Buch, chair of the Supervisory Board of the European Central Bank, 'Building a Resilient Future: How Europe's Financial Stability Fosters Growth and Competitiveness', speech, Budapest, 12 September 2024, https://www.bankingsupervision.europa.eu/press/speeches/date/2024/html/ssm.sp240912~72bbc94da5.en.html; John Sindreu, 'American Finance Has Left Europe in the Dust. The Tables Aren't Turning', *Wall Street Journal*, 11 January 2024, https://www.wsj.com/finance/investing/american-finance-has-left-europe-in-the-dust-the-tables-arent-turning-8c5fe07c; Peter Lee, 'US Banks Muscle In on the European Midmarket', *Euromoney*, 19 January 2024, https://www.euromoney.com/article/2cqb6mhe2i59kdmfufb4o/banking/us-banks-muscle-in-on-the-european-midmarket; and Harriet Agnew and Brooke Masters, 'The Relentless Advance of American Asset Managers in Europe', *Financial Times*, 17 December 2024, https://www.ft.com/content/bc1b6eaf-dd5f-4e63-b4dc-90a30e9bec58.

39 See Dominic Lawson, 'Vanguard Defends Dominance of US Equities in EU-domiciled Funds', *Financial Times*, 20 May 2024, https://www.ft.com/content/6b8b3c0b-bb4e-4ae6-970c-9972dbfb61ce.

40 Quoted in Thomas Moller-Nielsen, 'Letta: Europe Is a "Financial Colony" of the US', Euractiv, 2 October 2024, https://www.euractiv.com/section/economy-jobs/news/letta-europe-is-a-financial-colony-of-the-us/.

41 See Barry Eichengreen, Arnaud Mehl and Livia Chitu, *How Global Currencies Work: Past, Present, and Future* (Princeton, NJ: Princeton University Press, 2017), pp. 3–11.

42 While European banks' US-dollar liabilities have declined since the 2008 global financial crisis, they need more short-term funding. Furthermore, central-bank euro currency-reserve holdings also declined somewhat, according to IMF data. See Mareike Beck, 'Extroverted Financialization: How US Finance Shapes European Banking', *Review of International Political Economy*, vol. 29, no. 5, 2022, pp. 1,723–45; Dmitry Dolgin, 'Global De-dollarisation Takes a Pause, Embattled Euro Gives Room for Asian FX', ING Think, 10 April 2024, https://think.ing.com/articles/global-dedollarization-takes-a-pause-yuan-challenged-by-the-yen/; and European Central Bank, *The International Role of the Euro* (Frankfurt: European Central Bank, June 2024).

43 See Tooze, *Crashed*, pp. 206–19.

44 See Adam Tooze, *Shutdown: How Covid Shook the World's Economy* (New York: Viking, 2021), pp. 111–30.

45 Adam Tooze, 'The Forgotten History of the Financial Crisis', *Foreign Affairs*, vol. 97, no. 5, September–October 2018, pp. 199–210, especially p. 208. For the view that US Federal Reserve policies have been part of American statecraft for much longer, see Perry Mehrling, *Money and Empire: Charles P. Kindleberger and the U.S. Dollar System* (Cambridge: Cambridge University Press, 2022).

46 See John Cassetta, 'The Geopolitics of Swap Lines', Harvard Kennedy School, M-RCBG Associate Working Paper Series, no. 181, April 2022.

47 See Geoff Dyer, 'BNP Paribas's Record Fine Highlights Double-edged Sword for US', *Financial Times*, 2 July 2014, https://www.ft.com/content/6ef03624-01a5-11e4-bb71-00144feab7de; and Nate Raymond, 'BNP Paribas Sentenced in $8.9 Billion Accord over Sanctions Violations', Reuters, 1 May 2015, https://www.reuters.com/article/business/bnp-paribas-sentenced-in-89-billion-accord-over-sanctions-violations-idUSKBN0NM41J/.

48 See Jonathan Stearns and Helene Fouquet, 'U.S. Warns Europe That Its Iran Workaround Could Face Sanctions', Bloomberg, 29 May 2019, https://www.bloomberg.com/news/articles/2019-05-29/u-s-warns-europe-that-its-iran-work around-could-face-sanctions.

49 See Mohamed El-Erian, 'Why the West Should Be Paying More Attention to the Gold Price Rise', *Financial Times*, 21 October 2024, https://www.ft.com/content/b5fb1e6b-bb8d-4ab5-9c92-f1f6fc40a54b.

50 Serkan Arslanalp, Barry Eichengreen and Chima Simpson-Bell, 'The Stealth Erosion of Dollar Dominance: Active Diversifiers and the Rise of Nontraditional Reserve Currencies', IMF Working Paper WP/22/58, March 2022; and Serkan Arslanalp, Barry Eichengreen and Chima Simpson-Bell, 'Dollar Dominance in the International Reserve System: An Update', IMF Blog, 11 June 2024, https://www.imf.org/en/Blogs/Articles/2024/06/11/dollar-dominance-in-the-international-reserve-system-an-update.

51 See Zongyuan Zoe Liu, 'China Wants to Ditch the Dollar', *NOĒMA*, 11 January 2024, https://www.noemamag.com/china-wants-to-ditch-the-dollar/; and Zongyuan Zoe

Liu, 'China's Attempts to Reduce Its Strategic Vulnerabilities to Financial Sanctions', *China Leadership Monitor*, no. 79, March 2024, pp. 1–13. See also Daniel McDowell, *Bucking the Buck: US Financial Sanctions and the International Backlash Against the Dollar* (Oxford: Oxford University Press, 2023).

52 See Catherine Casanova, Eugenio Cerutti and Swapan-Kumar Pradhan, 'Chinese Banks and Their EMDE Borrowers: Have Their Relationships Changed in Times of Geoeconomic Fragmentation?', BIS Working Papers, no. 1213, September 2024.

53 See Hector Perez-Saiz and Longmei Zhang, 'Renminbi Usage in Cross-border Payments: Regional Patterns and the Role of Swap Lines and Offshore Clearing Banks', IMF Working Paper WP/23/77, March 2023.

54 See Kimberly Donovan and Maia Nikoladze, 'The Axis of Evasion: Behind China's Oil Trade with Iran and Russia', New Atlanticist, 28 March 2024, https://www.atlanticcouncil.org/blogs/new-atlanticist/the-axis-of-evasion-behind-chinas-oil-trade-with-iran-and-russia/.

55 See Summer Said and Stephen Kalin, 'Saudi Arabia Considers Accepting Yuan Instead of Dollars for Chinese Oil Sales', *Wall Street Journal*, 15 March 2022, https://www.wsj.com/articles/saudi-arabia-considers-accepting-yuan-instead-of-dollars-for-chinese-oil-sales-11647351541; William Sandlund, 'China's International Use of Renminbi Surges to Record Highs', *Financial Times*, 29 August 2024, https://www.ft.com/content/ae08b6ed-d323-4a95-a687-0172a98857f4; and Charles Chang et al., 'Saudi–China Ties and Renminbi-based Oil Trade', S&P Global, August 2024, https://www.spglobal.com/en/research-insights/special-reports/saudi-china-ties-and-renminbi-based-oil-trade. For a status quo perspective, see Javier Blas, 'The Myth of the Inevitable Rise of a Petroyuan', Bloomberg, 27 February 2023, https://www.bloomberg.com/opinion/articles/2023-02-27/pricing-petroleum-in-china-s-yuan-sounds-inevitable-not-for-saudi-arabia.

56 Niall Ferguson, 'The Second Cold War Is Escalating Faster than the First', Bloomberg, 21 April 2024, https://www.bloomberg.com/opinion/articles/2024-04-21/china-russia-iran-axis-is-bad-news-for-trump-and-gop-isolationists.

57 Congressional Budget Office, 'Monthly Budget Review: September 2024', 8 October 2024, Table 3.

58 See Chelsey Dulaney and Megumi Fujikawa, 'Where Have All the Foreign Buyers Gone for U.S. Treasury Debt?', *Wall Street Journal*, 17 November 2023, https://www.wsj.com/finance/investing/where-have-all-the-foreign-buyers-gone-for-u-s-treasury-debt-3db75625; Robin Wigglesworth, 'Treasury Market Liquidity: Fine but Fragile?', *Financial Times*, 24 September 2024, https://www.ft.com/content/53bbf63b-e9cb-483a-8a75-74b6ab5a9780; and Ian Smith and Harriet Clarfelt, 'Treasuries Sell-off Reverberates Through Global Markets', *Financial Times*, 25 October 2024, https://www.ft.com/content/d1452378-2980-42a4-877c-6a84b7ed6fcd.

59 Congressional Budget Office, 'An Update to the Budget and Economic Outlook: 2024 to 2034', June 2024, p. 5.

60 Quoted in Marc Trachtenberg, *A Constructed Peace: The Making of the European Settlement, 1945–1963* (Princeton, NJ: Princeton University Press, 1999), pp. 147–56.

61 On the interaction between military strategy and finance during the Cold War, see Gavin, *Gold, Dollars, and Power*.

62 See Robin Wigglesworth, 'Fitch Downgrades US on "Erosion of Governance"', *Financial Times*, 1 August 2023, https://www.ft.com/content/a7dfd132-ba8c-481f-aa7a-2f0731751559; and Hung Tran, 'Two Credit Downgrades in the US Are a Much-needed Warning', Econographics, 15 August 2023, https://www.atlanticcouncil.org/blogs/econographics/credit-downgrades-are-a-much-needed-warning/.

63 See Darrell Duffie, 'Structural Changes in Financial Markets and the Conduct of Monetary Policy', in Federal Reserve Bank of Kansas City, *Structural Shifts in the Global Economy: A Symposium Sponsored by Federal Reserve Bank of Kansas City* (Kansas City, MO: Federal Reserve Bank of Kansas City, August 2023), pp. 77–119; and Jon Sindreu, 'The Big Problem with Government Debt Isn't What You Think', *Wall Street Journal*, 6 November 2023, https://www.wsj.com/finance/the-big-problem-with-government-debt-isnt-what-you-think-b876c198.

64 See Alex Aronovich, Dobrislav Dobrev and Andrew Meldrum, 'The Treasury Market Flash Event of February 25, 2021', FEDS Notes, 21 May 2021, https://www.federalreserve.gov/econres/notes/feds-notes/the-treasury-market-flash-event-of-february-25-2021-20210514.html.

65 See Eric Wallerstein, 'How a Hack Shook Wall Street's Multitrillion-dollar Foundations', *Wall Street Journal*, 19 November 2023, https://www.wsj.com/finance/regulation/how-a-hack-shook-wall-streets-multitrillion-dollar-foundations-6a574bd7.

66 See Kate Duguid, Nikou Asgari and Costas Mourselas, 'The Radical Changes Coming to the World's Biggest Bond Market', *Financial Times*, 4 March 2024, https://www.ft.com/content/15fb1589-35ab-4b4e-9af7-b3abd44b7999.

67 A complicating factor in West Germany was that the US military presence there led to a massive outflow of dollars. See Duccio Basosi, 'Oil, Dollars, and US Power in the 1970s: Re-viewing the Connections', *Journal of Energy History*, vol. 3, May 2020, pp. 1–10, https://energyhistory.eu/en/node/192; and Jens Hofmann, 'Subsidizing US Hegemony: The Offset Agreements in US–West German Relations, 1960–1976', in Nobuki Kawasaki, Takeshi Sakade and Hubert Zimmermann (eds), *US Hegemony, American Troops Abroad and Burden-sharing: West Europe and East Asia During and After the Cold War* (New York: Routledge, 2025), pp. 93–110.

68 See Arshad Mohammed, 'Clinton Says U.S. and China Are in the Same Economic Boat', Reuters, 22 January 2009, https://www.reuters.com/article/world/clinton-says-u-s-and-china-are-in-the-same-economic-boat-idUSPEK282230/.

69 See Mateusz Morawiecki, 'Former Poland PM: Europe's Impossible Trinity', *Politico*, 10 June 2024, https://www.politico.eu/article/europe-future-decision-makers-

politics-military-spending-green-deal-climate-neutral-economy-policy/; and Lucio Pench, 'Should the European Union's Fiscal Rules Bend to Accommodate the Defence Transition?', Bruegel Analysis, 23 October 2024.

70   François Heisbourg, 'Planning for a Post-American Europe', *Survival*, vol. 66, no. 3, June–July 2024, pp. 7–20.

71   Jean-Jacques Servan-Schreiber, *Le défi américain* (Paris: Denoël, 1967).

72   See Segers, *The Origins of European Integration*.

73   See Diane Kunz, *Butter and Guns: America's Cold War Economic Diplomacy* (New York: Free Press, 1997), pp. 84–7.

74   See Leopoldo Nuti, 'The European Nuclear Dimension: From Cold War to Post-Cold War', in Mathieu Segers and Steven van Hecke (eds) *The Cambridge History of the European Union* (Cambridge: Cambridge University Press, 2023), pp. 366–92.

75   Communication with Renè Aninao, Managing Partner of CORBŪ, on 10 January 2025.

76   On this separation, see Paul Kennedy, *Strategy and Diplomacy, 1870–1945: Eight Essays* (London: George Allen, 1983), pp. 89–106.

77   Daleep Singh, 'Forging a Positive Vision of Economic Statecraft', New Atlanticist, 22 February 2024, https://www.atlanticcouncil.org/blogs/new-atlanticist/forging-a-positive-vision-of-economic-statecraft/.

78   For a general discussion on the development of nuclear strategy, see Lawrence Freedman and Jeffrey Michaels, *The Evolution of Nuclear Strategy*, 4th ed. (London: Palgrave Macmillan, 2019), pp. 65–277.

79   Francis Gavin, *Nuclear Statecraft: History and Strategy in America's Atomic Age* (Ithaca, NY: Cornell University Press, 2012), pp. 12–29.

80   The term 'geo-economics' was coined in 1990 by Edward Luttwak in 'From Geopolitics to Geo-economics: Logic of Conflict, Grammar of Commerce', *National Interest*, no. 20, Summer 1990, pp. 17–23. It was only in the mid-2010s, however, that it started to be commonly used. See Robert Blackwill and Jennifer Harris, *War by Other Means: Geo-economics and Statecraft* (Cambridge, MA: Belknap Press of Harvard University Press, 2016).

81   See Charles Kindleberger, *A Financial History of Western Europe*, 2nd ed. (Oxford: Oxford University Press, 1993).

82   Fernand Braudel, *La Dynamique du capitalisme* (Paris: Arthaud, 1985), p. 64.

83   See *ibid.*, p. 56; and Richard Ehrenberg, *Capital and Finance in the Age of the Renaissance: A Study of the Fuggers and Their Connections* (New York: Harcourt, 1928), pp. 23–32.

84   Braudel, *La Dynamique du capitalisme*, p. 64.

85   See Perry Mehrling, 'Financialization and Its Discontents', *Finance and Society*, vol. 3, no. 1, 2017, pp. 1–10.

86   See, for example, Gita Gopinath et al., 'Changing Global Linkages: A New Cold War?', IMF Working Paper WP/24/76, April 2024.

87   The term 'geofinance' was originally coined by Jacques Goldfinger, *La géo-finance: Pour comprendre la mutation financière* (Paris: Seuil, 1986).

88   See, for example, Giovanni Arrighi, *The Long Twentieth Century: Money, Power, and the Origins of Our Times* (London: Verso, 2009).

89 Mehrling, 'Financialization and Its Discontents'.

90 Edward Luttwak, *Strategy: The Logic of War and Peace* (Cambridge, MA: Belknap

Press of Harvard University Press, 2001), pp. 3–4, 13–15.

91 Isaiah Berlin, *Four Essays on Liberty* (Oxford: Oxford University Press, 1969).

Copyright © 2025 The International Institute for Strategic Studies

Forum: European Nuclear Deterrence and Donald Trump

Héloïse Fayet, Andrew Futter, Ulrich Kühn, Łukasz Kulesa, Paul van Hooft and Kristin Ven Bruusgaard

Europeans will soon experience the effects of the strategic realignment that US President Donald Trump has promised. America will prioritise Asia and, most importantly, its own interests. He will seek to reshape transatlantic relations, encompassing the Russo-Ukrainian war, America's relationship with Russia, its trade with Europe, NATO and corresponding US military commitments to European security. In his view, Europeans are mere 'clients' who 'owe' America, its commitment to NATO contingent on Europeans paying 'their bills'.[1] While US retrenchment is not a foregone conclusion, mitigating it depends on Europeans' willingness to take care of their own defence.

Whether they can and at what cost has been debated for many years.[2] Anticipating Trump's return, Héloïse Fayet, Andrew Futter and Ulrich Kühn examined what Trump's return could mean for European nuclear deterrence in *Survival* several months ago.[3] They concluded that neither French nor British nuclear forces, individually or in combination, could compensate for full US disengagement. Yet they did see options that could produce a viable European nuclear deterrent. Advancing them, however, would

Héloïse Fayet is a research fellow at the Security Studies Center and head of the deterrence and proliferation research programme at the Institut français des relations internationales (IFRI). **Andrew Futter** is Professor of International Politics at the University of Leicester. **Ulrich Kühn** is head of the Arms Control and Emerging Technologies programme at the Institute for Peace Research and Security Policy at the University of Hamburg, and a non-resident scholar at the Carnegie Endowment for International Peace. **Łukasz Kulesa** is Director, Proliferation and Nuclear Policy, at the Royal United Services Institute (RUSI). **Paul van Hooft** is a research leader at RAND Europe. **Kristin Ven Bruusgaard** is Director of the Norwegian Intelligence School.

Survival | vol. 67 no. 1 | February–March 2025 | pp. 123–142   https://doi.org/10.1080/00396338.2025.2459011

require a degree of national flexibility and European financial support that may be difficult to imagine. They assessed that, given the uncertain extent of American retrenchment under Trump, securing Europe called for enhancing practical Anglo-French deterrence cooperation, setting up a four-way discussion platform including Germany and Poland, and strengthening conventional deterrence.

This follow-up forum enlists voices from the continent's far north, east and west to discuss the requirements for and limits of a possible European nuclear deterrent. In their responses to Fayet, Futter and Kühn, they incorporate their respective national perspectives, which range from stark scepticism to heightened urgency.

A Nordic View of European Strategic Solutions

It has become a cliché to declare that Europeans must take greater responsibility for their own security. Debates routinely focus on the need for stronger European conventional capabilities, assuming that the US nuclear guarantee will be the last component of its contribution to Europe's defence to be withdrawn. Fayet, Futter and Kühn provided a cool and clear-eyed analysis of prospects for a European nuclear deterrent, taking into account existing economic, strategic and political constraints in Paris, London and Berlin. They covered the feasibility issue well, and this response will focus on the requirements for such a deterrent – in particular, the political and operational details of potential US nuclear disengagement, what Europe would face in terms of Russia's strategic posture and how European allies could combine forces to address those challenges in light of institutional, cultural and political obstacles.

Fayet, Futter and Kühn argued that 'for purely self-interested reasons … the US may never completely disassociate itself from European security'.[4] These self-interested reasons are much more acute in the nuclear arena than they are in the conventional arena. A full US pullback of nuclear as well as conventional operations in Europe would elevate the threat that Russian strategic nuclear forces based in the European and Arctic theatres pose to the US homeland. The US nuclear presence in Europe is therefore not only about extending deterrence to allies, but also about containing Russia's nuclear threat to America.

Russian nuclear forces based on the Kola Peninsula constitute one important element of Russia's assured retaliation against the United States: its submarines and novel capabilities there are survivable elements of its strategic nuclear force. During the Cold War, these forces posed a threat to the US homeland through land- and air-based missile trajectories, as well as through sea-based threats towards and across the Atlantic. During the latter part of the Cold War, the United States and its NATO allies developed maritime strategies that threatened Soviet nuclear-armed submarines within this strategic bastion protecting the Kola assets.[5] Although capabilities and concepts have evolved since then, the strategic challenge Russian forces present remains. For the United States, the ability to track and hold at risk such Russian nuclear forces remains paramount. Accordingly, complete US nuclear disengagement from the European theatre, leaving all aspects of nuclear deterrence to European allies, seems unlikely.

Nevertheless, full US disengagement – nuclear and conventional – is not impossible, and it would dramatically alter the European strategic landscape. It would place new demands on Europe, as described by Fayet, Futter and Kühn. But it would also prompt Russia to reassess its strategic problem set and reconsider how to prioritise its nuclear capabilities. Today, Russian nuclear forces have two key tasks: deterring large-scale nuclear war, traditionally a matter for the country's strategic nuclear forces, and deterring regional wars, traditionally a job for its sub-strategic nuclear forces. The two tasks are increasingly intertwined, and neither is confined to Europe. Russia deters large-scale war with the US, secondarily with the United Kingdom and France, and prospectively with China. Russia deters and would seek to manage regional wars first and foremost with NATO in Europe, but also prospectively in other theatres such as the Asia-Pacific.

In the event of a full US withdrawal from Europe, Russia would still have to devote some of its nuclear assets to deterring the threat from US nuclear forces, even if fewer US strategic assets were present in the European theatre. Deterring large-scale nuclear war in Europe would, however, become easier for Russia, which would then potentially enjoy significant nuclear superiority at the strategic level in Europe. But this superiority would be contingent on how Russia prioritised its nuclear forces to handle a new three-body problem for Moscow – deterring the US at home and in the Asia-Pacific while deterring NATO in Europe.

In the post-Cold War era, Russia's strategy for deterring regional war with NATO has emphasised the threat of limited nuclear strikes to compensate for its own perceived conventional inferiority.[6] With no US forces in Europe, the Russian estimation of its conventional inferiority would likely shift. A key question would be whether these changed perceptions would produce a re-examination of the role of nuclear weapons in Russian strategy. If it did not, Europeans would still need to deter a Russian threat of nuclear escalation in the face of conventional defeat, with a diminished nuclear force lacking US nuclear forces.

To deter Russia alone, Europe would need a repurposed deterrent with at least three components. The first would be the capacity for nuclear retaliation against a strategic Russian nuclear attack, which would probably entail a significant expansion of European strategic nuclear options. The scope and scale of such options would need to be calibrated to the strategic threat that Russia would pose to Europe in light of Russian reassessments of its options vis-à-vis the US, Europe and, prospectively, China. The second would be a credible nuclear response to limited nuclear use, alone or in combination with conventional means.[7] Thirdly, substantial conventional deterrent options would be required, potentially including a counterforce capability.[8]

Notwithstanding the constraints of current postures described by Fayet, Futter and Kühn, one could imagine alternative approaches to optimise a European nuclear force. One would centre on creating hubs around today's nuclear-armed European powers, each taking on a key task. The UK might constitute one hub, designated for handling the strategic-deterrence problem. Depending on whether the US continued nuclear operations in the European theatre, London could undertake the task in collaboration with the United States or France. Allies such as Germany, Poland and the Nordic countries could enhance conventional counterforce or defensive capabilities.

France would be a second hub, focused on escalation management and drawing on enhanced European sub-strategic capabilities, building on the future French arsenal or a European version of the dual-capable aircraft (DCA) mission, or with a heavier reliance on strategic nuclear forces or conventional deterrence. Such a role would necessitate a significant shift in French nuclear policy to extending nuclear guarantees to allies. As Fayet points out, such collaborative ideas have been floated before.[9] In renewed form, it could include allies such as Belgium, Italy, the Netherlands and Turkiye, or other states such as Poland or the Nordics.

Under another approach, combined European forces would again execute the two tasks, but in different combinations. The UK and France might take on strategic deterrence, with a carefully calibrated European strategic triad. A combination of states might tackle regional deterrence, with, say, the UK inheriting the DCA mission and France augmenting its sub-strategic capabilities with mission-specific weapons. Other allies could either continue with existing tasks or take on new nuclear or conventional ones. Either approach could involve a minimal nuclear force with expanded conventional deterrent elements to promote stability in Europe.

The viability of a future European nuclear deterrent hinges on several complex factors: the United States' future military posture, Russia's possible reconsideration of its strategic options in light of that posture, and Europe's novel political and strategic dynamics. Although a US withdrawal from Europe would significantly disrupt strategic stability, it could also produce fresh thinking about crafting a more durable strategic framework for Europe.

– Kristin Ven Bruusgaard

Poland: Sceptical but Interested

Polish decision-makers and experts have observed the debate about a European nuclear deterrent, encapsulated in *Survival*'s recent forum, with interest but also concern. Poland's clear preference has been for the continuation of NATO's nuclear-deterrence policy in its current form, with US nuclear capabilities at the centre and the independent capabilities of France and the UK providing additional protection. Poland sees the size and diversity of the US arsenal as providing the most credible response to Russia's nuclear challenges to European security, which may involve the threat of limited nuclear strikes using non-strategic nuclear weapons.[10] According to this view, British and French arsenals cannot replicate the political and military effects of US forward-deployed nuclear weapons in Europe, bolstered by NATO's nuclear-sharing arrangements. Britain relies on a single submarine-based delivery system, and France, for doctrinal and operational reasons, is not likely to embrace nuclear sharing or the deployment of nuclear weapons beyond its territory.

Consequently, increasing the credibility of NATO's nuclear posture in general and pushing for the closer involvement of Poland in the Alliance's nuclear mission in particular have been Warsaw's foci in recent years. Between 2022 and 2024, Polish President Andrzej Duda and then-prime minister Mateusz Morawiecki publicly raised the option of including Poland in NATO nuclear sharing, including hosting US nuclear weapons on Polish soil.[11] Short of the deployment of US nuclear weapons in Poland, they also mooted nuclear certification of Polish F-35 fighters.[12] The current Polish government led by Donald Tusk seems more restrained, but has still manifested interest in closer involvement with NATO's nuclear mission. Note, however, that deployment of nuclear weapons on Polish soil would require changing NATO's so-called 'three nuclear nos' policy, under which allies have 'no intention, no plan and no reason' to deploy nuclear weapons, including storage sites, on the territory of members that joined the Alliance after the end of the Cold War.[13]

From Warsaw's perspective, raising the option of a European nuclear deterrent publicly could be harmful insofar as it could be read as acquiescing to decoupling US and European security and creating unrealistic expectations regarding the potential Europeanisation of French and British capabilities. As with various proposals for a European army, serious obstacles involving joint decision-making procedures and financial contributions could arise. Many Polish analysts also see the German debate on European nuclear deterrence beyond the NATO context as a potential distraction from what they consider Germany's prime task: building up its conventional capabilities.

Furthermore, France's long-term political reliability as a bulwark of European nuclear deterrence appears dubious, as French elections in 2027 could yield a president who opposes France's nuclear outreach to European partners. Polish doubts extend to the operational level. Without US engagement, a European nuclear deterrent would initially rely on combined British and French nuclear capabilities, since introducing new nuclear capabilities would take time. While British nuclear weapons are clearly assigned to the defence of NATO, it is still unclear what the 'European dimension' of the French nuclear deterrent would mean in practice, particularly in an acute security crisis. Poland and other directly affected countries would need to gain insight into French planning and decision-making to be able to coordinate deterrent actions. In the short and medium terms, a European nuclear deterrent would turn on the threat of retaliatory strikes from British and French ballistic-missile submarines, which could inflict considerable damage on Russia

Poland would need to gain insight into French planning

but also prompt massive Russian nuclear retaliation. While the air leg of the French nuclear dyad would offer some capacity for nuclear signalling during a crisis and the option of conducting a warning strike, these capabilities are limited compared to Russia's. In this light, the mere 'pooling' of French and British capabilities would not be enough to assure deterrence.

That said, there is increased interest in Warsaw in strengthening the bilateral relationship on security and defence matters with France, encouraged by French President Emmanuel Macron's boosting of France's military presence in Central and Eastern Europe and upping French support for Ukraine. This openness extends to nuclear-deterrence issues, but with the clear understanding that such a dialogue could lead to complementing rather than undermining NATO's nuclear-deterrence policy. A Franco-Polish exchange platform could be established to discuss Polish expectations regarding the French deterrent and to consider specific steps to enhance bilateral military–technical cooperation within the boundaries set by the French nuclear doctrine.[14] This could include, among other things, scenario-based discussions of nuclear crises, observation and participation of Polish armed forces in the French nuclear exercises, and visits or deployments of the French air force's nuclear squadrons to NATO's eastern flank.

With a defence budget totalling 4.7% of its GDP and a massive military-modernisation programme under way, Poland is one of several European countries with strong credentials for constructively engaging and influencing a new Trump administration determined to exact greater defence contributions from European NATO members.[15] Poland supports shoring up European security and defence, and Tusk recently stressed that 'the era of geopolitical outsourcing is over'.[16] At the same time, Warsaw sees Trump's return as a challenge rather than a shock.

It is hardly inevitable that Trump will decline to extend US nuclear deterrence to European allies. He may choose to maintain and potentially even increase America's ability to deter aggression by nuclear-armed adversaries at the regional level. One possible scenario is the reduction of the United States' conventional military presence in Europe coupled with a strengthened nuclear umbrella, less restrained by NATO's 'three nuclear nos'.[17] The Trump administration may even be open to including Poland in NATO nuclear sharing, or in other forms of cooperation in the nuclear domain, such as pilot training or hosting nuclear-storage sites. Washington may also consider broader changes to US theatre nuclear-force posture, which could include the development of a new nuclear-tipped sea-launched cruise missile and non-strategic air-launched and ground-based platforms capable of carrying a nuclear payload. Such novel systems could ultimately reinforce regional deterrence in Europe.[18]

Fayet, Futter and Kühn all highlighted the importance of conventional deterrence. Clearly, Poland can be a valuable partner, as its military-modernisation programme includes the development of offensive capabilities designed to deter as well as fight. Poland plans to increase the range of its rocket artillery with the introduction of both US High Mobility Artillery Rocket System (HIMARS) and South Korean K239 *Chunmoo* systems, with missiles in the 300-kilometre range and possibly longer. In May 2024, Poland signed an agreement with the United States to acquire several hundred additional JASSM-ER air-launched cruise missiles with ranges up to 1,000 km for Polish F-16 and, in the future, F-35 fighter aircraft. In July 2024, Poland, France, Germany and Italy set up a new programme for the development of a deep precision-strike capability – initially, a 1,000 km-range ground-based cruise missile – known as the European Long-range Strike Approach (ELSA). They have since been joined by the Netherlands, Sweden and the UK.[19] Finally, Poland's *Orka* programme will introduce a new class of submarines capable of launching land-attack cruise missiles. Poland could also host exercises, as well as episodic or crisis deployments of US long-range fires, like those slated to be deployed in Germany from 2026 onwards. Collectively, these capabilities can contribute important non-nuclear elements to European deterrence.

Any indication that the Trump administration plans to reduce US extended nuclear-deterrence commitments to European allies would be a major test for Poland. If Warsaw perceives such signalling as a bargaining tactic to get Europeans to increase their contribution to common defence, it might argue that Trump should look favourably on those countries already contributing well over NATO's benchmark of 2% of GDP to defence – like Poland. A firm US decision to withdraw some or all of the forward-deployed nuclear weapons from Europe would be more challenging, especially if it were to be part of a more general US disengagement from NATO. If Warsaw assessed such a move as definitive, it would probably be compelled to refocus its attention on a European nuclear deterrent by, for instance, participating in discussions of this prospect through either a reformed post-NATO security arrangement or a multilateral format with key European states, likely including France, Germany, Italy, Spain and the UK. Only the irreversible break-up of the transatlantic relationship and the disintegration of the post-war European security architecture could stimulate interest in Poland in developing its own nuclear options.

– Łukasz Kulesa

Dutch Atlantic Pragmatism

European alternatives or 'back-up options' for US extended nuclear deterrence – as explored by Fayet, Futter and Kühn – are also discussed in the Netherlands. The very existence of these discussions is remarkable and presents a canary in the coal mine of sorts. Historically, the Netherlands has been consistently pro-European Union but sceptical of attempts to establish European defence or strategic autonomy parallel to NATO. It is one of the most pro-US and pro-Alliance NATO allies, at least in Western Europe, and one of the five nuclear-sharing states. Yet, in The Hague too, behind closed doors, civilian and military policymakers are questioning long-standing dogma. In parliamentary committees and private meetings, Dutch politicians are inquiring about France's deterrent, its small arsenal of non-strategic nuclear weapons and possible financing options by European allies. These questions would have been unthinkable a decade ago, or even during Trump's first term.

The Netherlands has been sceptical of strategic autonomy

Like other European NATO states, the Netherlands has increased its defence spending and shifted its stance on European defence options, settling on the formula of 'strengthening the European pillar in NATO'. Many Dutch officials and politicians are deeply unsettled by the combination of Russia's invasion of Ukraine, Trump's rhetoric, and clear signs of the United States' seriousness about refocusing on the Indo-Pacific. But NATO remains the linchpin of Dutch security and defence deliberations. Dutch officials and politicians are seeking to maintain the transatlantic relationship even if the rhetoric from the White House again turns antagonistic. But they, like their German counterparts, understand that something must be done in case these attempts fail. In particular, a nuclear fallback option is needed, and this realisation leads to questions about French and British capabilities.

So far, the national debate has focused on strengthening conventional deterrence, or deterrence-by-denial. The Dutch air force is acquiring advanced US JASSM-ER cruise missiles and *Tomahawk*s, will be joining ELSA, and is contributing substantively to NATO's Integrated Air and Missile Defence mission. While these and related Europe-wide efforts, such as the establishment of an EU-wide €500 billion defence fund, would not diminish Russia's nuclear advantage, if they continued, NATO Europe could develop conventional capabilities that match, if not exceed, Russia's within a decade.

There is a bipartisan consensus in the United States that its strategic focus should be on the Indo-Pacific.[20] Should the United States be distracted or overtaxed in that region, or substantially disavow its commitment to NATO Europe, Russia would retain the nuclear upper hand over NATO Europe. This is simply because Russia outmatches deployed cumulative French and British strategic and especially non-strategic nuclear weapons by a significant factor, and because France and the UK cannot achieve escalation dominance with non-strategic weapons, though France retains the option of a sub-strategic nuclear 'warning shot'.

How then could European nuclear deterrence, centred on France and the UK, be made credible? The credibility of deterrence turns on three elements: the capability to cause unacceptable damage, the willingness to do so and the communication of these facts. Yet nuclear deterrence is not a mathematical certainty. Taken together, the 500+ French and British warheads should be sufficient for what British planners used to call the 'Moscow criterion' – the ability to destroy Moscow and other important Russian population centres whose loss would outweigh any Russian gains through aggression. On the other hand, neither France nor the UK has enough non-strategic nuclear weapons to escalate gradually if Russia resorts to high-end conventional or non-strategic nuclear options that remain below the threshold of an existential threat to France, the UK or their allies. This discontinuity makes their nuclear threat in limited contingencies more ambiguous. Accordingly, the French and British arsenals may not feel sufficient to European allies, including the Netherlands.

During the Cold War, of course, European doubts about the US commitment to Europe persisted right up to the dissolution of the Soviet Union, even though the US continually readjusted its conventional and nuclear postures to reassure them.[21] Something similar would hold for the UK and France. Even if their deterrents should theoretically deter Russia, their allies would likely call upon them repeatedly to confirm and reinforce their promises. The number of French and British warheads might need to be increased – not out of operational necessity, but as a political signal of resolve. At the same time, because Britain and France are not on the far side of the Atlantic and are likewise existentially threatened by a European war that could go nuclear, the

Europeans need not insist on US levels of warheads or launchers. This line of thought underlies French statements about the European dimension of French deterrence, and why it would not be extending its deterrent as explicitly as the United States, because it would remain focused on direct threats to France itself.[22] It is worth noting that France, to increase the escalatory potential of its arsenal, is strengthening the air leg of its deterrent and is developing air-to-ground hypersonic missiles. The UK may reconsider adding an air leg as well, though without joint financing from other European allies, expansion is likely not feasible in light of other defence objectives.[23]

To address the dearth of escalation options in the French and British arsenals, and to strengthen conventional deterrence, NATO Europe should invest in advanced conventional weapons, such as long-range precision-strike missiles, fifth-generation airpower, and air and missile defence. Improved NATO European conventional deterrence would raise the nuclear threshold, easing the burden on French and British nuclear weapons. Furthermore, should Russia elect to engage in conventional or hybrid aggression backed by nuclear threats – in line with a military doctrine that tilts towards constant pressure rather than stepwise escalation – advanced conventional weapons held by NATO European states could hold Russian assets at risk.[24] Thus, Europeans could perhaps manage Russian escalation without relying on non-strategic nuclear weapons.

France especially, but also the UK, would need to include European allies in their deterrence missions. The US deterrent became credible because it did this continuously over decades. Convincing the EU and the front-line states in the northern and eastern sectors of the Alliance – it's more important to assure Poland than Germany – would be the main challenge. One key means would be increased information sharing among European officials, preferably through NATO.[25] From the Netherlands' standpoint, the UK's integration of its deterrent activities into NATO's Nuclear Planning Group (NPG) lends credibility to its commitment. Were France to follow suit, it would send a powerful signal that Paris was constructively re-examining its nuclear doctrine. If French domestic politics make this politically infeasible, an Anglo-French nuclear-deterrence group that included key NATO European states would be the next best option.[26]

Joint exercises could also build trust. French participation in NATO's *Conventional Support for Nuclear Operations* (formerly known as SNOWCAT) and the Alliance's *Steadfast Noon* exercise, or dispersal of the French air force, would affirm the positive evolution of France's Europe-wide outlook. For their part, European allies, including the Netherlands, should accept Macron's offer to take part in the French annual *Poker* exercise.

As a bonus, European investments in deterrence might do more to advance non-proliferation and arms-control efforts than an attempt to restore the more normative multilateralist approaches prevalent in the 1990s and 2000s by diminishing pressure on the US to provide extended deterrence. This would help tame the three-way arms-race dynamics between the United States, Russia and China, and reduce incentives for other European states to go nuclear. Non-nuclear-armed European states should consider a more substantial role for advanced conventional weapons in fostering stable deterrence than they had during the Cold War. All involved should note that the Cold War was not nearly as stable as some remember, and that establishing the credibility of the US extended nuclear deterrent took time. The same will go for nuclear deterrence on the part of Europeans. Yet time may be their scarcest resource.

– Paul van Hooft

European Deterrence, the Right Way

When Donald Trump pressured European NATO allies to spend more on defence in his first term, they reacted with a mixture of outrage and accommodation. Some publicly expressed offence, while others placated the American president with measured increases in defence spending. By the end of Trump's first term, German chancellor Angela Merkel was inured to his hectoring. Confident that the US military would not be able to quickly replace Germany as the main regional hub for US operations in Africa and the Middle East, and convinced that Joe Biden would win the presidential election in 2020, Merkel shrugged off the United States' announcement that year that it would downsize conventional forces in Germany, which Biden promptly countermanded once in office.[27] Trump will likely continue where he left off, and there will be no staunch Atlanticist to rescue Europe anytime soon. Europeans will have to adapt quickly and decisively if they want to ensure their continued freedom and security.

As we wrote in *Survival* several months ago, whether or not there is full or partial US withdrawal from Europe, on nuclear and conventional deterrence 'better coordination between Berlin, London and Paris is urgently needed, and they need to net in other capitals'.[28] But what is the right way to do so, given the range of European views on the issue?

Kristin Ven Bruusgaard, Łukasz Kulesa and Paul van Hooft agree that Europe needs to invest in conventional deterrence assets. Ven Bruusgaard argues that a future European deterrent aimed at Russia would require substantial conventional options. She proposes a dual nuclear hub, with France and the UK taking on different tasks in the strategic and sub-strategic realms, accompanied by enhanced conventional counterforce and defensive capabilities fielded by Germany, Poland and the Nordic countries. We concur that conventional deep-strike precision capabilities will be key for deterring Russia, for two reasons. Firstly, they might help Europeans avoid a fully fledged sub-strategic nuclear-arms race for which Europeans are technically and economically ill-prepared. Secondly, they could better enable Europeans to manage escalation at the nuclear threshold. It is doubtful that the newly established ELSA initiative will be up to the task if it remains focused on medium-range ground-launched cruise missiles. To compete with the Russians on missiles, Europeans need to invest more and broaden the production lines under ELSA. The US approach of tailored conventional-deterrence options, with different sets of long-range fires slated for deployment in Germany, might serve as a blueprint for Europe.

Ven Bruusgaard, Kulesa and Van Hooft also concur on the need to increase the French and British arsenals should America fully withdraw from Europe. Kulesa correctly points out that the combined British and French capabilities fall well short of the Russian arsenal in size and diversity and cannot offset full US disengagement. As Van Hooft notes, however, the credibility of a country's deterrent hinges on its stakes in a conflict as well as comparative numbers. It would still be useful for France and the

UK to signal increased commitment, both to European allies and to Russia, with larger arsenals. As a practical matter, these would require joint financing. It is imperative for a dedicated group of European states to explore the legal, economic and political aspects of generating it. One possibility would be for Germany and like-minded states to co-finance the expansion of the French and British arsenals, especially given that Germany may soon have a conservative chancellor who may be willing and able to amend the German debt-brake law and increase German defence spending.[29] According to a study by the Bundestag, German co-financing might not contradict Germany's legal obligations under the Non-Proliferation Treaty.[30]

In turn, France and Britain could do more to share critical information about their nuclear capabilities and plans with their European allies. This is a sensitive matter for Paris and London as nuclear-armed powers. France has demonstrated laudable openness in recent years, inviting allied participation in its *Poker*

France has demonstrated laudable openness

exercises. A more substantive step would be for Paris to drop its aversion to participating in NATO's internal nuclear deliberations and finally joining the NPG. This is a prerequisite to deepening the nuclear dialogue with NATO's eastern-flank countries because it would signal that France views its deterrent as a contribution to Europe's security and not merely as a national insurance policy. A Franco-Polish exchange platform for discussing Polish expectations about the French deterrent, suggested by Kulesa, could be an important building block, possibly within the framework of the Nancy Treaty that is supposed to be signed between Paris and Warsaw in 2025.[31] Another plausible step would be the political activation of the Franco-German Treaty of Aachen, signed in 2019, which stipulates that the two countries 'shall afford one another any means of assistance or aid within their power, including military force, in the event of an armed attack on their territories'.[32] This is even firmer language than NATO's Article 5 commitment. A joint public declaration that 'military force' could include the French nuclear forces would send a strong message to Europe as well as to Russia.[33]

As for Britain, the new UK–Germany Trinity House Agreement on Defence, signed by the two countries in October 2024, established a dedicated sub-group on nuclear issues, which will regularly bring together representatives of the respective defence and foreign ministries.[34] The two governments could publicly announce their meetings and complement discussions by joint visits to key UK nuclear facilities to show how the UK deterrent works and to increase confidence in the system. In addition, London should consider replicating the Franco-German approach of issuing bilateral security guarantees, perhaps to key partner nations on the continent.

Any discussions and proposals must ultimately account for Russian reactions, as Ven Bruusgaard reminds us. Without the United States in Europe, would Russia re-examine the role of nuclear weapons in its defence strategy, and, if so, could this benefit Europeans? This central question points to the need for painstakingly developing the overall programme that Europe needs for dealing with Russia, beyond immediate and necessary containment. To durably deter Russia, Europe needs a long-term political strategy for stabilising the relationship. A key component would be a careful evaluation of the potentially perverse effects of bolstering European conventional and nuclear deterrence, such as an unbridled arms race or misperceived signals, as highlighted by Van Hooft. Policymakers in Berlin, London, Paris and Warsaw will have to think about devising a viable arms-control strategy to accompany Europe's inevitable arms build-up. And Europeans will have to set up functioning communication channels with Russia to mitigate avoidable misperceptions. Unfortunately, however, arms-control and confidence-building measures cannot be Europe's top priorities in the short term.

Despite Trump's return, complete US disengagement from Europe is not inevitable. America will continue to have strategic interests in Europe. Building a separate European nuclear deterrent is not yet necessary. But Europeans have little choice but to anticipate that the Trump administration, as it has amply indicated, will devalue transatlantic relations and turn its strategic attention starkly to the Indo-Pacific. Accordingly, European governments must invest jointly in conventional deterrence and defence assets while building cooperative clusters around the French and British nuclear hubs. Increased information sharing and deepened military exchanges and trust-building dialogue platforms are necessary tools. Europe should also mount bolder efforts to overcome French reluctance to join the NPG and engineer the co-financing of French and British arsenals. Trump will soon test how far Europeans are willing to go to meet his burden-sharing demands. On defence, it is in their interests to go quite far indeed. A Europe that contributes significant resources to NATO's conventional deterrent, such as a robust arsenal of deep-strike stand-off weaponry, would be safer from Russian attack and safer from complete US withdrawal.

– Héloïse Fayet, Andrew Futter and Ulrich Kühn

Notes

1   Peter Nicholas, 'Trump Details Sweeping Changes He'll Carry Out on Day One and Beyond in an Exclusive Interview', NBC News, 8 December 2024, https://www.nbcnews.com/politics/donald-trump/trump-details-sweeping-changes-ll-carry-day-one-exclusive-interview-rcna182858.

2   See Barry R. Posen, 'Europe Can Defend Itself', *Survival*, vol. 62, no. 6, December 2020–January 2021, pp. 7–34.

3   See Héloïse Fayet, Andrew Futter and Ulrich Kühn, 'Forum: Towards a European Nuclear Deterrent', *Survival*, vol. 66, no. 5, October–November 2024, pp. 67–98.

4   *Ibid.*, p. 68.

5   See Christopher A. Ford and David A. Rosenberg, 'The Naval Intelligence Underpinnings of Reagan's Maritime Strategy', *Journal of Strategic Studies*, vol. 28, no. 2, April 2005, pp. 379–409.

6   See Dmitry (Dima) Adamsky, 'If War Comes Tomorrow: Russian Thinking About "Regional Nuclear Deterrence"', *Journal of Slavic Military Studies*, vol. 27, no. 1, January 2014, pp.

163–88; Clint Reach, Vikram Kilambi and Mark Cozad, *Russian Assessments and Applications of the Correlation of Forces and Means* (Santa Monica, CA: RAND Corporation, 2020); and Kristin Ven Bruusgaard, 'Russian Nuclear Strategy and Conventional Inferiority', *Journal of Strategic Studies*, vol. 44, no. 1, January 2021, pp. 3–35.

7   Even Larsen discusses four options available to states seeking to escape paralysis: a countervalue punishment strategy; a conventional pause strategy; a damage-limitation strategy; and a tit-for-tat strategy. Each would require different nuclear and conventional capabilities. See Even Hellan Larsen, 'Escaping Paralysis: Strategies for Countering Asymmetric Nuclear Escalation', *Security Studies*, vol. 33, no. 3, February 2024, pp. 439–75.

8   South Korea is one potentially illustrative example. See Ian Bowers and Henrik Stålhane Hiim, 'Conventional Counterforce Dilemmas: South Korea's Deterrence Strategy and Stability on the Korean Peninsula',

International Security, vol. 45, no. 3, Winter 2020/21, pp. 7–39.

9   See Fayet, Futter and Kühn, 'Forum: Towards a European Nuclear Deterrent', pp. 73–6.

10 See Artur Kacprzyk, 'Debating Perspectives of European Nuclear Deterrence', *PISM Bulletin*, no. 56, 8 April 2024, https://pism.pl/ publications/debating-perspectives-of-european-nuclear-deterrence.

11 See 'Poland's Bid to Participate in NATO Nuclear Sharing', *IISS Strategic Comments*, vol. 29, no. 7, September 2023, https://www.iiss.org/ publications/strategic-comments/2023/ polands-bid-to-participate-in-nato-nuclear-sharing/; and 'Poland Ready to Host NATO Members' Nuclear Weapons to Counter Russia, President Says', France24, 22 April 2024, https://www.france24.com/en/ europe/20240422-poland-ready-to-host-nato-members-nuclear-weapons-to-counter-russia-president-says.

12 See Jakub Palowski, 'Polish F-35 to Be Nuclear Capable? Polish National Security Bureau Takes the Floor', Defence24, 11 July 2023, https:// defence24.com/defence-policy/ polish-f-35-jets-to-be-nuclear-capable-polish-national-security-bureau-takes-the-floor.

13 See NATO, 'Founding Act on Mutual Relations, Cooperation and Security Between NATO and the Russian Federation', 27 May 1997, https:// www.nato.int/cps/su/natohq/official_ texts_25468.htm.

14 See Łukasz Maślanka, 'President Macron Proposes a European Security Initiative', Centre for Eastern Studies Analyses, 29 April 2024, https://www.osw.waw.pl/ en/publikacje/analyses/2024-04-29/ president-macron-proposes-a-european-defence-initiative.

15 See 'Poland's Government Plans Record Defense Spending in Its 2025 Budget', AP News, 28 August 2024, https://apnews.com/article/poland-budget-2025-defense-spending-increase-d1b5d840876df2cb850a7 8348887473a.

16 'Tusk Says Poland Will Work on Strengthening Relations with US', Reuters, 7 November 2024, https:// www.reuters.com/world/tusk-says-poland-will-work-strengthening-relations-with-us-2024-11-07/.

17 For one such proposal, see Robert Peters, 'A Nuclear Posture Review for the Next Administration: Building the Nuclear Arsenal of the 21st Century', Heritage Foundation, 30 July 2024, https://www.heritage.org/defense/ report/nuclear-posture-review-the-next-administration-building-the-nuclear-arsenal-the-21st.

18 See Congressional Commission on the Strategic Posture of the United States, 'America's Strategic Posture: The Final Report of the Congressional Commission on the Strategic Posture of the United States', October 2023, pp. 48–9, available at https://www.ida.org/-/ media/feature/publications/a/am/ americas-strategic-posture/strategic-posture-commission-report.ashx.

19 See Timothy Wright, 'Europe's Missile Renaissance', IISS Analysis, 25 November 2024, https://www.iiss.org/online-analysis/online-analysis/2024/11/ europes-missile-renaissance/.

20 See Congressional Commission on the Strategic Posture of the United States, 'America's Strategic Posture'.

21 See Marc Trachtenberg, *A Constructed Peace: The Making of the European Settlement, 1945–1963* (Princeton, NJ: Princeton University Press, 1999).

22 See Emmanuel Macron, 'The Future of European Security – Speech by President Emmanuel Macron', Stockholm, 30 January 2024, available at https://www.youtube.com/watch?v=9utMpXOnMmA.

23 See Fayet, Futter and Kühn, 'Forum: Towards a European Nuclear Deterrent', pp. 83–4.

24 See Dmitry (Dima) Adamsky, *The Russian Way of Deterrence: Strategic Culture, Coercion, and War* (Stanford, CA: Stanford University Press, 2023); David Blagden, 'Strategic Stability and the Proliferation of Conventional Precision Strike: A (Bounded) Case for Optimism?', *Nonproliferation Review*, vol. 27, nos 1–3, October 2020, pp. 123–36; Paul van Hooft, 'Deter, Compete, and Engage: Europe's Responsibility Within the Arms Control Regime After Ukraine, With or Without the United States', in Nadezhda Arbatova, George Perkovich and Paul van Hooft (eds), *The Future of Nuclear Arms Control and the Impact of the Russia–Ukraine War* (Cambridge, MA: American Academy of Arts & Sciences, 2024), p. 75; and Joshua H. Pollack, Cristina Varriale and Tom Plant, 'The Changing Role of Allied Conventional Precision-strike Capabilities in Nuclear Decision Making', *Nonproliferation Review*, vol. 27, nos 1–3, October 2020, pp. 21–37.

25 See Fayet, Futter and Kühn, 'Forum: Towards a European Nuclear Deterrent', pp. 75–6.

26 The sharing of French nuclear weapons would be another option, though it is politically infeasible at present.

27 See Philip Oltermann, '"Regrettable": Germany Reacts to Trump Plan to Withdraw US Troops', *Guardian*, 6 June 2020, https://www.theguardian.com/world/2020/jun/06/regrettable-germany-reacts-to-trump-plan-to-withdraw-us-troops.

28 Fayet, Futter and Kühn, 'Forum: Towards a European Nuclear Deterrent', p. 92.

29 See Claus Hulverscheidt, 'Merz offen für Reform der Schuldenbremse' [Merz open to reform of debt brake], *Süddeutsche Zeitung*, 13 November 2024, https://www.sueddeutsche.de/politik/wirtschaftspolitik-schuldenbremse-friedrich-merz-olaf-scholz-neuwahlen-lux.LUC8f4BVMS6bi3vJBVHezH.

30 See 'Sachstand: Völkerrechtliche Verpflichtungen Deutschlands beim Umgang mit Kernwaffen: Deutsche und europäische Ko-Finanzierung ausländischer Nuklearwaffenpotentiale' [State of affairs: Germany's obligations under international law in dealing with nuclear weapons: German and European co-financing of foreign nuclear-weapons potentials], Bundestag, 23 May 2017, https://www.bundestag.de/resource/blob/513080/c9a903735d5ea334181c2f946d2cf8a2/wd-2-013-17-pdf-data.pdf.

31 See Adam Hsakou, 'Franco-Polish Rapprochement: A Window of Opportunity', German Marshall Fund, 13 November 2024,

https://www.gmfus.org/news/
franco-polish-rapprochement-
window-opportunity.

32   'Treaty Between the Federal Republic
of Germany and the French Republic
on Franco-German Cooperation and
Integration', 22 January 2019, available at https://www.diplomatie.gouv.
fr/IMG/pdf/19-0232-1900417_en_fin_
reinschrift_ws_aa105-0g_ck_010219__
cleo79d7b.pdf.

33   See Eckhard Lübkemeier, 'Voilà, ein
Plan B für Deutschland' [Voilà, a plan
B for Germany], *Frankfurter Allgemeine
Zeitung*, 16 February 2024, https://
www.faz.net/aktuell/politik/inland/
donald-trump-mit-nato-drohung-
deutschland-sucht-in-frankreich-
einen-partner-19524433.html.

34   See 'Agreement on Defence
Co-operation Between the Ministry
of Defence of the United Kingdom of
Great Britain and Northern Ireland
and the Federal Ministry of Defence
of the Federal Republic of Germany',
23 October 2024, available at https://
assets.publishing.service.gov.uk/
media/6718b947d94d2c219a5405d2/
Agreement_on_Defence_co-operation_
between__the_Ministry_of_Defence_
of_the_United_Kingdom_of_Great_
Britain_and_Northern_Ireland_and_
the_Federal_Ministry_of_Defence_of_
the_Federal_Republic_of_Germany.pdf.

Copyright © 2025 The International Institute for Strategic Studies

After Gaza: American Liberals and Israel

Steven Simon

The Gaza ceasefire is an inkblot onto which observers impose their views of Donald Trump and the outgoing Biden administration. On the one hand, Trump's gnomic outbursts, such as there being 'hell to pay' if a ceasefire were not agreed to, which raised the question of what residual and as yet unexperienced ordeal there might be for Gazans to endure, and endorsing a description of Israeli Prime Minister Benjamin Netanyahu as a 'dark son of a bitch', which might well have been a grudging compliment, are somehow deciphered as evidence of his commitment to an Arab–Israeli peace and Palestinian statehood.[1] Rumours that his representative to the peace talks, real-estate broker Steve Witkoff, told Netanyahu not to 'fuck this up' reinforces this interpretation of Trump's responsibility for the long-awaited ceasefire. On the other hand, Biden partisans insist that the ceasefire plan was his and that his administration, spearheaded by Biden administration CIA director William J. Burns, had been working with recalcitrant belligerents to get it since May 2024.

The first 42-day phase of the agreement is the one most likely to be carried out. Israel will not be required to withdraw its forces from Gaza right away, but only to remove them to the perimeter. If fighting restarts, Israelis won't have to defend their re-entry into the strip. Moreover, the Israel Defense

Steven Simon is a Distinguished Fellow and Visiting Professor at Dartmouth College and senior fellow at the Quincy Institute for Responsible Statecraft. He spent 20 years in the US government, holding senior positions in the State Department and at the National Security Council.

Survival | vol. 67 no. 1 | February–March 2025 | pp. 143–158   https://doi.org/10.1080/00396338.2025.2459022

Forces (IDF) will have the opportunity to return to training cycles, restock munitions spare parts and consumables, and rotate and refresh combat personnel. It also provides breathing space in which to assess options in the north, where a ceasefire with Hizbullah was holding at time of writing and a new technocratic government had been formed; and in western Syria, where the IDF was positioned to the east of the Golan Heights and may need to plan for a clash with Turkish forces. Hamas is keen to retrieve Palestinians from Israeli jails, which requires the release of some of the Israeli hostages they hold, and Mohammed Sinwar, the late leader Yahya Sinwar's brother and legatee, gets to live another 42 days. Both sides will retain plenty of fodder for future trades.

As for the question of to whom the Gaza ceasefire should be attributed, the answer must be Netanyahu. This is one version of a classic ceasefire, where the party that had resisted it has temporarily run out of targets and largely achieved its war aims. Two-thirds of Gaza's built infrastructure is now a mountain of rubble that will take 15 years to clear, between 2% and 3% of its population is dead, the Hamas leadership and forces that carried out the 7 October 2023 assault have been wiped out, and the Gaza enclave is effectively cordoned off from the rest of the world and no longer a security threat to Israel, under intensive, relentless surveillance and penetration by the Shin Bet. A significant proportion of Hamas's tunnel network has been mapped and neutralised. Polls still indicate that most Gaza residents believe armed resistance is the path to independence, but support for Hamas itself is wobbly. Of countries that had diplomatic relations with Israel before the war, only one, Turkiye, has broken them, despite International Criminal Court warrants and accusations of genocide. Having shrunk the opportunity cost of a ceasefire to insignificance after 15 months, Netanyahu decided it was time.

In any event, American policy towards Israel will be Trumpian for at least the next four years. With the return to office of the most illiberal president certainly since the Second World War, American liberals are left to wander in the political wilderness and consider the implications of their defeat. Gaza, in the end, did not play a significant role in that defeat. But liberals' troubled and, it now appears, dysfunctional relationship with Israel calls for some constructive reflection in preparation for their eventual return to power.

On account of the war, the prospect of a continuing US relationship with Israel has become a vexing challenge to American liberal voters. Liberals are not an undifferentiated mass, of course. They are situated along a spectrum of varying age groups, concerns about foreign policy versus domestic issues, attitudes towards the conflict and the belligerents involved, activist inclinations, and susceptibility to social media and peer pressure. At one end of the spectrum are older liberals, who tend to favour Israel but harbour sympathies towards Palestinians, at the other mobilised students on campuses with little or no comprehension of the idea of a Jewish state. Many American blacks liken the plight of Palestinians to the struggle for civil rights at home, much as liberal Jews in the 1960s equated the enslavement of blacks in the United States to that of Israelites in Egypt and marched with them in Alabama and elsewhere and, in Mississippi, were killed by segregationists. Arab Americans are angry at what they perceive as Democrats' disregard for their horror at events in Gaza, though Republican politicians seem to have escaped their ire.[2]

Discourse has been especially heated due to claims of genocide, which have transformed an ugly war into an existential moral crisis for all humanity that therefore demand a firm response. As a result, the demand issued by some younger Democrats and Arab Americans that the Biden administration impose sanctions on Israel in the midst of an extraordinarily consequential and bitter election campaign has pitted the future of American democracy against the imperative to punish the alleged genocidaires and settler-colonial malefactors. Looking ahead, the ongoing Middle East conflicts compel us to think more constructively about how to deal with divided democracies like Israel — as opposed to, say, annihilationist Nazis under the spell of a dictator — that commit war crimes in response to awful provocations.

Present at the creation and beyond

These are important questions in a general sense, and, in the case of the US–Israel relationship, urgent and consequential. The relationship is old and deep. The Zionists' declaration 'that Palestine be established as a Jewish

Commonwealth', as against a British mandate or a minority in an Arab state, emerged from New York's Biltmore Hotel in 1942.[3] Despite opposition from the State Department and the Pentagon, in 1947 US president Harry Truman decided to support the partition of Palestine into Arab and Jewish states. The United States was the first country to recognise the state of Israel when it declared independence in 1948. On that score, the United States was truly present at the creation.

Truman's decision had a redemptive character in the wake of the Holocaust, whose intended victims the United States, like other countries in the West, had done nothing to help. It was important too for a post-war government perceiving the need to square the deaths of 400,000 soldiers, marines, sailors and airmen with noble principles. This is not to say that the Zionists would not have had their state if Truman had taken the sensible if bloodless advice of his national-security team and balked at partition and eventual recognition of the Jewish state. The Jews had their backs to the wall and were going to fight until the bitter end. They were also well organised, relatively well equipped and seeded with combat-tested soldiers. The Arab forces lacked these advantages and lost. As a material factor, the United States was insignificant.

The Jews had their backs to the wall

The refugee crisis triggered by the war of independence, or *Nakba*, depending on one's perspective, 'disgusted' Truman, who seemed to experience buyer's remorse.[4] But there was nothing the administration could do about it. Arab objectives were maximal and expressed by some in what would certainly be classed now as genocidal terms. The Jews were defending indefensible boundaries established by the United Nations partition committee, and the only strategy that was going to work for them after the disastrous fight in winter 1947 was to expand the territory under their control.

The close US–Israel relationship endured despite serious tensions.[5] Israel and the Soviet Union abandoned each other, and Israel threw its lot in with the West. Although the liberal temper of late New Deal, post-war America offered black Americans as little as Israel's supposed liberalism offered Jews of Middle Eastern or North African origin, it worked in favour of Israel and Jewish immigrants, even if many wanted to return to their homelands.[6] Compared to the pre-war world, the US and Israel were liberal and democratic, and they shared a Western heritage. As a character in the Apple TV+ miniseries *Lady in the Lake* observes, American Jews had been declared white, as it were, and could therefore exercise their political influence without fear of retribution.[7] The Arabs, who had oil and the oil majors at their side, had to settle for an uneasy stand-off with the emerging pro-Israel lobby.

There followed a succession of crises in the US–Israel relationship. The two countries found it hard to align their strategic objectives even during the Cold War, when Washington sought to enlist Israel as a combatant in a potential war with the Soviet Union that many in the Reagan administration thought likely. The US and Israel fought over Israel's role in the 1956 Suez War, various peace initiatives, the question of arms transfers, Israel's nuclear-weapons programme, the establishment of settlements in captured territory following the 1967 Six-Day War, Israel's invasion of Lebanon in 1982, the quest for an Israeli–Egyptian peace treaty after the 1973 Yom Kippur War, Israel's attempt to interfere in the 1991 Gulf War, and more.

Throughout, the relationship remained fundamentally strong owing to Cold War dynamics and the political strength of American Jewish voters. And as America moved rightward, Israel moved with it. Israeli leader Menachem Begin's redirection of Israel's political economy from social democracy to unfettered – by Israeli standards – capitalism mirrored Ronald Reagan's repudiation of the New Deal. US public support for the relationship was almost overdetermined, as Israel and the US seemed to be evolving in sync. Both took a tough stance towards terrorists and shared what came to be called a 'Judeo-Christian tradition' during the Cold War. This was left imprecisely defined, since it never really existed in the sense of a shared religion. Of course, it was invoked during the Second World War and the post-war era to suggest that the two countries were united against fascism, and then behind social and economic reform, especially civil rights. But by the 1960s, the left was already questioning the validity of the term because it seemed to reinforce the view that public policy had to be grounded in religious doctrine. By the 1980s, the religious right had captured the phrase to convey wall-to-wall societal support for conservative social reforms favoured by Christian evangelicals.[8]

The relationship got a significant boost with the new Christian evangelical activism of Pat Robertson, Jerry Falwell and John Hagee, who focused their massive congregations on God's pledge to Abraham and David that the Israelites would possess the Holy Land, and interpreted the establishment of Israel as the fulfilment of this covenant and therefore a vindication of sacred scripture. American liberals weren't keen on this development, but, with the Labor Party's return to power in Israel under Yitzhak Rabin, advent of the Oslo Accords, Israeli and Palestinian mutual recognition, and Yassir Arafat's rejection of terrorism, they reckoned they'd won. The old Israel was back, swords were beaten into ploughshares, and liberals could redirect their activist instincts to more pressing causes.

A new Israel

Unfortunately, the old Israel was not back for long. In 1995, Rabin was shot dead leaving a peace rally in Tel Aviv by a religious Jewish student deranged by the prospect of surrendering Jewish land to non-Jews. A brutal wave of Palestinian terrorism followed, finishing what Rabin's assassin had started: the demolition of the Oslo Accords. The peace process, which had become central to liberal support for a shifting Israeli state and society, was dead. The Israeli left declined slowly, then rapidly, and the Israeli right has governed with only a few interruptions ever since.

For older Americans, especially Jewish ones, this new dispensation did not really register. Perceptions generally lag behind change. Voters might not realise that inflation has dropped, or that a recession is over, until months after these positive changes have occurred. In the case of American liberals and Israel, a blend of denial, nostalgia, loose observation and sheer gullibility produced a delayed reaction to deep changes under way in Israeli society and politics.

Bestsellers like *The Start-up Nation,* which valorised Israel's tech prowess, contributed to this lag by presenting contemporary Israeli society as cutting-edge, creative, focused on technology and, crucially, global in outlook. In short, Israel was cast as an epitome of Westernised modernity that was far more secular than it really was. Strange as it might seem now, in the era of Elon Musk and Peter Thiel, the prevailing belief among American liberals 20 years ago was that secularism and liberalism went hand in hand. The projection of this belief on to Israel's tech elite reinforced the sense of a liberal affinity connecting the two countries. The old joke about Israel was that it was a defence ministry with a symphony orchestra; by the 2000s it was fast becoming a cyber lab with a symphony orchestra. As the nonpartisan Shoresh Institution documents, however, Israel's educational system had imploded, starved of funding and knowledgeable teachers. Israeli teenagers were at the low end of Western standards for basic problem-solving and maths skills, while opinion surveys of 18-year-old Jewish Israelis showed that they distrusted democracy, wanted a 'strong leader' and thought Israeli Arabs' civil rights should be curtailed.[9] As *The Start-up Nation* concedes, the tech sector was strong only because it was populated by experts who had been handpicked by the IDF, given intensive training, funnelled into elite cyber-warfare units, and after their service in the IDF released into the capitalist wild.

To be sure, Israeli society remains remarkably liberal in important ways. It has a free press, elections that are essentially free, fair, and orderly, and a functioning, independent judiciary system that largely guarantees civil liberties, at least for Israeli Jews. Its Jewish population is ethnically diverse, discrimination against Jews from the Middle East and North Africa having faded. A glance at statistics on intermarriage between Ashkenazic and Mizrahi Jews, or 20 minutes of crowd-watching in central Tel Aviv, makes this abundantly clear. Tel Aviv and Haifa boast an array of Western urban features. LGBTQ+ individuals do not face organised harassment or proscription, and abortion is not criminalised. There are still plenty of liberal voters, judging by the size of demonstrations against the right-wing move to neuter the country's supreme court and by opinion-survey returns that align with the size of the street protests. One can be a liberal, Jewish or otherwise, and see Israel as a place one could feel at home. Yet Israeli society is starkly divided politically and ideologically. Accordingly, the number of liberal Israelis emigrating to the US and other Western countries is greater than the number of immigrants to Israel. Liberalism and university education are linked, better-educated Israelis are disproportionately liberal, and they are leaving Israel in search of economic opportunities elsewhere because their superior education and overseas links allow them to do so. The newcomers to Israel who are partially replacing the leavers bring a more conservative, less conciliatory set of values.[10]

In full context, Israel's transformation is understandable. Americans think they have been waging 'forever wars' after 20 years, but Israeli society has had to evolve amid a perpetual battle with regional states and indigenous Palestinians since the state's inception 75 years ago, which followed savage violence in Europe that culminated in the Holocaust. That a militant society would materialise was always likely.[11] Mainstream Zionists in the 1930s and 1940s were focused on creating the structure and institutions of a state. They were less concerned about reanimating an ancient map of an Israelite kingdom that had faded by the advent of the Common Era. Other factions subordinated the construction of an administrative state to building a religiously observant society on land promised to their ancestors by God.

Zvi Yehudah Kook, the son of Israel's first Ashkenazic Chief Rabbi Abraham Isaac Kook, famously bridged the gap between the secular posture of the mainstream Zionists and those whose commitment was to 'the land and the Lord'.[12] In 1967, in commemoration of Israel's nineteenth year of independence, he laid out his version of salvation history in an impassioned speech. It was three weeks before the outbreak of the Six-Day War. Emotions were at a high pitch. Deploying biblical references and exegesis, he deplored the partition of Palestine by the UN in 1947, which denied the future state of Israel the West Bank and lands east of the Jordan River. Secular Zionists had exulted in partition, but their focus had been the creation of a state rather than redeeming land to usher in a messianic era. Kook's dirge asked rhetorically where, in the context of partition, were 'our' Hebron, Shechem (Nablus) and so forth. Then, riffing on Psalm 19 – linking the text to the anniversary of independence – he preached that redemption had been started by secular Zionists who acquired and developed Palestinian land and defended it in battle, but could be completed only by religious Jews committed to the recovery of all the territory ruled by the last independent Jewish kingdom at its greatest extent in the late second and early first century BCE. He then encouraged his students to do the unthinkable and cheer a passing military parade because these were the troops who would liberate the land that pious Jews would sanctify.[13] A month later, the episode was held to be prophetic as the IDF took all the territory between Israel and the Jordan River, including the Temple Mount in Jerusalem.

Other prominent rabbis, as well as lay religious leaders, elaborated or revised these themes in various ways. Especially after the trauma of the 1973 war with Egypt and Syria, the religious imperative to settle the territories gradually eclipsed the security rationale for settlements confined to the Jordan Valley, along the green line and around Jerusalem. Settlement activity branched out to areas of biblical import in the highlands of Samaria and to the south in Judean hill country. The ascendance of right-wing Israelis to power in 1977 gave this activity political ballast. The religious settler movement went from strength to strength. The movement anathematised Rabin and gave rise to his assassination, growing in its wake.

In 2022 the religious right became the state

For a while, the movement was more a pressure group than a successful political party capable of executing policy. It acted more like an insurgency, contesting the status of occupied territory with the state, which faced constraints – especially those involving diplomacy and security – that the movement did not. The modern movement's roots in the mandate era could be seen in its adversarial posture vis-à-vis the state. The religious settlements movement, having been largely excluded by the pre-state pioneers, were energised after 1967 not only by Kook's passion, but also by the opportunity to be in the vanguard themselves. In this respect, just as the pre-state settlers had to create facts against the will of the British government, the post-1967 settlers needed to create facts in opposition to the wishes of the Israeli government.

In November 2022, the dog caught the car: the religious right became the state. This was scarcely inevitable. Netanyahu might never have been born, or he might have chosen different coalition partners. The counterfactuals are infinite. Why mainstream Israeli politicians defaulted is complicated, but one reason was their own perceptual lag, and perhaps their sublimi-nal sympathy towards the neo-pioneers, which prevented them from recognising the threat posed by land fetishists. The political ruthlessness of the centre-right has now led to their inclusion in the government itself. Palestinian society ran a parallel risk of militancy, already clear in 1929, when Palestinians launched an assault on Zionist enclaves which in retro-spect was eerily similar to the 7 October attack.[14]

The loneliness of the American Jewish liberal

It can take a serious shock to eliminate perceptual lags. For American lib-erals, Israel has now delivered one by way of the Gaza war. Some liberals expected excessive violence, perhaps because it would validate their crystal-lising perception of the Israeli state under Netanyahu. Others could scarcely believe that Israelis would respond so violently and indiscriminately to an assault even as sadistic as the one Yahya Sinwar unleashed on 7 October, and wilfully kill so many civilians. There was no real precedent. There had been local massacres, including one in Jordan, in the early years of the state, a terrible slaughter of Palestinians by Israel's Maronite Christian allies in Lebanon, an errant artillery strike that killed over 100 internally displaced people there, and the intense assault on Lebanese civil infrastructure in the 2006 Israel–Hizbullah war, but never anything like the systematic destruc-tion that the IDF has wrought in Gaza over the past 13 months. The pager and walkie-talkie bombs targeting Hizbullah in Lebanon in September 2024, which the moral philosopher Michael Walzer has defined as a war crime, followed by the invasion of Lebanon and the intense aerial attacks carried out in the environs of Beirut, have rattled liberals even more.[15]

Older American liberals, especially Jewish ones, have now awakened to a more complex tableau that evolved during the roughly five decades they thought Israel was still frozen in the amber of 1967. But they are still at a loss to explain the radically punitive character of Israel's military campaign in Gaza. To some extent, it is attributable to secular factors. The artificial-intelligence-driven targeting system used by the IDF is one proximate cause of the high civilian death toll. It enables the Israelis to claim with super-ficial validity that they do not deliberately target civilians. But of course, the IDF deliberately chooses the targeting methodology that makes civilian deaths inevitable.[16] More defensibly, civilian casualties are unavoidable in urban combat, especially when there's no place for the civilian population to shelter. The probable ratio of civilian to combatant deaths, about 1:1, is the same as that in the US-led actions against the Islamic State in Syria and Iraq. This assessment will unavoidably remain provisional until the exact number of deaths is known.[17] As for the disgraceful actions of individual soldiers, such as tossing Palestinian bodies off rooftops, the IDF is a conscript force, a citizens' army, whose soldiers' behaviour reflects the attitudes of the communities from which they are drafted. In an all-volunteer force like the United States', discipline is much tighter and offences by individual soldiers are more likely to be punished. Finally, Sinwar's barbaric way of war was an intentional stimulus to the worst instincts of the IDF soldiers.

In considering Israel's conduct of the war, American liberals could find extenuating circumstances. Their quandary has arisen before. In 2016, there was a serious internecine quarrel over the plank in the Democratic Party's platform on US support for Israel. Netanyahu's address to a joint session of Congress in March 2015, during Barack Obama's presidency, had been designed to undermine the president, mobilise Republicans and stampede scared Democrats to the right. By 2016, liberals had had enough time to ponder that event and arrive at an effective response. The platform fight was resolved in favour of the status quo, however, and there the issue remained. Netanyahu's rococo friendship with Trump, who many believe flirts with anti-Semitism and without doubt maintains ties to openly anti-Semitic public figures, led some liberals to conclude that Israelis were trading the security of diasporic Jews for the territorial ambitions of the Israeli right.[18]

Netanyahu's disregard for American Jews was especially hard to face because they have so little to fall back on. Years ago, the late Rabbi Jacob Neusner, a Talmud professor at Brown University, wrote a carefully considered essay, condensed in an op-ed in the *Washington Post*, asking 'Is America the Promised Land for the Jews?'.[19] Neusner's piece argued that Zionism could not sustain Jewish identity in the United States. If Jews in the diaspora failed to cultivate their own garden in the way that Jews in exile succeeded in doing in the wake of their expulsion from Palestine after the

Bar Kokhba revolt against Rome in 135 CE, then American Judaism – and Jews – would fade from the scene. While many American Jews became more secular and less likely to believe in God, they continued to look to Zionism and Israel as the focus for their identity and community. Some still relied on Israel for a sense of religious identity. But Neusner made it clear that Israel's transformation into a state whose policy towards Palestinians rejects values American Jewish liberals cherish confronted them with a serious dilemma.

It has gotten worse. The burden of intersectionality does not lie on non-Jewish left-liberal shoulders. Their identity is unitary. They are free to deny Israel's legitimacy, or even its existence, with a clear conscience and still maintain their liberal credentials. It's a cost-free position. For mainstream Jewish liberals, however, it emphatically is not. Condemning Israel poses an agonising conflict of interest. For them to deny Israel's legitimacy is to deny a critical aspect of their own identity. Whatever sense of righteousness they gain is offset by a sense of betrayal. The costs rise as their repudiation by the left, with its unabashed denunciations of Israel and its diaspora, intensify. A segment of the broader non-sectarian American left has come to perceive liberal American Jews as part of an undifferentiated mass of murderous Zionists with an easy vehemence that is chilling.[20] And it only validates the Israeli far right's world view. Meanwhile, the illiberal cast of the Netanyahu government increasingly undermines Jewish liberals while fuelling the indignation of their erstwhile non-Jewish liberal comrades.

New rules

Trump's policy towards Israel is impossible to predict with high confidence because of his mercurial nature, uncertain dominance over Congress on key issues – NATO and Israel come to mind – and cabinet, subcabinet and White House personnel choices that appear to undermine his own instincts. But it is probably safer to assume that his administration will not try, at least not very hard, to derail Netanyahu and the direction he's taking his own country. If so, tensions between liberal American Jews and both Israel and non-Jewish American liberals are likely to persist. The onus is on liberal American Jews to propose policies that, say, signal considered disapproval for Israeli treatment of Palestinians so long as they are unlikely to endanger

Israel's security, as opposed to its government stability. This alone would be a tall order, but they must also work to form coalitions with other liberal factions that may seem less concerned with the safety of Israel's Jewish population than with seeing Israel experience pain comparable to that suffered by Gazans.

It is not difficult to identify policy proposals that would distance the United States from punitive or destabilising Israeli government action without compromising the security of Israelis. Washington has got to walk this tightrope in part because of history and ethics, but also as a strategic proposition. The US has treaty allies that would be seriously disconcerted if the US punished Israel by weakening its self-defence capabilities. On a less formal level and in the domestic context, Jewish liberals should not acquiesce in the self-righteous, anti-Israel posturing of non-Jewish liberals. But their most effective recourse would be dialogue rather than confrontation. The purpose would be to focus on values and objectives that Jewish and non-Jewish liberals still share despite differences over the Gaza war, while working towards a common set of propositions about the nature of the conflict and how best to influence the parties, as well as Washington.

*   *   *

Optimism would be imprudent. The available evidence suggests that liberals in Israel will be further sidelined over time and that demographic change will not do them any favours. Continuous war yields militant societies. In Israel's case, it will strengthen the messianic, territorially focused religious right. If the Haredi population decides to opt for military service or the government decides to enforce existing law, the composition of the IDF elite will become more militant and reinforce current trends.

American liberals of a certain age were inculcated with the belief that Israel's army was devoted to *tohar haneshek*: 'purity of arms'. With occupation having become the primary mission of IDF ground troops, however, operational realities have corroded the possibility of a moral army. The prospect of an Israeli 'long war' combined with disinvestment in education and other domestic-policy choices the current government is prone to make will render Israel increasingly unrecognisable to Jewish and non-Jewish American liberals alike. The latter will have a structure of vindicated beliefs to fall back on. Their Jewish compatriots will not.

Notes

1   See Joseph Gedeon, 'Trump Shares Inflammatory Video with Crude Reference to Netanyahu', *Guardian*, 9 January 2025, https://www.theguardian.com/us-news/2025/jan/08/trump-video-crude-reference-netanyahu.

2   See Masood Farivar, 'In Historic Shift, American Muslim and Arab Voters Desert Democrats', Voice of America, 7 November 2024, https://www.voanews.com/a/in-historic-shift-american-muslim-and-arab-voters-desert-democrats/7854995.html.

3   'Declaration Adopted by the Extraordinary Zionist Conference at the Biltmore Hotel of New York City, 11 May 1942', available from the United Nations, https://www.un.org/unispal/document/auto-insert-206268/.

4   US Department of State, Office of the Historian, 'The President to Mr. Mark F. Ethridge, at Jerusalem, April 29, 1949', Foreign Relations of the United States, 1949, The Near East, South Asia, and Africa, vol. VI, document 617, https://history.state.gov/historicaldocuments/frus1949v06/d617, cited in John B. Judis, *Genesis: Truman, American Jews, and the Origins of the Arab–Israeli Conflict* (New York: Farrar, Straus and Giroux, 2015), p. 343.

5   For a general account, see Dana H. Allin and Steven N. Simon, *Our Separate Ways: The Struggle for the Future of the U.S.–Israel Alliance* (New York: PublicAffairs, 2016).

6   See Shai Hazkony, *Dear Palestine: A Social History of the 1948 War* (Stanford, CA: Stanford University Press, 2021).

7   *Lady in the Lake*, directed and co-written by Alma Har'el, Apple TV+, 2024.

8   See James Loeffler, 'The Problem with the "Judeo-Christian Tradition"', *Atlantic*, 1 August 2020, https://www.theatlantic.com/ideas/archive/2020/08/the-judeo-christian-tradition-is-over/614812/; and David Tal, 'The Judeo-Christian Tradition and the US–Israel Special Relationship', *Diplomacy & Statecraft*, vol. 34, no. 4, November 2023, pp. 755–76.

9   See Ralf Hexel and Roby Nathanson, 'All of the Above: Identity Paradoxes of Young People in Israel', Friedrich-Ebert-Stiftung, 2010, https://israel.fes.de/fileadmin/user_upload/All_of_the_Above-_final_for_print_31.5.2011.pdf.

10   See 'Israel's Population Growth Slows as Emigration Soars, with 83,000 Leaving in 2024', *Haaretz*, 31 December 2024, https://www.haaretz.com/israel-news/2024-12-31/ty-article/.premium/israels-population-growth-slows-as-emigration-soars-with-83-000-leaving-in-2024/00000194-1cf3-db03-a1f6-1cfb5dcf0000.

11   See Bernard Avishai, *The Tragedy of Zionism: How Its Revolutionary Past Haunts Israeli Democracy* (New York: Allworth Press, 2002).

12   Ian S. Lustick, *For the Land and the Lord: Jewish Fundamentalism in Israel*

(New York: Council on Foreign Relations Press, 1988).

13 *Ibid*.

14 See 'Report of the Commission on the Palestine Disturbances of August, 1929', March 1930, pp. 26–69, https://balfourproject.org/bp/wp-content/uploads/2021/01/shaw-commission-reducedpdf_compressed-1.pdf.

15 See Michael Walzer, 'Israel's Pager Bombs Have No Place in a Just War', *New York Times,* 21 September 2024, https://www.nytimes.com/2024/09/21/opinion/lebanon-pagers-israel-gaza-war-crimes.html.

16 See, for example, Beth McKernan and Harry Davies, '"The Machine Did It Coldly": Israel Used AI to Identify 37,000 Hamas Targets', *Guardian*, 3 April 2024, https://www.theguardian.com/world/2024/apr/03/israel-gaza-ai-database-hamas-airstrikes.

17 See Stephanie Nolen, 'Estimated Gaza Toll May Have Missed 25,000 Deaths, Study Says', *New York Times*, 14 January 2025, https://www.nytimes.com/2025/01/14/health/gaza-death-toll.html.

18 See Steven Simon and Aaron David Miller, 'Can This "Special Relationship" Be Saved?', *New York Times*, 14 February 2017, https://www.nytimes.com/2017/02/14/opinion/can-this-special-relationship-be-saved.html

19 See Jacob Neusner, 'Is America the Promised Land for the Jews?', *Washington Post*, 7 May 1987, https://www.washingtonpost.com/archive/opinions/1987/03/08/is-america-the-promised-land-for-jews/9ac69b8f-0642-4e0f-8379-7237e4e208c2/.

20 See Joshua Zeitz, 'Anti-Israel Progressives Are Handing Liberal Jews an Impossible Decision, Just Like in 1967', *Politico*, 23 October 2023, https://www.politico.com/news/magazine/2023/10/23/anti-israel-left-jewish-politics-00122848.

Copyright © 2025 The International Institute for Strategic Studies

The Fourth Industrial Revolution and International Security

Dennis Murphy and Lawrence Rubin

The buzzphrase 'Fourth Industrial Revolution' (4IR) broadly refers to the disruptive effects of connecting data, artificial intelligence (AI), human–machine interaction and robotics to transform virtually any industry. However, it tends to conceal a lack of understanding on the part of those that use it about what this revolution can actually accomplish. A consequence is that the discourse regarding 4IR often defaults to broad generalisations about future developments, or more robust but insular niche discussions around the transformations in the business or tech sectors. This means that less serious attention has been paid to how 4IR might affect international security dynamics more broadly.

We raise three questions that illuminate ways to think about how 4IR might affect international security. Firstly, how might the rapid increase in innovation promised by 4IR disrupt how states understand the offence–defence balance? Secondly, how could 4IR cause us to rethink how we define national sovereignty? Thirdly, how could 4IR transform military operations?

What is 4IR?

Klaus Schwab, in a much-cited 2015 article in *Foreign Affairs*, said that 4IR is characterised 'by a fusion of technologies that is blurring the lines between the physical, digital, and biological spheres'. This is not, in his view, a mere

Dennis Murphy is a PhD candidate at the Sam Nunn School of International Affairs at the Georgia Institute of Technology. **Lawrence Rubin** is an associate professor at the Sam Nunn School of International Affairs at the Georgia Institute of Technology and an associate fellow at the International Institute for Strategic Studies.

Survival | vol. 67 no. 1 | February–March 2025 | pp. 159–172   https://doi.org/10.1080/00396338.2025.2459023

continuation of an earlier revolution in computing, but rather an exponential leap wholly different in terms of its 'velocity, scope, and systems impact'. Schwab described 4IR as expansive, interacting with advances across many domains of development and 'emerging technology breakthroughs in fields such as artificial intelligence, robotics, the Internet of Things, autonomous vehicles, 3-D printing, nanotechnology, biotechnology, materials science, energy storage, and quantum computing', on top of an already massive expansion in computing power and interconnection around the world.[1] Although Schwab discussed the potential for increased surveillance and its intersection with cyber conflict, his principal focus was the transformative effects 4IR would bring to society, discussing the possibility that it would displace a large percentage of the working population as well as revolutionising manufacturing.

Some have dismissed 4IR as a tendentious and overhyped concept hawked by think-tankers and academics.[2] Certainly, exaggerations about current and future technological advancements have arisen in public discourse. Nevertheless, there are serious reasons to investigate and interrogate the implications of 4IR for international security, even if it is less than it appears. Lawrence Freedman has argued that the field could benefit from temporary surges of interest that allow new ideas and insights to filter into the discipline. Not only do they help shape how future thinkers might better handle later ideas, but the process of engaging them can also ensure that the discipline retains policy relevance.[3]

Digital engineering

Underpinning 4IR is the capability to represent any physical asset in a digital environment and then apply AI and machine learning to that environment to gain a rapid understanding of the asset's properties and to discover new ways of using it. This methodology is perhaps most familiar in the realms of biology and bioengineering, but an instructive example can be found in the possibly more accessible world of Formula 1 racing.

As Will Roper, former assistant secretary of the US Air Force for Acquisition, Technology, and Logistics, has noted, Formula 1 racing presents serious technical challenges. It requires an advanced understanding of mechanics, aerodynamics and human capabilities to execute effectively. Yet the racing environment is self-contained and lends itself readily to proof-of-concept engineering projects linked to 4IR and digital-transformation efforts.[4] Racing involves thousands of moving parts, almost all of which need to be replaced at some point in a vehicle's lifespan. Formula 1 engineers have been able to create digital representations of their vehicles in a virtual environment and to conduct numerous experiments, producing significant improvements in cars' performance on the racetrack. The higher the quality of the digital asset, and the more rigorous the testing, the better the engineers can understand and identify which parts need replacing and how best to optimise the design of their cars.[5] High-quality models like these are sometimes referred to as 'digital twins'.[6] Companies can use them to try out thousands of designs a day, each to varying specifications related to weather, speed and other stressors that influence the performance of various technologies. Roper is convinced this is the key to rapid development and innovation in sectors far beyond racing, including in matters of security and defence.[7]

Unsurprisingly, the US Department of Defense has taken a keen interest in digital engineering.[8] For over half a century, the US armed forces have advanced the objective of greater domain awareness through the linkages of sensors, communications and platforms throughout a theatre of combat. The aim of 'mosaic warfare', an early iteration of this concept, was for the US to take the increasing complexity of the battlefield and turn that into an advantage.[9] Joint All-Domain Command and Control (JADC2), the current vision for future US military operations, seeks to combine all earlier concepts for integrating command-and-control systems among the services into a single cohesive framework that unifies battlespace awareness.[10] Fully realised, this would bring the Internet of Things to the battlefield and help to enable the development of a digital representation of the entire battlespace in near real time.

The Fourth Industrial Revolution has transformed how US military services acquire and equip soldiers with technology for use in combat. The US Air Force has been in the forefront of this change as its Materiel Command has adopted digital transformation to drive its acquisition processes.[11] Digital engineering and modelling have reduced the time it takes to assemble and develop new aircraft, with Boeing estimating that such tools 'slashed assembly hours by 80% and halved the time needed for software development'.[12] Roper has also called for a new strategy of digital acquisitions for the US Air Force, arguing that the engineering environment itself could be represented in a digital model. This would allow tools the military needs to be created virtually, and tested and validated in a model long before they are actually produced.[13]

4IR and the strategic environment

China and Russia have invested in 4IR technologies that could affect the balance of power even before they are applied in actual operations. 4IR technologies can be difficult to assess and are certain to drive misperceptions among strategic competitors. As Elsa Kania has noted, 'the disparate and qualitative character of how AI can enhance various military capabilities may create a degree of uncertainty that could impede assessments of relative advances' such that 'the military balance may be merely perceived, rather than adequately evaluated'.[14]

China's People's Liberation Army has expressed an interest in applications related to 'education, decision making, training, research and development, maintenance and finally, logistics' with the goal of creating a more capable 'military that adapts and improves rapidly'.[15] AI in particular could assist China's revolution in military affairs by leveraging emerging technologies. Roper has suggested that the United States needs to employ digital engineering aggressively to stay ahead of China.[16]

Russia also recognises the importance of 4IR. In modernising its defence sector, it has manifested an 'intent to push forward the development of breakthrough military technologies', according to Katarzyna Zysk, who further notes that Russia views 4IR technologies as important for their potential to 'change the character of future warfare'. Because new technologies identify vulnerabilities that can be exploited among their less technologically sophisticated rivals, the Russians' approach to military innovation in 4IR appears to be defensive in character – less a choice than an 'existential inevitability'.[17] Russian President Vladimir Putin has warned that those who effectively harness 'this technological wave will be far ahead', while those who do not 'will simply be overwhelmed and drowned'.[18]

The diffusion of 4IR is not limited to strategic competitors of the United States. Israel's assimilation of 4IR technologies has coincided with and at times facilitated changes in its military doctrine.[19] It replaced large ground operations with more precise and lethal strikes against the adversary's vital capabilities both in wartime and between wars. Small states – particularly Denmark, Norway and Sweden – have the potential to strengthen their security by integrating 4IR technologies through autonomous weapons systems and AI.[20] The use of novel technologies such as additive manufacturing – also known as 3D printing – and drones could improve their freedom of action, as could the use of AI for targeting purposes.

Beyond offence and defence

The transformation of the battlefield via technological innovation is a complex and often non-linear process. Michael Horowitz and Shira Pindyck argue that 'technological innovation alone does not have the "self-sustaining momentum" to produce effective military innovation'.[21] Military innovation requires change, but the nature and significance of any given change is open to debate. Some scholars emphasise long-term, evolutionary change, which highlights the importance of technological innovation in warfare over the span of centuries.[22] Others choose to explore a single change or period, delving deeper into the relationship between a specific advancement and military innovation.[23]

Whether the process is fast or slow, militaries eventually adapt to technological change. It is reassuring to think that innovation occurs during peacetime and adaptation in wartime.[24] But the integration of 4IR technologies holds the potential to blur the lines between adaptation and innovation, while also affecting the balance between offence and defence by enabling one side to gain an advantage in the midst of an arms race or even an armed conflict.

Many advanced military establishments are feeling pressure not just to innovate, but to innovate faster. The US Department of Defense's 2019 'Digital Modernization Strategy' noted that 'preserving and expanding our military advantage depends on our ability to deliver technology faster than our adversaries and the agility of our enterprise to adapt our way of fighting to the potential advantages of innovative technology'.[25] The 2022 US Nuclear Posture Review, which laid out a blueprint for a sector that has been relatively slow to innovate, called for 'faster development of technologies and system concepts through digital engineering and open architecture designs'.[26] If novel weapons can be introduced within a year, or even several months, from their first conception, innovation and adaptation will be difficult to distinguish.

Such a dynamic could profoundly affect international stability. New military equipment and technological innovations come with benefits for battlefield use, but they may also present new vulnerabilities for opponents to exploit. This occurred in the 1990s, when network-centric warfare emerged as the dominant precept for modern military operations, and the digital architectures that powered it became targets.[27]

New capabilities and vulnerabilities affect the real and perceived balance of power. Furthermore, one state's misperceptions about a rival state's technological innovation can further increase instability by impeding accurate assessments of relative advantage.[28] The 4IR suggests that novel equipment and software will arise at a rapid pace, cyclically generating new capabilities for exploiting new vulnerabilities. It may seem reasonable to assume that the advantage would accrue to players that robustly embrace 4IR. But if this cycle of innovation were very rapid, it could become difficult for peer competitors to accurately assess whether the international system or relative technological balance were offence- or defence-dominant. International competition might be offensively dominant for a couple of months, then shift to defence. The utility of theoretical frameworks based on one balance or the other would diminish, rendering the strategic landscape chaotic, uncertain and prone to escalation.

Digitalising sovereignty

Digital engineering, a key feature of 4IR, raises important questions about sovereignty and borders. It can provide the capability to coordinate sensors along a border and create a single, overarching system to monitor traffic into and out of a given state or other formally designated area. In China, this capability has given rise to a surveillance state that offers Beijing an upgraded means of social management.[29] While the potential for authoritarian states to expand political control is palpable, democratic states could also employ the capabilities offered by 4IR for more legitimate purposes. In the United States, the defence contractor Anduril has established a broad range of sensory capabilities that enable real-time border monitoring, offering the ability to identify, detect and monitor people, vehicles and other 'objects of interest'.[30]

Digitalised sovereignty too creates vulnerabilities. Hamas's surprise invasion of Israel on 7 October 2023 showed what can happen when a powerful military relies too heavily on 4IR technologies. Israel, which has the most sophisticated military in the Middle East, fell victim to a land, sea and air invasion by nearly 4,000 fighters using wire cutters, bulldozers and paragliders, in addition to some limited cyber activities. The invaders killed more than 1,200 Israelis and foreign nationals and kidnapped 200, which led to an ongoing war in which more than 40,000 Palestinians, most of them civilians, have died. Hamas's low-tech penetration overcame Israel's state-of-the-art 'smart border', which relied on sensors, drones, automated weapons, robots and cameras. Preliminary analysis suggests that the Israel Defense Forces (IDF) had become overly reliant on technology and convinced that their 'smart fence' – a system of integrated sensors and concrete barriers – was impenetrable, and that this complacency induced them to reduce IDF personnel numbers along the border.[31]

It seems clear that high technology could not overcome incorrect assumptions about the adversary's intentions, military shortsightedness and the politicisation of intelligence.[32] It is worth noting that the United States uses similar technologies to monitor NATO countries' borders with Russia. For example, the United States supports Poland's East Shield initiative, which uses physical barriers, advanced surveillance systems, electronic-warfare and anti-drone measures.[33]

Enhanced battlespace awareness and war gaming

Commercial firms such as Anduril provide border-monitoring technology to the US military.[34] It was selected along with Palantir to create additional sensor capabilities in support of US command-and-control systems to advance the United States' modern vision of war.[35] The idea is to use AI to integrate sensors and weapons systems across all relevant battlefield domains in near real time.[36] These developments are merely the next step in a long series of changes designed to bring about JADC2. Its purpose is to inform command-and-control systems and decision-makers in as close to real time as possible about events going on in an operational theatre.[37]

Although 4IR has the potential to realise this vision, the problems it seeks to solve are as old as warfare itself. Warfighters have always needed to manage uncertainty and ambiguity in combat. Carl von Clausewitz famously characterised this challenge as the 'fog of war'. Cutting through that fog by way of technological advancement remains a high priority for contemporary war planners.[38] The same capabilities that yield a digitalised border offer the promise of a digital twin of the battlefield whereby the sensor integration can afford commanders centralised and comprehensive mastery over the battlefield and greater control over the course of a military campaign, including, for example, more precise coordination of air support with ground operations.[39] Digital twins could also prove useful as forecasting and diagnostic tools, alerting operational commanders to problems as they arise or even, under certain circumstances, beforehand.[40]

Should 4IR technologies reach their full potential, digital engineering and AI could conceivably implement real-time war gaming, allowing for the creation of a virtual representation of the battlefield that is manipulable through a dashboard. Commanders in an operational theatre of battle could try out multiple combat scenarios, gaming out the optimal course of action and adjusting tactics in near real time to maximise the chances of battlefield success while minimising casualties. Such a capability is not purely speculative, as there are several initiatives that could support such an effort. In 2015, US deputy secretary of defense Robert O. Work and Admiral James A. Winnefeld, Jr, then vice chief of the Joint Chiefs of Staff, advocated revitalising war gaming within the Defense Department.[41] The US Air Force has fielded an experimental uncrewed aircraft controlled by AI, and staged exercises in which this 'robot wingman' flew alongside a traditionally piloted F-15.[42] In September 2023, the Pentagon established AI battle labs to design and test 'data analytic and AI capabilities with warfighters'.[43]

While there will inevitably be challenges in the development and implementation of digital-engineering techniques, states that excel in this sphere are likely to enjoy a significant edge over those that do not. It is easy to see why the United States has pursued 4IR capabilities as much as it has, and why rivals such as Russia feel compelled to keep up. Failure to do so could compel the laggards to rely increasingly on unconventional – including nuclear and cyber – threats to maintain deterrence or coercion as traditional approaches to warfare fall by the wayside.

*   *   *

It has always been necessary for strategic analysts, international-relations scholars and diplomats to be conversant with technological innovation to ensure that scientists, engineers and military planners do not take them by surprise. This generation will need to manage the complications brought about by the emergence of AI and 4IR in a multipolar nuclear world. As advances in computing power and AI continue at unprecedented rates, the need for scientific competence among non-technical security analysts and practitioners will only grow.

It is important to think through the implications of the advances promised by 4IR for international security, chief among them the intensification of uncertainty about how countries might understand the capabilities of their competitors, and the potential to build accurate digital models of the real world to inform border and battlefield management. Failing to think through the implications of technological advancements, as well as the long practical journeys required to realise them, can only leave us all more vulnerable.

Acknowledgements

Thank you to Nicholas Nelson for his insights.

Notes

[1] Klaus Schwab, 'The Fourth Industrial Revolution', *Foreign Affairs*, 12 December 2015, https://www. foreignaffairs.com/world/fourth-industrial-revolution. Schwab's article builds on the findings of Erik

Brynjolfsson and Andrew McAfee, *The Second Machine Age: Work, Progress, and Prosperity in a Time of Brilliant Technologies* (New York: W. W. Norton & Co., 2014).

2   See Chris J. Barton, 'The Fourth Industrial Revolution Will Not Bring the Future We Want', Technology and Society, 21 December 2021, https://technologyandsociety.org/the-fourth-industrial-revolution-will-not-bring-the-future-we-want/; and Ian Moll, 'The Myth of the Fourth Industrial Revolution', *Theoria*, vol. 68, no. 167, January 2021, pp. 1–38.

3   See Lawrence Freedman, 'In (Qualified) Praise of Fads and Fashions', *Journal of Strategic Studies*, vol. 46, no. 4, June 2023, pp. 881–90.

4   See Daniel Pereira, 'The Future of the Pentagon Is Digital Engineering – and Formula One Racing-style "Prowess at This New Statecraft"', Oodaloop, 9 November 2023, https://www.oodaloop.com/archive/2023/11/09/the-future-of-the-pentagon-is-digital-engineering-and-formula-one-racing-style-prowess-at-this-new-statecraft/.

5   See Jeff Koyen, 'How Data Analytics Automation Is Powering McLaren Racing's Formula 1 Success', *Forbes*, 18 October 2021, https://www.forbes.com/sites/alteryx/2021/10/18/how-data-analytics-automation-is-powering-mclaren-racings-formula-1-success/.

6   See Peter van Manen, 'Digital Twins in F1 and the Built Environment', Institution of Civil Engineers, Civil Engineer Blog, 11 July 2019, https://www.ice.org.uk/news-insight/news-and-blogs/ice-blogs/the-civil-engineer-blog/digital-twins-in-f1-and-the-built-environment; and Tolga Erol, Arif

Furkan Mendi and Dilara Doğan, 'Digital Transformation Revolution with Digital Twin Technology', 4th International Symposium on Multidisciplinary Studies and Innovative Technologies (ISMSIT), Istanbul, Turkiye, October 2020, pp. 1–7.

7   See Michael Marrow, 'Why Will Roper Still Believes the Pentagon Should Work More Like Formula One', Breaking Defense, 14 August 2023, https://breakingdefense.com/2023/08/formula-one-will-roper-air-force-digital-design/.

8   Frank Kendall, the current secretary of the US Air Force, is more cautious but recognises the benefits of digital engineering. See John A. Tirpak, 'Kendall: Digital Engineering Was "Over-hyped", but Can Save 20 Percent on Time and Cost', *Air & Space Forces Magazine*, 23 May 2023, https://www.airandspaceforces.com/kendall-digital-engineering-over-hyped-20-percent/.

9   See Defense Advanced Research Projects Agency, 'DARPA Tiles Together a Vision of Mosaic Warfare: Banking on Cost-effective Complexity to Overwhelm Adversaries', https://www.darpa.mil/work-with-us/darpa-tiles-together-a-vision-of-mosiac-warfare.

10 See John R. Hoehn, 'Joint All-domain Command and Control: Background and Issues for Congress', Congressional Research Service, 18 March 2021, https://crsreports.congress.gov/product/pdf/R/R46725/2.

11 See Air Force Materiel Command, 'AFMC's Digital Transformation: Digital Materiel Management', https://www.afmc.af.mil/About-Us/Digital/.

12 Courtney Albon, 'How One Air
    Force Office Eliminates Barriers to
    Digital Transformation', *Defense
    News*, 6 September 2022, https://www.
    defensenews.com/air/2022/09/06/
    how-one-air-force-office-eliminates-
    barriers-to-digital-transformation/.

13 See Will Roper, 'There Is No Spoon:
    The New Digital Acquisition Reality',
    Department of the Air Force, 7
    October 2020, https://www.af.mil/
    Portals/1/documents/2020SAF/There_
    Is_No_Spoon_Digital_Acquisition_7_
    Oct_2020_digital_version.pdf.

14 Elsa B. Kania, 'Artificial Intelligence
    in China's Revolution in Military
    Affairs', *Journal of Strategic Studies*, vol.
    44, no. 4, May 2021, pp. 515–42.

15 Joshua Baughman, 'Enhancing the
    Battleverse: The People's Liberation
    Army's Digital Twin Strategy', *Military
    Cyber Affairs*, vol. 6, no. 1, 2023, article 1.

16 See Marrow, 'Why Will Roper Still
    Believes the Pentagon Should Work
    More Like Formula One'.

17 Katarzyna Zysk, 'Defence Innovation
    and the 4th Industrial Revolution in
    Russia', *Journal of Strategic Studies*, vol.
    44, no. 4, May 2021, pp. 543–71.

18 President of Russia, 'Message from the
    President to the Federal Assembly', 1
    March 2018, http://kremlin.ru/events/
    president/news/56957.

19 See Yoram Evron, '4IR Technologies
    in the Israel Defence Forces: Blurring
    Traditional Boundaries', *Journal of
    Strategic Studies*, vol. 44, no. 4, May
    2021, pp. 572–93.

20 See Magnus Petersson, 'Small
    States and Autonomous Systems –
    the Scandinavian Case', *Journal of
    Strategic Studies*, vol. 44, no. 4, May
    2021, pp. 594–612.

21 Michael C. Horowitz and Shira
    Pindyck, 'What Is a Military
    Innovation and Why It Matters',
    Journal of Strategic Studies, vol. 46, no.
    1, March 2022, pp. 85–114.

22 See Paul Lockhart, *Firepower: How
    Weapons Shaped Warfare* (New York:
    Basic Books, 2021); and William
    H. McNeill, *The Pursuit of Power:
    Technology, Armed Force, and Society
    Since A.D. 1000* (Chicago, IL:
    University of Chicago Press, 1982).

23 See Geoffrey L. Herrera, 'Inventing
    the Railroad and Rifle Revolution:
    Information, Military Innovation
    and the Rise of Germany', *Journal
    of Strategic Studies*, vol. 27, no. 2,
    June 2004, pp. 243–71; and David
    Kirkpatrick, 'Logistics of the American
    Civil War', *RUSI Journal*, vol. 152, no.
    5, November 2007, pp. 76–81.

24 See David Barno and Nora Bensahel,
    *Adaptation Under Fire: How Militaries
    Change in Wartime (Bridging the Gap)*
    (Oxford: Oxford University Press, 2020);
    and Horowitz and Pindyck, 'What Is a
    Military Innovation and Why It Matters'.

25 US Department of Defense, 'DoD Digital
    Modernization Strategy', 12 July 2019,
    p. 14, https://media.defense.gov/2019/
    jul/12/2002156622/-1/-1/1/dod-digital-
    modernization-strategy-2019.pdf.

26 US Department of Defense, '2022
    Nuclear Posture Review', 2022,
    p. 22, https://fas.org/wp-content/
    uploads/2023/07/2022-Nuclear-
    Posture-Review.pdf.

27 See Jacquelyn Schneider, 'The
    Capability/Vulnerability Paradox and
    Military Revolutions: Implications for
    Computing, Cyber, and the Onset of
    War', *Journal of Strategic Studies*, vol.
    42, no. 6, August 2019, pp. 841–63.

28 See Kania, 'Artificial Intelligence in China's Revolution in Military Affairs'.

29 See David Karpa, Torben Klarl and Michael Rochlitz, 'Artificial Intelligence, Surveillance, and Big Data', in Lars Hornuf (ed.), *Diginomics Research Perspectives: The Role of Digitalization in Business and Society* (Cham: Springer International Publishing, 2022), pp. 145–72.

30 Hilary Beaumont, '"Never Sleeps, Never Even Blinks": The Hi-tech Anduril Towers Spreading Along the US Border', *Guardian*, 16 September 2022, https://www.theguardian.com/us-news/2022/sep/16/anduril-towers-surveillance-us-mexico-border-migrants.

31 See Yaakov Katz, 'Israel Must Fix Its Deadly Overreliance on Defensive Technologies', *Newsweek*, 4 December 2023, https://www.newsweek.com/israel-must-fix-its-deadly-overreliance-defense-technologies-opinion-1849315; and James Risen-Birch, 'How Changes in the Israeli Military Led to the Failure of October 7', *New Lines Magazine*, 20 May 2024, https://newlinesmag.com/argument/how-changes-in-the-israeli-military-led-to-the-failure-of-october-7/.

32 On the politicisation of Israeli intelligence, see Ehud Eiran, Ofer Guterman and David Simantov, 'Israel's Oct. 7 Early Warning Failure: Who Is to Blame?', *War on the Rocks*, 4 October 2024, https://warontherocks.com/2024/10/israels-oct-7-early-warning-failure-who-is-to-blame/.

33 See David Brennan, 'Poland Starts Building Fortifications on NATO's Border with Russia', *Newsweek*, 30 May 2023, https://www.newsweek.com/poland-starts-building-fortifications-natos-border-russia-1978499; and

Sebastian Sprenger, 'Poland's New East Shield Plan Mixes Modern ISR with Old-school Physical Barriers', *Breaking Defense*, 1 May 2024, https://breakingdefense.com/2024/05/polands-new-east-shield-plan-mixes-modern-isr-with-old-school-physical-barriers/.

34 See Joe Gould, 'Anduril Debuts Wheeled Version of Sentry Surveillance Tower', *Defense News*, 10 October 2022, https://www.defensenews.com/industry/2022/10/10/anduril-debuts-wheeled-version-of-sentry-surveillance-tower/.

35 See 'Army Selects Anduril and Palantir to Deliver TITAN Deep Sensing Capability for Long Range Fires', *ASD News*, 8 March 2024, https://www.asd-news.com/news/defense/2024/03/08/army-selects-anduril-palantir-deliver-titan-deep-sensing-capability-long-range-fires.

36 See Hoehn, 'Joint All-domain Command and Control'.

37 *Ibid.*

38 See, for example, Dennis Murphy, 'Sorting Through the Noise: The Evolving Nature of the Fog of War', *Strategy Bridge*, 10 September 2022, https://thestrategybridge.org/the-bridge/2022/9/10/sorting-through-the-noise-the-evolving-nature-of-the-fog-of-war; and Rodger S. Pitt, 'Realities of the Space Age & the Realities of Carl von Clausewitz's Theories of "Fog and Friction"', *Army Space Journal*, vol. 7, no. 2, Spring 2008, pp. 54–9.

39 See Daniel J. Adams, 'Staying Alive: Air Power in Support of Ground Operations in the Contested Environments of 2035 and Beyond', master's dissertation, US Marine Corps

Command and Staff College, approved 8 April 2021, https://apps.dtic.mil/sti/trecms/pdf/AD1177919.pdf.

40 See Grant S. Schlichting et al., 'Contested Logistics Operating Under Digital Support', conference paper, AIAA SCITECH 2024 Forum, January 2024.

41 John T. Hanley, Jr, 'Changing DoD's Analysis Paradigm', *Naval War College Review*, vol. 70, no. 1, Winter 2017, p. 66.

42 See Eric Lipton, 'A.I. Brings the Robot Wingman to Aerial Combat', *New York Times*, 27 August 2023 (updated 28 August 2023), https://www.nytimes.com/2023/08/27/us/politics/ai-air-force.html.

43 US Department of Defense, 'DoD to establish AI Battle Labs in EUCOM, INDOPACOM', 27 September 2023, https://www.defense.gov/News/Releases/Release/Article/3540283/.

Copyright © 2025 The International Institute for Strategic Studies

Review Essay

Big Tech and the Brussels Effect

Paul Fraioli

Digital Empires: The Global Battle to Regulate Technology
Anu Bradford. Oxford and New York: Oxford University Press,
2023. £30.99/$39.95. 608 pp.

The titans of America's largest technology companies were busy in the
initial weeks of 2025. The chief executive of Apple, the largest US firm by
market capitalisation, contributed $1 million personally to support the 20
January inauguration of Donald Trump to a second term as US president.
The leaders of Alphabet, Amazon, Meta, Microsoft and OpenAI did the
same, either individually or on behalf of their firms.[1] Meanwhile, Elon Musk
took up an extended residence at Trump's private club in Florida while
inserting himself into wide-ranging debates about domestic political issues
in Germany and the United Kingdom, all while making a play to acquire
TikTok from the Chinese firm ByteDance.

On 7 January, in a video posted to his Facebook account, Meta CEO
Mark Zuckerberg announced several surprise policy changes at the social-
media platform, including greatly relaxed content-moderation standards.
In 2016, after the passage of the Brexit referendum in the UK and Trump's
first election as president, Facebook faced widespread accusations in both

Paul Fraioli is IISS Senior Fellow for Geopolitics and Strategy, and Editor of *Strategic Comments*.

Survival | vol. 67 no. 1 | February–March 2025 | pp. 173–182   https://doi.org/10.1080/00396338.2025.2459024

Europe and the United States that it had served as a major hub for electoral propaganda. It responded to these criticisms by integrating third-party fact-checkers into its process for reviewing contested posts. In 2021, after friction with the Biden administration over the standards for censoring posts related to the COVID-19 pandemic, the company decided to reduce the amount of civic and political content shown on the platform.[2] Zuckerberg's January statement undid these changes, sending the fact-checkers home and heralding the return of political content to Facebook feeds.

A reporter asked Trump whether Zuckerberg's policy changes had come directly in response 'to the threats that you have made to him in the past', to which he responded, 'probably yes'.[3] The tone of Zuckerberg's statement was, in fact, notably accommodating towards arguments made on the right in recent years about perceived censorship online. The statement also expressed hope that the new administration would help Meta and other tech companies in their intensifying battles with foreign governments over free expression and content moderation:

We're going to work with President Trump to push back on governments around the world. They're going after American companies and pushing to censor more. The US has the strongest constitutional protections for free expression in the world. Europe has an ever-increasing number of laws institutionalizing censorship, making it difficult to build anything innovative there. Latin American countries have secret courts that can order companies to quietly take things down. China has censored our apps from even working in the country. The only way that we can push back on this global trend is with the support of the US government, and that's why it's been so difficult over the past four years when even the US government has pushed for censorship.[4]

In a nearly three-hour podcast interview with Joe Rogan on 10 January, Zuckerberg said that his company has had a very adversarial relationship with the Biden administration, which did little to help it with its many regulatory challenges internationally. The same week, Musk raised the ire of regulators in the European Union by broadcasting his interview with Alice Weidel, the candidate for German chancellor representing the far-right Alternative für Deutschland party in February 2025 snap elections, on his X platform. Brussels is now investigating whether X, by algorithmically boosting content posted by Musk, may have benefitted Weidel's candidacy and run afoul of the EU's expansive Digital Services Act, adopted in 2022.[5] Musk responded by criticising former EU commissioner Thierry Breton, who led the development of the 2022 law, in extremely harsh terms.[6]

The realignment of Big Tech at the dawn of a second Trump term is a prudential move to placate a government that will be much more personalistic than the Biden administration. But it also responds to deep dissatisfaction with that administration, during which firms faced robust antitrust actions launched by the Federal Trade Commission and withering criticism – sometimes well deserved, sometimes reflexive and unfounded – from the US and international media. They also spent billions of dollars to comply with laws and regulations developed by the European Commission, most notably the General Data Protection Regulation (GDPR) of 2018, the Digital Markets Act of 2022 and the Digital Services Act. This serves as critical context for understanding Musk's nascent partnership with Trump – beginning as it did less than four months before the general election – and presages a significant transatlantic battle over trade, technology and security issues that is likely to be joined early on in Trump's second term.

Trade and technology

On trade issues, Trump has claimed that 'the European Union treats us … worse than China, they're just smaller'.[7] He thinks about foreign relations primarily through the lens of trade balances, not national security or defence alliances. This explains his dismay at the fact that, on the one hand, the US provides security guarantees to Germany while, on the other, General Motors has great difficulty exporting automobiles to the EU single market. His new administration seems poised to disrupt the transatlantic trade relationship in unprecedented ways, likely featuring the use of unilateral tariffs. Musk and others now offering support to Trump are probably hoping that digital-trade issues – and the conditions under which US tech firms must operate in the European single market – will be subject to renegotiation as part of this process. Yet it will be extraordinarily difficult politically for Brussels to retreat from the personal-privacy standards currently protected by EU laws and regulations.

There is a significant risk that the looming EU–US battle over technology will exacerbate a rupture in transatlantic relations in 2025 over broader trade issues. These disputes will also distract Brussels and Washington from the reality that technologies and regulatory concepts developed in China are quite attractive to many countries globally for cost or ideological reasons, and are becoming more widespread. Anu Bradford's *Digital Empires*, published in September 2023, significantly illuminates these issues from a legal and digital-trade perspective. Bradford, a professor at Columbia Law School, had earlier coined and popularised the term 'Brussels Effect', arguing that the EU was an underrated global power given its expertise in developing and implementing laws and regulations. The argument is essentially that because the EU single market is large and relatively wealthy, ambitious EU rules and standards tend to be spread internationally because foreign firms feel obliged to comply to sell to Europeans.

Digital Empires offers a comprehensive picture of how the regulatory instincts of the European Commission that gave rise to the Brussels Effect are affecting innovation, global technology usage and standard-setting, particularly by firms based in China and the US. It proceeds by distinguishing regional approaches to regulating technology: the American market-driven model, the Chinese state-driven model and the European rights-driven model.

The limitations of models

The American model for regulating technology has the deepest roots, given the US role in shepherding the emergence of the internet as a global public good. In 1997, then-president Bill Clinton released a Framework for Global Electronic Commerce describing the early US approach. 'Because the Internet has such explosive potential for prosperity, it should be a global free-trade zone … We want to encourage the private sector to regulate itself as much as

possible. We want to encourage all nations to refrain from imposing discrim-
inatory taxes, tariffs, unnecessary regulations, cumbersome bureaucracies
on electronic commerce.'[8] Bradford calls this approach 'techno-libertarian'
and 'techno-optimist', and argues that it endures and continues to define
the American model today. While the book is measured in tone, on balance,
Bradford applies these terms critically. She acknowledges, however, that the
American model has enabled an explosion of technological innovation. In
Europe, by contrast, there is no significant indigenous technology industry.[9]

Bradford summarises the main differences between her three models as
follows: 'Unlike the United States, whose market-driven regulatory model
leaves tech companies in charge, or China, whose state-driven model is
aimed at regulating its tech industry to preserve the political power of the
state, the EU has pursued a third path by adopting its own human-centric
and rights-driven approach to digital regulation' (p. 105). Technically, the
American model is also rights-driven in character, but it focuses exclusively on the right to free speech, whereas the European model balances
this right against other 'fundamental rights, including human dignity and
the right to privacy' (p. 9).

Bradford's models – operating like protagonists or antagonists rather than
as constructed categories – play an outsize role in the book, which is a weak-
ness. Bradford tends to characterise every action taken by the Americans,
Chinese or Europeans as something that either reinforces the national model
or pushes it closer to one or another alternative model. The cumulative effect,
over the course of a long book, is noisy rather than enlightening.

The tendency to speak primarily in terms of models also obscures some
important, finer-grained distinctions that might have been explored more
constructively, given the considerable care with which Bradford approaches
her topic. The book highlights the fact that the US and the EU, despite both
being mostly liberal and democratic in character, often see technology issues
very differently, the one emphasising free speech and the other privacy. A
more focused discussion of the development of these biases in both juris-
dictions could have provided valuable comparative insights for interpreting
ongoing transatlantic disputes. She might have asked, for instance, what
factors explain the relative social passivity of Americans towards the vampiric

demands of some tech companies for personal data, particularly compared with expansive Germanic conceptions of privacy. Conversely, what might have explained the emergence in Europe of a broad 'fundamental rights' doctrine, including protections for privacy and human dignity, that gives notably less consideration to free expression than the US dispensation does?

These issues touch on aspects of political contestation within the geographical domains discussed in the book. The model construct, however, makes it too easy to overlook domestic political disputes and treat each locality as a unitary actor, maximising techno-libertarianism in the US and rights-protecting, global standard-setting in Europe. The laissez-faire American model seems less coherent given that political factors since 2016 have produced a significantly less congenial domestic regulatory climate for American tech firms. Bradford portrays Europeans as united behind the regulatory approach that has yielded the Brussels Effect, but downplays how these factors contributed to Brexit, and how brain drain to the US and free-speech issues have helped strengthen right-wing movements in many member states.[10]

Lastly, the book's China-focused sections, while providing excellent primers on the thrust of Beijing's approach to technology issues during the Xi Jinping era, sit somewhat uncomfortably beside the sections on the EU and the US. The latter focus almost exclusively on issues related to social-media companies. The China material is centred on hardware, infrastructure and surveillance, and efforts to export these technologies, in light of the party-led crackdown in 2021–22 on the Chinese technology sector, mostly on firms focused on fintech, e-commerce, education and online gaming (p. 95). Indeed, Xi appears to have decided as a matter of national strategy to prioritise China's achieving a dominant global position as a manufacturer of phones, batteries, drones, automobiles and robots. This fact undermines Bradford's argument that the models describe phenomena that are similar enough to afford ready comparisons.

*   *   *

While she is broadly a proponent of the European rights-based approach to technology regulation, Bradford should be credited for noting many of its drawbacks, including the extraordinary burdens that Brussels places on small European firms in its efforts to target American Big Tech. She is slightly more equivocal on the issue of innovation. She writes that 'the EU model does not inevitably compromise innovation' and that there is only a 'potential trade-off' the US might face in choosing to adopt a more European approach (p. 369). I would contrast this with the conclusions of the 2024 report by Mario Draghi on EU competitiveness, in which he portrayed the bloc as caught in 'a vicious circle of low investment and low innovation'.[11] His diagnosis of the problem was that winner-takes-most dynamics have prevailed in many domains and that 'the EU faces now an unavoidable trade-off between stronger ex ante regulatory safeguards for fundamental rights and product safety, and more regulatory light-handed rules to promote EU investment and innovation'.[12]

The innovation–regulation trade-off is perhaps most salient in the context of how Europe has chosen to regulate artificial intelligence (AI). The EU adopted the Artificial Intelligence Act in August 2024, and the law features strong personal privacy protections that overlap with those of the GDPR. Draghi and others have noted the potential complexity and difficulty for tech firms in launching consumer products relying on large-language models in the EU in compliance with the GDPR, the AI Act and other regulations. In 2024, for example, Apple and Meta refused to release their latest AI products in the EU out of concern that they did not comply with the Digital Services Act and other measures, showing that the reach of the Brussels Effect is limited.[13]

One striking revelation from Bradford's book is the alarming degree to which Brussels and Washington, even under Joe Biden, have regarded each other with mutual resentment on many technology issues. On 13 January, for instance, the Biden administration announced new export controls on semiconductors essential for training cutting-edge AI models that apply to 17 of 27 EU member states, among others.[14] Under Trump – with his protectionist instincts, lack of sentimentality regarding US allies in Europe, and unified support from American tech executives at least concerning the EU regulatory landscape – it may prove impossible to prevent further trade fragmentation. It thus seems likely that new barriers will be raised and that technical standards applying to social media, e-commerce, hardware and AI will continue to diverge.

Notes

1 See Gustaf Kilander, 'Who Pays for the Presidential Inauguration? These Are Some of the Major Donors', *Independent*, 10 January 2025, https://www.independent.co.uk/news/world/americas/us-politics/donald-trump-presidential-inauguration-donors-b2676886.html.

2 See, for example, Zuckerberg's account of this period in '#2255 – Mark Zuckerberg', *The Joe Rogan Experience*, 10 January 2025, transcript available from Happyscribe, https://www.happyscribe.com/public/the-joe-rogan-experience/2255-mark-zuckerberg.

3 Geoff Bennett, 'As Meta Drops Fact-checking, Critics Fear It Could Pave the Way for a Misinformation Spike', PBS News Hour, 7 January 2025, https://www.pbs.org/newshour/show/as-meta-drops-fact-checking-critics-fear-it-could-pave-the-way-for-a-misinformation-spike.

4 Mark Zuckerberg, 'It's Time to Get Back to Our Roots Around Free Expression', remarks on Facebook, 7 January 2025, https://www.facebook.com/zuck/videos/1525382954801931.

5 See Gian Volpicelli and Oliver Crook, 'EU Considers Expanding Probe into Musk's X, Digital Chief Says', Bloomberg News, 13 January 2025, https://www.bloomberg.com/news/articles/2025-01-13/eu-considers-expanding-probe-into-musk-s-x-digital-chief-says.

6 The exchange between Musk and Breton in January 2025 followed a heated one in August 2024 regarding the Digital Services Act. See 'Elon Musk Calls Former EU Digital Chief Breton "Tyrant of Europe"', *Brussels Times*, 11 January 2025, https://www.brusselstimes.com/1388595/elon-musk-calls-former-eu-digital-chief-breton-tyrant-of-europe-tbtb; and Elon Musk (@elonmusk), post to X, 12 August 2024, https://x.com/elonmusk/status/1823076043017630114?s=46.

7 'Trump Says EU Treats U.S. Worse than China Does on Trade', Reuters, 17 May 2019, https://www.reuters.com/article/world/trump-says-eu-treats-us-worse-than-china-does-on-trade-idUSKCN1SN2FC/.

8 William J. Clinton, 'Remarks by the President in Announcement of Electronic Commerce Initiative', 1 July 1997, https://clintonwhitehouse4.archives.gov/WH/New/Commerce/remarks.html.

9 Bradford does not blame this fact on Brussels's proclivity for regulation but rather on fragmentation among EU member states, insufficient markets for funding start-ups, brain drain to the US and other factors.

10 Regarding Brexit, escaping from laws and regulations imposed by Brussels and ending the jurisdiction of the European Court of Justice over the UK were major themes of the Vote Leave campaign in 2016. See, for example, Estelle Shirbon and Philip Blenkinsop, 'Hands Off Our Teabags!

Britons Chafe at EU Rules Despite Myth-busting Drive', Reuters, 22 June 2016, https://www.reuters.com/article/world/us/hands-off-our-teabags-britons-chafe-at-eu-rules-despite-myth-busting-drive-idUSKCN0Z80WE/.

11 European Commission, 'The Future of European Competitiveness – Part A: A Competitiveness Strategy for Europe', September 2024, p. 28, https://commission.europa.eu/document/download/97e481fd-2dc3-412d-be4c-f152a8232961_en.

12 European Commission, 'The Future of European Competitiveness – Part B: In-depth Analysis and Recommendations', September 2024, p. 79, https://commission.europa.eu/document/download/ec1409c1-d4b4-4882-8bdd-3519f86bbb92_en?filename=The%20future%20of%20European%20competitiveness_%20In-depth%20analysis%20and%20recommendations_0.pdf.

13 See Arthur Sullivan, 'Europe's AI Bosses Sound Warning on Soaring Compliance Costs', Deutsche Welle, 25 September 2024, https://www.dw.com/en/europes-ai-bosses-sound-warning-on-soaring-compliance-costs/a-70243489.

14 See US Department of Commerce Bureau of Industry and Security, 'Biden–Harris Administration Announces Regulatory Framework for the Responsible Diffusion of Advanced Artificial Intelligence Technology', 13 January 2025, https://www.bis.gov/press-release/biden-harris-administration-announces-regulatory-framework-responsible-diffusion.

Copyright © 2025 The International Institute for Strategic Studies

Book Reviews

Africa
Karen Smith

Responding to Mass Atrocities in Africa: Protection First and Justice Later
Raymond Kwun-Sun Lau. Abingdon: Routledge, 2023.
£41.99. 256 pp.

The ongoing Israeli military action in Gaza has again highlighted the question of how populations can be protected from genocide and other atrocity crimes, and – in view of South Africa's case against Israel at the International Court of Justice – what role international law can play. In that vein, the focus of *Responding to Mass Atrocities in Africa* is the relationship between the responsibility to protect (R2P) principle – developed in the aftermath of the Rwandan genocide against the Tutsi to address the tension between the impetus to protect populations from atrocity crimes and arguments around the inviolability of state sovereignty – and the International Criminal Court (ICC), which author Raymond Kwun-Sun Lau refers to as representative of the responsibility to punish. Lau notes that, because they share a normative underpinning and were developed during the same period, they are often assumed to be mutually reinforcing. He quotes former ICC chief prosecutor Fatou Bensouda, who described the court as the 'legal arm of the responsibility to protect' (p. 3). At the same time, Lau emphasises what he calls their different motivating logics: R2P is focused on preventing atrocities and saving lives, while the mandate of the ICC is to prosecute perpetrators following the commission of crimes.

Seeking to determine the extent to which R2P and the ICC are complementary, the book provides a systematic analysis of potential sources of tension. A quote from former United Nations secretary-general Kofi Annan elucidates the dilemma: 'there cannot be real peace before justice. Yet the relentless pursuit of justice may sometimes be an obstacle to peace' (pp. 93–4). Employing three case studies from Africa – northern Uganda, Darfur (Sudan) and Kenya – Lau sets out to argue that the order in which R2P is invoked and legal proceedings are initiated can make a difference in situations where mass atrocities are being committed. Through detailed research, he shows that a 'protection first, justice later' approach, as exemplified by the Kenyan case, makes for a complementary relationship between R2P and the ICC.

While the argument is persuasive, in practice, the dynamics of a given situation can complicate matters, and the prevention–protection–response cycle is not always linear. As the author points out, announcing that the chief prosecutor of the ICC is monitoring a situation or has started a formal investigation may have a deterrent effect on the commission of atrocity crimes, though empirical evidence for the deterrent effect of prosecutions remains disputed. Lau's argument is based on a clear analytical separation between the two responsibilities, yet one could argue that the potentially deterrent effect of an ICC investigation and prosecution is part of the R2P toolbox. It is beyond question, however, that preventing atrocities and protecting vulnerable populations must precede prosecution and justice.

The book is timely given that there is a growing trend among states and multilateral bodies such as the UN's General Assembly and Human Rights Council to resort to legal mechanisms, such as independent investigative processes, to collect evidence to be used in future trials, often in the absence of, and sometimes at the cost of, preventive and protective action. While holding perpetrators accountable for crimes is undoubtedly important, Lau's plea for protection first and justice later should be taken seriously. *Responding to Mass Atrocities in Africa* should be of interest to scholars of mass atrocities, conflict, human rights, international criminal justice and the responsibility to protect, but this book is perhaps most relevant for policymakers who are grappling with ongoing instances of mass atrocities.

Revolutionary Movements in Africa: An Untold Story
Pascal Bianchini, Ndongo Samba Sylla and Leo Zeilig, eds.
London: Pluto Press, 2023. £22.99. 326 pp.

Intellectual histories of the post-Second World War radical left have typically centred on movements in Europe, Latin America and the United States, with Africa being largely left out of the discussion. Yet neglecting African experiences not only impairs our understanding of leftist revolutionary movements, but also inhibits understanding of the interconnected nature of global events, with many African activists seeing their struggles in regional or global terms. This edited volume offers a collection of 15 case studies of African revolutionary movements in the 1960s and 1970s that highlight the frequently overlooked ways in which African actors have contributed to the shaping of global governance and order, and engaged with global political, social and economic trends.

The book responds to persistent stereotypes about African actors' lack of agency and the dismissal of radical movements as Soviet proxies or wholesale expressions of Marxist–Leninist thinking. Such limited views fail to recognise the myriad ways in which African activists rejected, adapted and created revolutionary ideas. Zeyad el Nabolsy's chapter, for example, discusses the radical debates on political economy that took place at the University of Dar es Salaam as an example of African Marxism, and highlights the multiple views on anti-colonial Marxism in post-independence Africa. These are important stories to tell not only for their own sake, but also because they can improve our understanding of the wider scope of such movements. While there are many similarities between the African revolutionary left and its counterparts in other places, there are also significant differences that challenge universalist assumptions. For example, the legacy of colonialism had implications for class relations that were not based on the familiar proletariat–bourgeoisie divide seen in Western societies. Radical organisations in Africa emerged not primarily from labour movements, but from students, the diaspora and the petty bourgeoisie, who had been victims of colonial discrimination. The book highlights how cities such as Dar es Salaam, Algiers and Brazzaville became meeting places for the exchange of ideas. Héloïse Kiriakou and Matt Swagler's chapter focusing on Congo-Brazzaville, for example, illustrates how exiled activists from elsewhere in Africa not only shaped the country's own revolutionary process and became essential to the survival of leftist movements in the region, but also made a difference at the international level, including by affecting the Cold War dynamics of Central Africa.

In telling the untold stories of African activists and radical movements, books such as this one improve our understanding of how global processes often have multiple beginnings, play out differently in relation to local conditions, and are interconnected in ways that produce mutual interaction and the cross-pollination of ideas. *Revolutionary Movements in Africa* will be of interest to scholars of African politics and pan-African Marxism, but should also be required reading for anyone interested in gaining a global perspective on radical leftist movements.

South African Foreign Policy Review Volume 4: Ramaphosa and a New Dawn for South African Foreign Policy
Lesley Masters, Philani Mthembu and Jo-Ansie van Wyk, eds.
Boulder, CO: Lynne Rienner Publishers, 2023. $45.00. 406 pp.

This fourth instalment of what has become a regular overview of trends in South Africa's foreign policy focuses on the administration of President Cyril Ramaphosa. It argues that his track record in delivering on his promise of a 'new dawn' for South Africa's international relations displays both continuities and changes, the latter illustrated by his focus on trade and foreign direct investment. Most of the chapters are predominantly descriptive, which has the benefit of making them accessible for a lay audience. This can sometimes mean that they lack academic rigour and analytical depth, however, with limited theoretical engagement for readers interested in understanding *why* South Africa takes certain policy decisions. Readers expecting to see the application of familiar foreign-policy analytical models will also be disappointed.

Bianca Naude's chapter is one of the exceptions. With an emphasis on the influence of relationships and identity in the making of foreign policy, she highlights how historical processes and existing, routinised relationships shape the way states behave as they attempt to maintain stable identities. Offering examples of South Africa's relationships with what might be considered its allies and enemies, she helps to shed light on policies that appear to contradict the national interest, including combative stances vis-à-vis important trading partners and displays of solidarity with known violators of human rights.

There are brief mentions of groupings such as BRICS and specific cases such as the Russia–Ukraine war, but no chapters dedicated to these topics. While the editors justify the exclusion of some important topics on the grounds that these have received attention in previous volumes or in other publications, their absence remains noticeable. On the other hand, the collection includes chapters on new themes such as health, maritime affairs and candidature diplomacy. The contributions were written before recent events in Gaza, so the volume does not contain reflections on South Africa's stance on Israel–Palestine. The country's decision to bring a case of genocide against Israel at the International Court of Justice is arguably a significant development that has not only affected South Africa's relations with Western capitals, but also raised questions about what is in the country's national interest.

Making sense of how South Africa's colonial and apartheid history affects how it views its place in the world, and the way in which foreign-policy actions also shape, rather than simply reflect, the national interest, are important puzzles for scholars, analysts and policymakers alike. While the volume as a whole does not engage with these more theoretical questions, it provides a compendium of different topics that constitute the foreign policy of a state that, due to its particular history, transition to democracy and leadership role in Africa, remains of interest to observers beyond its borders.

The Foreign Policy and Intervention Behavior of Africa's Middle Powers: An Analytic Eclecticism Approach
Olumuyiwa Babatunde Amao. Lanham, MD: Lexington Books, 2023. £81.00/$105.00. 248 pp.

Despite the ambitious title, the focus of the book is on the intervention behaviour of South Africa and Nigeria in the Democratic Republic of the Congo (DRC) and Sierra Leone respectively, based on a broad definition of intervention that encompasses diplomacy and military force. Whether South Africa and Nigeria can usefully be termed 'middle powers' is a debate author Olumuyiwa Babatunde Amao discusses only in the penultimate chapter, where he admits that 'the concept of a middle power is quite problematic' (p. 178). Otherwise, Amao draws on the regional-powers literature, so it is never entirely clear why he opted for the middle-power concept instead. Also left unexplained is the decision to describe only interventions sanctioned by the United Nations Security Council as multilateral. This means that Nigeria's participation in the Economic Community of West African States (ECOWAS) Monitoring Group and South Africa's contribution to African Union peacekeeping are regarded as unilateral. Similarly, reference is made throughout to the responsibility to protect (R2P), but the interventions discussed took place before the R2P concept was developed and adopted.

While there is much emphasis on the analytical eclecticism the author claims to have employed in this study, it is applied in a limited and selective manner. Analytical eclecticism, which finds value in engaging with multiple theoretical traditions, promotes the combination of different causal explanations. What the author does in this book, however, is to separately apply rather than combine two alternative theoretical frameworks. Moreover, the value of analytical eclecticism arguably remains limited if its scope is restricted to the triad of theories – realism, liberalism and constructivism – outlined in Rudra Sil and Peter Katzenstein's original elaboration of the approach, leaving out a multitude of other potential explanations. Amao's justification for his own choice of theories (structural realism and social constructivism) is also not entirely convincing. Viable alternatives, such as liberal institutionalism (given the emphasis on the way these states work through regional and multilateral institutions) and post-colonialism (the legacy of colonialism looms large in the foreign policies of both countries), are dismissed out of hand. Amao also does not question whether Eurocentric theories can be unproblematically applied to Africa.

In his analysis, Amao does not credibly defend why shared identity is a more convincing explanation than other factors, such as economic profit. Perhaps most significantly, individual leadership and personalised foreign policy are emphasised in both cases. With regard to South Africa, for example, Amao writes of an 'inextricable relationship between the leadership orientation of South Africa's post-apartheid leaders and its foreign policy formulation' (p. 127), and concedes that the role of leadership is an area where both structural realism and constructivism fall short. Why then was a framework that takes the role of leaders into account not considered?

The Foreign Policy and Intervention Behavior of Africa's Middle Powers provides some interesting insights about the interventionist behaviour of Africa's leading states, but its declared focus on analytical eclecticism is more of a distraction. The book is worth reading for information on the case studies, but less so for its theoretical analysis, and is a missed opportunity to think more critically about the foreign policies of two African powerhouses that continue to perplex commentators and policymakers.

The Ideological Scramble for Africa: How the Pursuit of Anticolonial Modernity Shaped a Postcolonial Order, 1945–1966
Frank Gerits. Ithaca, NY: Cornell University Press, 2023. $67.95. 318 pp.

Viewing Africa's international relations in the second half of the twentieth century solely through the lens of the Cold War provides an incomplete understanding of events, according to historian Frank Gerits, who offers an alternative framework that raises questions about how we make sense not only of the past, but also of Africa's contemporary global engagements. Based on extensive archival research, *The Ideological Scramble for Africa* convincingly argues that the ideological struggle between the East and West, or communism and capitalism, was not the only, or even the most important, battle from the vantage point of African states. Of greater concern to Africans was the North–South anti-colonial struggle. Indeed, this struggle continues to shape the continent's outlook. Through meticulous research, Gerits builds his argument by showcasing efforts by post-independence African leaders to develop anti-colonial modernisation projects through engagement with the legacy of the Haitian Revolution as a corrective to European modernity, rather than limiting themselves to positions that either opposed or agreed with American or Soviet ideology.

Gerits emphasises the agency of African actors in the face of severe structural constraints and ongoing external intervention, making the case that the pan-Africanist project not only competed with but also shaped Northern projects for the continent. Adopting a chronological approach, he weaves together events that show how different African leaders were engaging with anti-colonial and pan-African modernity. While external actors were competing for African hearts and minds, African nationalists were simultaneously attempting to achieve modernity on their own terms, presenting pan-Africanism as an alternative to imperialist, capitalist and communist development models. The focus is unapologetically on Africa, including African rejection, selective adoption or adaptation of external ideas, and creation of original ideas. Conclusions are also drawn about the impact of ideological deliberations among anti-colonial leaders on the international system as a whole as they devised innovative diplomatic and cooperative practices to advance their shared interests.

The book foregrounds the dangers of histories that prioritise events of significance to the West (such as the Cold War) while overlooking how differently the same period may have been experienced elsewhere. We should be alert to these dangers not only when interpreting history, but also when considering contemporary events, such as the foreign-policy decisions of African states in relation to the Russia–Ukraine and Israel–Hamas conflicts.

Asia-Pacific
Lanxin Xiang

**Beyond Power Transitions: The Lessons of East Asian
History and the Future of U.S.–China Relations**
Xinru Ma and David C. Kang. New York: Columbia University
Press, 2024. £30.00/$35.00. 280 pp.

In *Beyond Power Transitions*, Xinru Ma and David C. Kang ask a fundamental question: 'are power transitions between a rising power and a declining hegemon particularly volatile?' (p. 3). They further ask whether 'a war between China and the United States [is] possible or even likely as a power transition draws near' (p. 3). These questions have become a key preoccupation of scholars and policymakers, who often examine the events of the past to draw lessons for today. Thucydides' classic *History of the Peloponnesian War*, for example, is today very much in vogue. Yet the authors argue that East Asian history is routinely overlooked in the literature on power transitions. This is an oversight they seek to correct in their own analysis as they explore whether different world regions have experienced different kinds of transitions as great powers have risen and fallen.

Ma and Kang find that there is one key difference between the historical experience of Europe and East Asia: whereas Europe has been home to a multipolar, balance-of-power system, East Asia has been dominated by a hegemonic system (p. 43). This may not be new information, but the implications for power-transition theory are important. The authors argue that throughout East Asian history, power transitions have been better explained by internal dynamics than by external relations.

One example they cite is the Manchu conquest of the Ming dynasty in China. Although Japanese leader Toyotomi Hideyoshi attempted to topple the Ming dynasty in the late sixteenth century, it was the Manchus who accomplished this in the seventeenth century, ruling China for 250 years after peasant revolts fatally weakened the Ming. Thus, the power transition was accomplished by internal actors, without a conflict in the traditional sense. Likewise, China's replacement of Japan in the early twenty-first century as East Asia's pre-eminent economic power was accomplished without any violence. According to the authors, internal dynamics are also relevant in the case of US–China relations, as societal divisions in the United States and splits within China's ruling party are identified as key factors in the deterioration of the countries' bilateral ties.

The authors conclude that if scholars had begun 'with East Asian history, they would never have developed a theory of power transitions, and indeed the theory does not appear to apply in the premodern East Asian context' (p. 187). Asian dynasties have risen and fallen, but almost always for reasons of internal dynamics, not external wars of conquest. Culture has thus been more important in explaining war, stability and peace in East Asia than international relations.

Hedging the China Threat: US–Taiwan Security Relations Since 1949
Shao-cheng Sun. Boulder, CO: Lynne Rienner Publishers, 2024.
$125.00. 373 pp.

In *Hedging the China Threat*, Shao-cheng Sun, a Taiwanese military-intelligence officer turned academic, explores the evolution of, and recent developments in, the US–Taiwan relationship from the Truman administration through to Joe Biden's White House. The book's strength lies in the comprehensive and detailed historical survey it offers, but its analysis is weak, especially because it presents an interpretation reflecting the official thinking in Taipei and Washington, but not in Beijing.

Sun never explains clearly how Washington's current Taiwan policy is being used to 'hedge the China threat'. Hedging can be defined as the practice of establishing multiple positions at the same time to protect against risk or uncertainty. Losses resulting from one position are offset by gains from another. The United States' use of 'hedging' in relation to Taiwan could once be seen in its policy of strategic ambiguity towards the island, a policy that was first established in the 1970s. Under this policy, the US had a legal obligation to provide Taiwan with the means to defend itself (through the Taiwan Relations Act), but Washington did not explicitly guarantee to intervene militarily in any conflict between Taiwan and mainland China. Thus, strategic ambiguity served a double-deterrence purpose by preventing a declaration of independence by Taiwan as well as pre-emptive military strikes against Taiwan by Beijing.

The author effectively admits that, under the Biden administration, strategic ambiguity has been all but replaced by strategic clarity, a shift encouraged by the Taiwanese government (p. 307). Yet he argues that the Taiwanese government's purpose is merely to prevent mainland China from launching military attacks. This is an untenable argument, since neither Washington's nor Taipei's stance can reasonably be described as 'hedging' – their support for Taiwanese independence now seems clear. This leaves Beijing with little choice but to lean towards the conviction that the US is collaborating with Taiwan's independence agenda.

Sun asks the key question of why Taiwan matters to the United States. His answer, which cites common values, economic interests, strategic interests, and science and technology (p. 15), is fully in line with the official claims of both Taipei and Washington. But it is also worth asking why Taiwan, as a lesser power caught in the middle of the competition between China and the US, has not upheld a hedging strategy, given that a majority of its population favours the status quo. Instead, Tsai Ing-wen, who was elected president of Taiwan in 2016, chose to bank on a new American policy of containment to manage China's rise. Thus, cross-Strait relations have reached a cold impasse, and may be heading towards a hot confrontation.

Decolonisation in the Age of Globalisation: Britain, China, and Hong Kong, 1979–89
Chi-kwan Mark. Manchester: Manchester University Press, 2023. £85.00. 280 pp.

This is a timely book that explores the relationship between Margaret Thatcher's neo-liberal Britain and Deng Xiaoping's reformist China as each sought to manage the decolonisation of Hong Kong – a story that has been largely forgotten or deliberately distorted in relation to more recent events in Hong Kong. The prevailing view today is that Thatcher's naivety and a typically British appeasement policy sold Hong Kong, a former neo-liberal paradise, down the river to a communist dictatorship.

Author Chi-kwan Mark believes that Thatcher's Hong Kong policy had two main goals: to promote a neo-liberal model of globalisation and to manage decolonisation in a pragmatic way. Unfortunately, pragmatism in British foreign policy is often linked to the less appealing prospect of appeasement (pp. 6–7). Thus, Thatcher's Hong Kong deal with China is often compared to the 1938 Munich Agreement, however absurd that comparison may be.

Based on original archival materials, the author discusses in considerable detail London's decolonisation efforts with respect to Hong Kong. This was a unique case in British history because, by the time Sino-British negotiations were taking place in the early 1980s, Hong Kong had already developed into a 'global city' – a major player in international trade and finance. Thus, Britain's challenge was not the traditional one of spurring development in a 'backward' territory, but of maintaining Hong Kong's prosperity and momentum as a means of bringing China into the globalisation process and helping Britain to maintain its own international position. Thatcher's Hong Kong policy duly connected her faith in free markets to her vision of a 'Global Britain' that was a major player beyond Europe. Meanwhile, Deng's economic reforms 'provided a golden opportunity for Britain to integrate China into the global economy'(p. 37). This convergence of national interests allowed the countries to devise the One Country, Two Systems formulation.

Thatcher has been accused of assuming that with economic liberalisation, China would eventually move towards political liberalisation, but neither she nor her top advisers on China, such as Percy Cradock, Murray MacLehose, David Wilson and Edward Youde, were under the illusion that a Hong Kong deal would jump-start the democratisation of China. Deng was clear that he only wanted perestroika – a 'market economy with Chinese characteristics' – but not glasnost, or political opening up.

As Mark points out, 'there is a danger of using the past to serve the present' (p. 244). Now that a once positive narrative about 'China's rise' has been replaced by ubiquitous warnings of the 'China threat', the real history of the British–Chinese Hong Kong settlement deserves our attention.

Xi Jinping's China: The Personal and the Political
Stig Stenslie and Marte Kjær Galtung. Boulder, CO: Lynne
Rienner Publishers, 2023. $95.00. 179 pp.

Xi Jinping's China tries to answer what has become a key question among Westerners: why Xi Jinping, once a presumed 'reformer', has since sought to make himself into a 'new Mao' (p. 143). Stig Stenslie and Marte Kjær Galtung rightly point out that many China experts made two incorrect predictions when Xi came to power in 2012. The first was that, because Xi's father, a senior Communist Party official, had been brutally persecuted during the Cultural Revolution, his son would have a natural tendency against despotism. Nicholas Kristof, for example, said that 'reform was in Xi's genes'. A second false prediction was that Xi would be the weakest leader in the history of the People's Republic. The reason for this, according to Willy Lam, was that the party was too divided for Xi to handle, while Cheng Li of the Brookings Institution suggested that the new generation of Chinese leaders lacked a 'power base within the party' (p. 7). Not only did these predictions miss the mark, they misled Western policymakers into designing a tough policy towards China.

Why did so many China hands get Xi wrong? The authors blame the methodologies many of them used in studying China, in particular the 'Beijingologist' approach that focuses narrowly on what's happening in Beijing, and the social-science approach that draws broad conclusions from quantitative data. Neither of these is sufficient to explain either Xi's leadership or Chinese politics more generally. Instead, the authors of this study suggest that a serious psychoanalytical biography is needed to make sense of Xi and contemporary Chinese politics (p. 9).

Unfortunately, the authors' bold attempt to provide such a biography fails. To begin with, they make too many factual mistakes in the chapter 'Xi's Climb Through the Ranks' to sustain their later arguments. Two mistakes in particular could be deemed fatal. The first is the authors' claim that Xi rose through the ranks because he was 'clean' or non-corrupt (pp. 15–16). In fact, Xi did not need to directly participate in the kinds of commercial activities or lucrative 'kickback' schemes that were widespread during the reform period because his family had sufficient connections and power to allow its members to engage in rent-seeking, as the Panama Papers later exposed. Secondly, the authors endorse the official story that Xi rose through the ranks by his own merits, for example by claiming that Xi's 'cave-dwelling years' paved the way to his future success. In fact, there were 20 million 'cave-dwellers' or 're-educated youth' who were sent to the countryside during the Cultural Revolution – Xi's experience was by no means unique. What *did* set him apart was his father's political rehabilitation and return as a senior party figure just as Xi was starting his own career. Hence, from the beginning, Xi enjoyed a privileged career path guaranteed by the crony system.

In their discussion of Xi's efforts to establish a cult of personality, the authors claim that these efforts have been largely successful, writing that 'ordinary people appreciate that Xi is a strong leader who gets things done. He is someone they can be proud of' (pp. 83–4). In truth, Xi's personality cult is the least effective way through which he has sought to shore up his power, given that personal charisma has never been a defining attribute of his leadership. On Xi's assertive 'wolf-warrior diplomacy', the authors fail to identify it as a strategic miscalculation based on a belief in the decline of the West and the United States in particular (pp. 123–4).

As a biographical study, *Xi Jinping's China* leaves much to be desired. As a work of political analysis, it relies too much on speculative judgements. But the authors are right to point out the mistakes of the West's so-called China hands, and to note that there is no decent biography of Xi, arguably one of the most powerful men on Earth.

Russia and Eurasia
Angela Stent

Goodbye to Russia: A Personal Reckoning from the Ruins of War
Sarah Rainsford. London: Bloomsbury Publishing, 2024.
£22.00. 368 pp.

Sarah Rainsford, the BBC's correspondent in Moscow from 2014–21 and lifelong aficionado of all things Russian, was deemed a 'threat to national security' and expelled from Russia in 2021. In this trenchant personal memoir, she chronicles Russia's descent into repression and militarism under Vladimir Putin. She also spends time at the Ukrainian front and interviews Ukrainians affected by the brutal war there.

Rainsford first arrived in Moscow just as the Soviet Union imploded, and she witnessed the initial flowering of a sense of excitement, opportunity and hope on the heels of the Soviet collapse. But she also saw the dark side of Moscow's 'Wild East', describing Russia as 'a land of immense opportunity that became a deadly scramble for wealth' (p. 57). Visiting St Petersburg during this period, she came to understand that Putin, a former KGB agent who was then the city's deputy mayor, aimed 'not to stamp out crime and corruption, but to control it' (p. 129).

Returning to Russia in 2000, she covered the sinking of the *Kursk* nuclear submarine in the Barents Sea. The authorities provided no information about what had happened for several days and refused offers of help from Western countries. By the time rescue operations began, it was too late to save any of the 118 people on board. Putin showed up a few days after the explosion and only met with the bereaved families ten days after the disaster. His handling of this first major crisis of his presidency showcased traits that would define his rule: 'an instinctive dishonesty, wariness of the West and a chilling disregard for human life' (p. 154).

Putin has always feared independent journalists, and his 'war on truth' began early in his tenure, when Gazprom took over Vladimir Gusinsky's NTV channel, which had broadcast critical stories about the war in Chechnya and the *Kursk* disaster. According to Rainsford, the taming of Russian television was complete by 2003. All independent media organisations inside Russia have since been eviscerated, although some continue to broadcast from outside Russia. The last remaining independent media outlet, the Echo of Moscow radio station, was closed after the full-scale invasion of Ukraine. Several independent journalists have been assassinated during Putin's 25-year rule, the most prominent of

Survival | vol. 67 no. 1 | February–March 2025 | pp. 195–200   https://doi.org/10.1080/00396338.2025.2459027

whom was Anna Politkovskaya, whose critical coverage of Chechnya infuriated the Kremlin. She was killed on Putin's birthday.

Since her expulsion from Russia, Rainsford has spent time in different parts of Ukraine, witnessing the destruction in bombed-out cities and villages and the aftermath of Russian atrocities in Bucha and other places. She has spoken to Ukrainian children who were abducted by Russians and sent to live with Russian families, only to be returned to their own relatives after an arduous process. She has also interviewed Russophone Ukrainians who decided to move to Russia for safety, as well as those who left for Europe.

Rainsford concludes that, for now, she has said goodbye to Putin's Russia, although she still hopes that future generations could bring positive change.

Midnight in Moscow: A Memoir from the Front Lines of Russia's War Against the West
John J. Sullivan. London and New York: Little, Brown and Company, 2024. £28.00/$32.50. 416 pp.

John J. Sullivan served as US ambassador to Russia from 2019–22, under the Trump and Biden administrations. In this compelling and dramatic memoir, he recounts the downward spiral of US–Russian relations prior to Russia's full-scale invasion of Ukraine in 2022, the unsuccessful US attempts to deter Vladimir Putin, and the struggle to find an appropriate response to Russia's attack and ongoing aggression. His observations about the challenges of dealing with the Kremlin are a sobering reminder of how difficult it will be for the West to interact with Russia for the foreseeable future.

Sullivan is an avid hockey player and had planned to engage with ordinary Russians by attending their games and playing with them. But COVID-19 hit soon after he arrived, and he spent his three years largely holed up in the Moscow embassy as the frosty US–Russian relationship cut off most of his official contacts. By the end of his tenure, the embassy was reduced to a skeleton staff.

The most important thing to know about Putin, argues Sullivan, is that 'he was, and proudly called himself, a Chekist' (p. 122). His KGB background largely defines him, but 'Putin is also a savvy gangster, unbound by facts, law, morals or truth – he is motivated not only by power and money, but also by the grandiose ambitions of the most powerful and fierce Tsars in history' (p. 185). This combination of an intelligence mindset, a Mafia-style code of conduct and messianic imperial ambitions, writes Sullivan, makes him both difficult and dangerous to deal with. He likens Putin's rationale for invading Ukraine and subsequent aggression to Adolf Hitler's actions in 1939 leading to the invasion of Poland.

How could the West forge a more effective strategy towards Russia? Westerners must recognise, writes Sullivan, that the Kremlin is a self-declared enemy of the United States that believes it is at war with Washington. It must also be understood, he says, that the Russian government cannot be trusted in any context. He doubts that Russia will ever renounce the goals of its 'special military operation' in Ukraine, and is convinced there is no 'off ramp' to defuse the situation. Even if Putin were somehow removed, that would not solve the problem. Only Russians themselves can decide to change their form of government and their leadership.

Sullivan has extensively studied George Kennan's writings about Russia and the USSR, and he concludes that the only viable strategy for the West is the twenty-first-century containment of Russia. The first step is to ensure that Ukraine is not defeated, because Sullivan is convinced that Russian aggression will not stop at Ukraine. He rejects regime change, but urges the West to moderate and restrain Russia's disruptive actions. Ultimately, that will depend on the health of Western societies and their ability to act consistently and concertedly to deter Russia from further acts of aggression against its neighbours.

Punishing Putin: Inside the Global Economic War to Bring Down Russia
Stephanie Baker. New York: Scribner, 2024. $29.99. 368 pp.

In this informative and absorbing book, Stephanie Baker highlights the challenges of sanctioning a globally integrated country as large as Russia, with its ample natural resources. Informed by a wealth of interviews with key players, she details how the United States and its allies devised unprecedented financial and trade sanctions after Russia's full-scale invasion of Ukraine in 2022, and explains why the sanctions have not been as successful as the West had hoped.

After Russia's 2014 annexation of Crimea and the launch of a war in the Donbas, the US and its allies faced a dilemma: 'How to coerce an opponent without the costs of direct military conflict?' (p. 81). The United States, Baker points out, had never imposed sanctions on a country as large as Russia or with such extensive links to global financial markets. Sanctions were placed on some of Putin's inner circle, on some banks, and on foreign oil companies involved in energy projects in the Arctic. The value of the rouble tumbled and the Russian economy shrank 3.7% in 2015. Yet, as one of the sanctions' architects told Baker, 'what we didn't anticipate was how little Putin seemed to care about the economy's decline' (p. 89).

When US intelligence agencies became aware of Russia's massive troop build-up in 2021 and concluded that a full-scale invasion of Ukraine was imminent, CIA director William Burns travelled to Moscow and warned Putin that he would pay a 'heavy price' (p. 17) if he launched an invasion. At the same time, US officials began preparing to impose sanctions that were more far-reaching than those in 2014, believing that the West enjoyed asymmetric advantages in capital and cutting-edge technology.

After Russia launched its invasion, the US persuaded its European allies to remove selected Russian banks from the SWIFT international-payments system, freeze $300 billion of Russian assets in Western banks and restrict Russian banks from using foreign reserves. Since then, additional rafts of sanctions have been imposed on Russian banks, Putin's inner circle and Russian enterprises. Europe has largely weaned itself off Russian hydrocarbons. And yet the Russian economy – now on a wartime footing – is experiencing high growth rates while oil revenues from India and China continue to pour in. Why have Western sanctions not achieved their objectives?

The US has been pursuing Russian oligarchs and seizing their assets in the vain hope that this might turn them against Putin. Baker details the hunt for tycoons' superyachts, bank accounts and properties. She also highlights how oligarchs have been able to evade sanctions, exploiting the loopholes in open Western societies. Many countries have helped Russia circumvent sanctions, and shadow fleets transport Russian oil. Cyprus and Dubai remain havens for Russian money-laundering and sanctions evasion.

So far, Baker argues, Western sanctions have not brought the Russian economy to its knees. 'The single most important thing the West can do to deny Putin resources to fund the war', she concludes, 'is to lower the price cap on Russian oil and enforce it rigorously' (p. 281).

Legitimating Nationalism: Political Identity in Russia's Ethnic Republics
Katie L. Stewart. Madison, WI: University of Wisconsin Press, 2024. $89.95. 312 pp.

In justifying Russia's invasion of Ukraine in 2022, Vladimir Putin insisted that Russians and Ukrainians are one nation. Yet he told his Security Council that, as the ruler of a country with more than 300 nationalities and ethnic groups, 'I am proud to be … part of our powerful and strong multinational people of Russia' (p. 5). This highlights a challenge which Russian rulers have faced since Russia began colonising its neighbours centuries ago: how to create an acceptable national narrative for its diverse subjects that will legitimise and guarantee the Kremlin's control over them.

In her deeply researched study, Katie L. Stewart examines how Putin's nation-building policies have fared among the non-Russian subjects of the

Russian Federation. She focuses on three republics – Karelia, Tatarstan and Buryatia – that have very different histories and ethno-religious traditions, all of which have had to navigate the competing claims of Putin's Russo-centric rule and the demands of their own indigenous populations. She concludes that, for now, Putin's authoritarian rule has managed to co-opt the leadership of these republics into accepting the narrative about Russia's greatness and its existential fight in its 'special military operation' in Ukraine. But local resentment against Russian nationalist policies continues to simmer.

Boris Yeltsin told the non-Russian republics to 'seize as much sovereignty' as they could after the Soviet collapse. Tatarstan, an oil-rich, Sunni-majority republic, took him at his word and signed its own treaty with the Kremlin, giving it broad political and economic autonomy and enabling it to establish strong ties with Turkiye and other Turkic states. Putin came to power determined to reverse this devolution of authority and recentralise power. His 'vision of the nation now places ethnicity, traditional values, and Orthodoxy at the fore' and seeks to 'remasculinize' the Russian nation (p. 10).

Stewart evaluates the state of identity politics in the three republics by examining four questions: what monuments exist in the capital city, what holidays are celebrated in the republic, how museums are organised and how history is taught. The last issue is particularly sensitive, since the Putin regime has introduced new school textbooks that embody the president's particular view of historical facts, especially those surrounding the Great Patriotic War (1941–45) and its aftermath. The textbooks stress the importance of patriotism and warn against the 'falsification' of history. As the regime has worked to centralise education, the republics face the challenge of incorporating the history of Russian colonisation into their own textbooks.

Authoritarian states, argues Stewart, rely on nationalism for legitimacy, but given Russia's ethnofederal and imperialist legacy, Putin has to recognise the interests of the country's ethnic minorities. The war with Ukraine has exacerbated his dilemmas. Ethnic Buryats and Tartars have suffered a disproportionate number of casualties on the battlefield. In the words of the Buryat anti-war movement, 'Buryats insist that the war for the "Russian world" is not their war' (p. 210).

Uncommon Company: Dissidents and Diplomats, Enemies and Artists
William H. Luers. New York: Rodin Books, 2024. $35.00. 472 pp.

In 1986, as he ended his tour as American ambassador to Czechoslovakia, William H. Luers experienced first-hand the wrath of the Czech communist authorities after he made a speech commemorating the US liberation of

Southern Bohemia from Nazi rule. An old woman approached him offering the traditional greeting of bread and salt. He ingested the bread, only to become quite ill. German doctors who examined him in Munich shortly thereafter concluded that the bread offering had likely been laced with arsenic.

Luers, an American diplomat with a distinguished career both in the Foreign Service and as president of the Metropolitan Museum of Art (the Met), has written a compelling memoir stressing how important diplomacy and strategic empathy are in dealing with allies and adversaries alike. His experiences dealing with the Soviet Union remind the reader that there were far more contacts and channels of communication between the United States and the USSR during the post-Stalin Cold War era than there are between America and Vladimir Putin's Russia, a development which he laments and insists must be reversed.

Luers was a pioneer in promoting cultural diplomacy. Arriving in Moscow in 1963, he created the first US–Soviet exchanges, bringing American writers, artists and musicians to the USSR. Their meetings with their Soviet counterparts were at times awkward and tense. When the playwright Edward Albee told the Union of Soviet Writers of Leningrad that writers were treated worse under Josef Stalin than under Adolf Hitler, he received a frosty reception. Nevertheless, the exchanges became a centrepiece of US–Russian relations, complementing arms-control agreements and other measures to defuse tensions.

As president of the Met, Luers played a role in facilitating Ronald Reagan's trip to the USSR in 1988. When Reagan told him that he believed that Mikhail Gorbachev was a Christian and a capitalist, Luers pushed back (as did Margaret Thatcher), but Reagan persisted in these beliefs until the end. Reagan, writes Luers, 'left office obsessed with his relationship with Gorbachev' (p. 288).

Luers was a strong supporter of Václav Havel, both when he was a dissident writer in Czechoslovakia and after he became the country's president following the 1989 Velvet Revolution. Luers highlights the speech that Havel made to a joint session of the US Congress in 1990 in which he argued that the best way for the US to help Eastern Europe would be to 'help the Soviet Union on its irreversible but immensely complicated road to democracy' (p. 291). Luers implies that the American government failed to pursue policies that would have set Russia on a democratic path, without giving any details about how that might have been accomplished.

Luers concludes by urging the US government to talk to Putin to explore how the war with Ukraine might end. 'The demonization of Putin is fully understandable', he writes, 'but the need to converse with uncommon company, including your enemies, should override the hatred and hostility of the enemy' (p. 396).

Copyright © 2025 The International Institute for Strategic Studies

Ireland's Future: United, European and in NATO

Jonathan Stevenson

I

I lived in Belfast, as a freelance writer, from 1993 through 1999. It was a significant period of Northern Ireland's history, spanning the last year of the 25-year low-intensity conflict known as 'the Troubles' between mainly Protestant unionists (or 'loyalists' at the extreme), favouring the province's union with Great Britain, and largely Catholic nationalists ('republicans' at the extreme), favouring a united Ireland; the ceasefires undertaken by the Provisional Irish Republican Army (IRA) and the loyalist paramilitaries in late 1994; their breakdown triggered by the Provisional IRA's February 1996 bombing of Canary Wharf in London; the resumption of the ceasefires and the advance of peace talks, eventually American-mediated, after the electoral victory of a British Labour Party more receptive to Irish unity than the Conservative Party; and the signing in 1998 of the Belfast Agreement. Familiarly known as the 'Good Friday Agreement' and approved by 71% in Northern Ireland and 94% in the Republic of Ireland, it institutionalised power-sharing between nationalists and unionists in Northern Ireland and formalised a path to a united Ireland.[1]

The principal fruit of my labour was a book called *'We Wrecked the Place': Contemplating an End to the Northern Irish Troubles*, which drew on

Jonathan Stevenson is an IISS Senior Fellow and Managing Editor of *Survival*.

Survival | vol. 67 no. 1 | February–March 2025 | pp. 201–216   https://doi.org/10.1080/00396338.2025.2459028

the testimony of republicans and loyalists, most of whom had been in prison, at a time when both sides were free and eager to talk.[2] Ostensibly impartial, the narrative was, between the lines, tinged with a unionist point of view. My opinion has evolved over the past 30 years. Though hardly a Provisional IRA enthusiast, I now believe that Ireland should be united. Partitioning Ireland and establishing Northern Ireland as part of the United Kingdom made strategic and demographic sense in 1921 as a necessary means of ending the Anglo-Irish War; otherwise, a 32-county Irish Free State would have been left with a six-county enclave of angry and probably violent Protestant rejectionists. It was not certain then that Northern Ireland would, as it did, assert itself as a punitively Protestant bastion – 'a Protestant state for a Protestant people', as Sir James Craig, Northern Ireland's first prime minister, famously put it in 1934 – and a state that would marginalise its large Catholic minority, inspiring a gener-ationally enduring Catholic insurgency. At the time of the 1994 ceasefires, political and institutional reforms had ameliorated anti-Catholic discrimi-nation, and the Protestant and unionist majority was intact but dwindling. Whether Northern Ireland should indefinitely remain part of the UK was an open question. Assiduously negotiated by all interested parties and thereby internalising relevant Irish history, the Good Friday Agreement implicitly answered that question in the negative in contemplating referen-dums north and south in favour of unification when material demographic and political circumstances had changed.[3] In my view, they now have.

Girding this shift in my position, to some degree, is personal intellec-tual evolution. Immediately following the Cold War, some were inclined to ride the wave of optimism to right long-standing wrongs, but I took the view that a decent interval of calm would best maintain the uneasy peace. Having since witnessed abundant injustice consonant with this view, culminating in Russia's war against Ukraine and its spurious civilisational case for it, I now have less faith in the tolerability of historical inertia and precedent than I did in those halcyon days.

Parenthetically, I suppose I have also gained a grudging respect for a republican movement that moved from a baldly sectarian terrorist force in the early 1970s to a more strategic and selective insurgency in the 1980s, cleverly exploited its re-empowerment via the 1981 hunger strikes by devising the 'Armalite and ballot box' political–military strategy, and tilted that strategy steadily from Armalite to ballot box through the ceasefires and peace talks to the decommissioning of weapons and substantial peace. When I lived in Northern Ireland in the 1990s, my tacit unionism was in part motivated by my visceral abhorrence of republican violence and the grossly sectarian loyalist atrocities it prompted. With the hindsight of more than three decades, however, I and others can acknowledge the historical reality that terrorism, however disruptive and tragic at the time, has been part of the progress of history: from Jewish militants helping to create Israel, to Palestinian extremists setting the table for the Oslo Accords, to South African fighters paving the way to an end to apartheid. More substantively, the durability of the Provisional IRA's ceasefire has afforded Sinn Féin, its political alter-ego, firm legitimacy.[4]

It is mainly changed circumstances that have rebalanced the equities, though. Under the Good Friday Agreement, the British government is required to hold a referendum on a united Ireland – often referred to as a border poll – when 'it appears likely … that a majority of those voting would express a wish that Northern Ireland should cease to be part of the United Kingdom and form part of a united Ireland'.[5] While this criterion is intentionally vague and subject to wide interpretation, that moment appears to be drawing nearer. Whereas Protestants outnumbered Catholics in Northern Ireland by a little less than three-to-two during the Troubles, Catholics slightly exceeded Protestants as of 2021.[6] At present, the province's strongest party is Sinn Féin, which garnered barely 12% of the vote 30 years ago and now gets about 27%.[7] Furthermore, although the UK overall voted to leave the European Union in 2016, 56% of Northern Irish voters wanted to remain.[8] It was hardly fanciful for Gerry Adams – Sinn Féin president from 1983 to 2018 and the architect of its non-violent political strategy – to argue that this discrepancy, combined with the possible post-Brexit reimposition of a hard border with security checkpoints between Northern Ireland and the Irish Republic, justified border polls in both places.[9] Republicans genuinely consider the shared membership of the UK and the Irish Republic in the EU a fundamental premise of the

Good Friday Agreement that Northern Ireland's vote for remaining in the Union affirms and Brexit betrays. Politically if not juridically, this is a strong argument.[10]

Voters and politicians in the Irish Republic probably would not go that far. Most support Irish unification in principle but have not been in any great hurry to see it happen and in any event detested the Provisional IRA's armed campaign. At the same time, EU membership has indisputably become an important element of Ireland's national identity. Over the past 40 years, the republic has developed into an active, enthusiastic and progressive EU member, politically and culturally liberalising, economically expanding, and in the process casting off the neuralgic Anglophobia produced by centuries of subjugation.[11] The EU, for its part, has reciprocally embraced Ireland and, subtly but surely, its unification. Following the Brexit vote, EU members indicated that a united Ireland would automatically become a full EU member.[12] In a rousing December 2022 speech to the Irish parliament celebrating the fiftieth anniversary of Ireland's accession to the European Economic Community, European Commission President Ursula von der Leyen verged on making the endorsement explicit, extolling 'the heroes of the Easter Rising and the architects of the Good Friday Agreement' as 'optimists because they believed that they could change the course of history' and 'dared to look beyond the imperfection of what is to see the beauty of what could be'.[13] Commensurate national confidence has diminished the south's cultural and economic nervousness about absorbing the north, and Irish voters appear to be warming to the realisation of Irish unity sooner rather than later.[14] Sinn Féin – a marginal player in the Irish Republic a couple of decades ago – is now pushing long-dominant Fianna Fáil and Fine Gael for primacy in the Irish parliament, the Dáil Éireann. In the 2024 election, Sinn Féin won 19% of first-preference votes, which only Fianna Fáil exceeded and not by much.[15]

Taken together, these factors suggest that nationalists could, in the foreseeable future, prevail in border polls in Northern Ireland and the Republic of Ireland, meeting the Good Friday Agreement's requirement for Irish unification.[16]

II

Geopolitics have complicated the picture, but they too ultimately favour a united Ireland. Throughout the Cold War, the Irish Republic had remained neutral and refrained from joining NATO. The United States and its European allies regarded Northern Ireland as fulfilling NATO's need for an allied bulwark against the island's co-optation by the Soviet Union in any primarily naval battle for the Atlantic that might have materialised. In the Downing Street Declaration of December 1993, however, British prime minister John Major declared that the UK no longer had any 'selfish, strategic, political or economic interest' in Ireland. He and Irish taoiseach Albert Reynolds also publicly relaxed their countries' respective claims on Northern Ireland and left its constitutional future wholly to the electoral will of the province's population.[17] Meanwhile, Ireland's post-Cold War Europeanisation made the republican goal of a 32-county socialist siege state – Sinn Féin invariably muted the socialist part for American audiences – unrealistic. The Provisional IRA's ceasefire was to an extent premised on the calculation that the end of the Cold War had extinguished NATO's requirement of non-neutral Irish territory while the Irish Republic's evolving European vocation made it more inclined to advance peaceful unification.[18] This has been more or less the conventional wisdom since the Good Friday Agreement was signed, allowing Sinn Féin to acclimate voters in the south to unification and bide its time in the north.

Yet it is arguable that Russia's revanchism and reconstituted military threat to Europe, and more generally the rise of great-power competition, have revived the case for retaining the union between Great Britain and Northern Ireland. In a thorough and systematic paper published by the Policy Exchange, a centre-right British think tank, Marcus Solarz Hendriks and Harry Halem argue that because the Irish Republic's formal neutrality, meagre defence spending and substandard military and intelligence capabilities make it an unreliable and inadequate security partner, and because Russia has shifted the emphasis of its maritime security doctrine towards the Arctic and the Atlantic, the UK is compelled to resurrect the presence of the Royal Navy and the Royal Air Force in Northern Ireland – drawn down during the Troubles – for maritime-patrol operations along the British coastline and into the Greenland–Iceland–UK gap to protect transatlantic approaches to Europe.

Increasing the urgency of this claim, they add, is the fact that Sinn Féin will likely gain influence in the south, which means the UK and NATO should expect less rather than more defence cooperation from the Irish Republic. It's an understandable concern. Sinn Féin's republican forbears proclaimed 'neither king nor kaiser' when they staged the 1916 Easter Rising as the First World War raged, deeply rooting neutrality in what would become the Republic of Ireland.[19] To blunt the counter-argument that reintroducing British military forces into Northern Ireland could reignite the Troubles, Hendriks and Halem note that it was the active presence of British ground forces, not the defensive positioning of air and naval ones, that perpetuated the conflict.[20] UK ground forces deployed in the province have dropped from 9,000 immediately after the Good Friday Agreement was signed in 1999 to 1,580 at present, and none any longer patrol the streets.[21]

That the UK and Ireland are strategically inseparable on account of their geographical proximity is a valid point. Moreover, while the Russian threat that Hendriks and Halem perceive is not as dire as the one Finland and Sweden – NATO's two newest members – face, it is real. Since Russia's invasion of Ukraine, the Irish Defence Forces have periodically spotted Russian naval and commercial vessels, including warships, off the Irish coast inside Ireland's exclusive economic zone (EEZ).[22] Russia has dispatched attack submarines to the Irish Sea twice since the invasion.[23] The Irish naval vessel LÉ *James Joyce* escorted a Russian intelligence ship loitering near critical energy and communications infrastructure out of Ireland's EEZ in November.[24] But the authors elide the probability that Irish republicans would read the deployment of British air and naval assets in the north as a militarised British reassertion of unionism.

The prospect of the UK reintroducing a hard border manned by British military personnel between Northern Ireland and the Irish Republic that came with Brexit was aggravating enough.[25] The reinsertion of British military personnel – air, naval or ground – in Northern Ireland would almost certainly inspire at least some theretofore dormant Provisionals to

rethink their ceasefire, reach out to active dissident groups and reinvigor-
ate Irish republican arguments for a return to the armed struggle.[26] At the
conclusion of what is for the most part an admirably objective and analytic
argument, Hendriks and Halem themselves reveal an unabashedly unionist point of view, intoning that '*Northern Ireland is an integral part of the
Union*' and that any attempts to compromise or finesse that stance cater to
'the most corrosive, radical, and unfounded of historically revisionist Irish
nationalist premises' and 'serve to aggrandise the most radical elements of
the Irish political system'.[27] Tacitly but unambiguously, this view dispar-
ages the Good Friday Agreement and even Ireland's most non-violent and
constitutional nationalist aspirations.

The fact remains, however, that sustaining a neutral outpost in Western
Europe would be at best an obtuse response – at worst a pusillanimous
one – to Russian President Vladimir Putin's unprovoked neo-imperial
war against Ukraine, rising European NATO perceptions of the Russian
threat, and the increasing tenuousness of the US commitment to NATO
and Europe's strategic defence occasioned by Donald Trump's return
as US president.[28] The most elegant solution to the quandary of meeting
the demands of Europe's defence while maintaining peace in Northern
Ireland, in line with a decisive if unavoidably fraught tilt towards
European strategic autonomy as well as the Irish Republic's steady
advance as a European nation, would be for the Republic of Ireland to
join NATO.[29] This would alleviate Western worries about Ireland's strategic vulnerability to Russia, perforce defuse any British attempt to revive
unionism, and preserve the Good Friday Agreement's promise to Irish
nationalists of a plausible pathway to a united Ireland.

III

Ireland's pursuit of NATO membership would not proceed from a cold
start. It joined the Partnership for Peace, NATO's post-Cold War programme for facilitating cooperation between the Alliance and non-member
states, in 1999 and has steadily thickened its relationship with NATO
through the Individually Tailored Partnership Programme, which facili-
tates information- and intelligence-sharing.[30] Russia's invasion of Ukraine

prompted the Irish government to become, very tentatively, more open to discussing an end to neutrality in favour of collective security.[31] A poll taken by Dublin's *Business Post* newspaper and Red C shortly after the invasion indicated that 48% of Ireland's population believed the country should join NATO, 46% were willing to serve in a European army, and 59% supported an increase in national defence spending. Paradoxically, however, 57% wanted Ireland to retain its policy of neutrality, while only 30% endorsed dropping it. Yet the expanded voting base of Sinn Féin, which has historically opposed European military alliances as pernicious tools of capitalism and imperialism, showed roughly the same degree of support for Ireland's NATO membership – 46% – as the general population.[32] A small socialist minority in the Dáil still staunchly opposes Irish non-neutrality on anti-imperialistic and pacifist grounds.[33] A poll conducted five months later by Behaviour Wise, however, yielded results compatible with the *Business Post*/Red C poll: 52% favoured and 48% opposed NATO membership.[34]

Responding to the discernible migration of public opinion, the Irish government launched a Consultative Forum in June 2023 to explore the possibility of national policy changes in response to the burgeoning threats to Europe. In Ireland, such efforts are not merely decorative, having produced successful referendums on abortion rights and gay marriage in recent years. The forum's report, released in October 2023, endorsed more robust Irish partnerships with international security organisations including NATO and the EU as well as increased defence spending and procurement, but recommended that Ireland's neutral status continue.[35] The upshot is that the Irish population is ambivalent, arguably reluctant, but convincible with respect to joining NATO.[36] Given the depth and potency of the tradition of Irish neutrality, Irish membership would require a constitutional referendum as a practical matter if not a strictly legal one.[37] For a government in favour of joining NATO to win over Irish voters sufficiently to prevail in a referendum, it would probably need to secure the assent of a majority of Sinn Féin as well as Fianna Fáil and Fine Gael voters. This would call for a frank and nuanced public narrative that placed Ireland's prospective NATO membership in the context of both

Irish history and contemporary geopolitics, and detailed the practical changes – including costs – that NATO membership would entail.[38] With respect to Sinn Féin, whose core members remain invested in neutrality, it would also require a significantly more proactive national commitment to advancing Irish unification.[39]

The republic now spends only 0.2% of its GDP on defence and lacks basic military capabilities such as intelligence, surveillance and reconnaissance assets, air-defence systems and a fully operational navy.[40] Hendriks and Halem are theatrically dismissive of the Irish Republic's exploration of NATO membership and what they sarcastically call 'Ireland's security awakening'.[41] To be sure, to meet current NATO standards, Ireland would have to pledge to increase its defence expenditures tenfold. But it could do so gradually. Ireland's primary contribution to the Alliance would be unlike Finland's and Sweden's. Both of these countries had relatively healthy defence budgets even before joining the Alliance and offer significant substantive military capabilities – and in Sweden's case, an exceptionally strong defence-industrial base – in addition to logistical access to geostrategic areas.[42] By contrast, Ireland's paramount asset for NATO would be strategic access. The Alliance could establish small bases and headquarters in Ireland and liaison with Irish forces, integrating these elements into NATO plans and operations.[43] Ireland's build-up of military equipment and development of military inter-operability, presumptively modest, could proceed on a more relaxed timeline. Meanwhile, Dublin would gain a more active and credible voice on European security.

The nature of Ireland's membership in NATO might thus be more akin to that of Iceland, whose commitment is notably more passive than Sweden's or Finland's is anticipated to be. An original 1949 member, Iceland has no army and a small coastguard, spends 0.1% of its GDP on defence, operates only a few air-radar sites networked into NATO's air-defence system, and has focused on diplomatic and political aspects of the Alliance's mission (recall Ronald Reagan and Mikhail Gorbachev's historic 1986 arms-control summit in Reykjavík). It is also an island country with a pacifist tradition, as Ireland is, and has struggled with its role in a defence alliance over the past 75 years, but always arrived at accommodation.[44]

This record could provide Dublin and the Irish people with sound precedent and bolster the case that NATO membership would be a sensible philosophical and practical step in Ireland's national evolution.[45]

At the end of my 1996 book, I suggested that the Troubles were 'pointless heartache unrepaid'.[46] Thirty years on, I do not believe that they were, from a republican perspective, pointless. Absent the credible threat of political violence, it is doubtful that the non-violent 'constitutional' nationalists of Northern Ireland's Social Democratic and Labour Party (SDLP) could have persuaded an unperturbed British government, let alone Ulster unionists, to come to the table for the talks that eventually yielded the Good Friday Agreement. It is the Provisional IRA's legacy of mayhem that best explains the fact that Sinn Féin now polls 27% and the SDLP only 11% in Northern Ireland.[47] While the Provisional IRA attracted a fair few volunteers who simply welcomed a political pretext for inflicting pain and misery, most were acting on generational grievances for what they considered a noble cause and felt genuine guilt and remorse for having taken lives. When Adams persistently denied his membership in the Provisional IRA, as he continues to do, some of these true believers felt that he dishonoured them by cheapening their existential hardships as well as the suffering of their victims, and implied that the armed struggle had been essentially futile.[48] In turn, republican dissidents have disavowed the Good Friday Agreement as a sell-out that has not palpably advanced Irish unity, and they remain a threat to peace that the UK's remilitarisation of Northern Ireland could reactivate.[49] Ireland's NATO membership would mitigate that threat by removing a significant strategic obstacle – Irish neutrality – to a united Ireland while enhancing Ireland's contribution to European security at a critical moment in world history.

Notes

[1] Under the agreement, the Republic of Ireland also dropped its constitutional claim on Northern Irish territory in exchange for an institutionalised voice in Northern Irish governance through 'cross-border bodies'. The agreement stipulates that consent for a united Ireland must be 'freely and concurrently given' by the populations of both Northern Ireland and the Irish

Republic, and requires the British government to hold a referendum on Irish unity 'if at any time it appears likely … that a majority of those voting would express a wish that Northern Ireland should cease to be part of the United Kingdom and form part of a united Ireland'. 'The Belfast Agreement: An Agreement Reached at the Multi-party Talks on Northern Ireland', April 1998, available at https://assets.publishing.service.gov.uk/government/uploads/system/uploads/attachment_data/file/1034123/The_Belfast_Agreement_An_Agreement_Reached_at_the_Multi-Party_Talks_on_Northern_Ireland.pdf.

2   Jonathan Stevenson, *'We Wrecked the Place': Contemplating an End to the Northern Irish Troubles* (New York: Free Press, 1996).

3   For a précis of the relevant history, see *ibid*., pp. 6–30. See also R.F. Foster, *Modern Ireland* (New York: Penguin, 1990).

4   See, for example, Jonathan Stevenson, 'Irreversible Peace in Northern Ireland?', *Survival*, vol. 42, no. 3, Autumn 2000, pp. 5–26; and Jonathan Stevenson, 'The Two Terrorisms', *New York Times*, 2 December 2003, https://www.nytimes.com/2003/12/02/opinion/the-two-terrorisms.html. In a wider, post-9/11 security environment dominated by mass-casualty transnational jihadists with practically non-negotiable political objectives, an old-school ethno-nationalist group with defensible ends if not acceptable means that executed a well-conceived strategic retreat was perversely reassuring. Dissident republican groups – the Continuity IRA, the Real IRA

and most recently the New IRA – have often strained and sometimes threatened peace in Northern Ireland, but they have remained containable.

5   'The Belfast Agreement', Annex A, Schedule 1, paragraph 2.

6   See, respectively, Bob Rowthorn and Naomi Wayne, *Northern Ireland: The Political Economy of Conflict* (London: Polity Press, 1988), p. 17; and NISRA, 'Main Statistics for Northern Ireland: Statistical Bulletin – Religion', 22 September 2022, p. 2, https://www.nisra.gov.uk/system/files/statistics/census-2021-main-statistics-for-northern-ireland-phase-1-statistical-bulletin-religion.pdf.

7   Raymond Russell, 'Election Report: Westminster General Election, 4 July 2024', Research and Information Service Research Paper, Northern Ireland General Assembly, 9 July 2024, p. 3, https://www.niassembly.gov.uk/globalassets/documents/raise/publications/2022-2027/2024/statistics_gis/2524.pdf.

8   'EU Referendum: Northern Ireland Votes to Remain', BBC News, 24 June 2016, https://www.bbc.com/news/uk-northern-ireland-36614443.

9   See Gerry Adams, 'Brexit and Irish Unity', *New York Times*, 12 July 2016, https://www.nytimes.com/2016/07/12/opinion/brexit-and-irish-unity.html.

10 See Jonathan Stevenson, 'Does Brexit Threaten Peace in Northern Ireland?', *Survival*, vol. 59, no. 3, June–July 2017, pp. 111–28.

11 See Fintan O'Toole, *We Don't Know Ourselves: A Personal History of Ireland Since 1958* (London: Head of Zeus, 2021).

12 'EU Says United Ireland Would Be Automatic Full Member', Reuters, 29

April 2017, https://www.reuters.com/ article/world/eu-says-united-ireland-would-be-automatic-full-member-idUSKBN17V0HQ/.

13 Ursula von der Leyen, '"Ireland Lies at the Heart of Europe"', address to both houses of the Oireachtas, 29 December 2022, https://www.ireland.ie/en/eu50/news/news-archive/ireland-lies-at-the-heart-of-europe-ursula-von-der-leyen-eu50/.

14 See John Walsh, 'A United Ireland Is Growing Ever More Likely – Thanks to the Failures of Brexit Britain', *Guardian*, 26 February 2024, https://www.theguardian.com/world/commentisfree/2024/feb/26/ireland-unity-brexit-britain.

15 Edna McClafferty, 'Fianna Fáil Emerges as Largest Party in Irish Election', BBC News, 2 December 2024, https://www.bbc.com/news/articles/cpdnlv8n7580.

16 On Northern Irish views, see, for example, Katy Hayward and Ben Rosher, 'Political Attitudes in Northern Ireland 25 Years After the Agreement', ARK, Research Update no. 151, April 2023, https://www.ark.ac.uk/ARK/sites/default/files/2023-04/update151.pdf; and Ruari Casey, 'In Northern Ireland, a "Shift in Enthusiasm" for Irish Unity', Al-Jazeera, 9 March 2021, https://www.aljazeera.com/news/2021/3/9/irish-reunification-debate-looms-large-as-ni-nears-centenary. For nuances and complicating factors – in particular, Northern Irish voters' development of hybrid identities – see Patrick Diamond and Barry Colfer, 'Irish Unification After Brexit: Old and New Political Identities', *Horizons*, no.

23, Spring 2023, pp. 92–106, https://www.cirsd.org/files/000/000/010/58/6a353a1f3f730b170554e84c74d9c2ccdee8af22.pdf.

17 'The Joint Declaration of 15 December 1993 (Downing St. Declaration)', avaialble at https://www.dfa.ie/media/dfa/alldfawebsitemedia/ourrolesandpolicies/northernireland/peace-process--joint-declaration-1993.pdf.

18 See Michael Cox, 'Bringing in the "International": The IRA Ceasefire and the End of the Cold War', *International Affairs*, vol. 73, no. 4, October 1997, pp. 671–93; Michael Cox, '"Cinderella at the Ball": Explaining the End of the War in Northern Ireland', *Millennium*, vol. 27, no. 2, June 1998, pp. 325–42; and Jonathan Stevenson, 'Peace in Northern Ireland: Why Now?', *Foreign Policy*, no. 112, Fall 1998, pp. 41–54. Anticipating these developments was Joseph P. O'Grady, 'The Strategic Value of Ireland After the Cold War', *Canadian Journal of Irish Studies*, vol. 16, no. 2, December 1990, pp. 7–20.

19 Ireland's predisposition to neutrality, of course, long preceded the Easter Rising and Anglo-Irish War. See Ronan Fanning, 'Irish Neutrality – An Historical Review', *Irish Studies in International Affairs*, vol. 1, no. 3, 1982, pp. 27–38.

20 Marcus Solarz Hendriks and Harry Halem, 'Closing the Back Door: Rediscovering Northern Ireland's Role in British National Security', Policy Exchange, 2024, https://policyexchange.org.uk/wp-content/uploads/Closing-the-Back-Door.pdf. See Ben Quinn, 'Russia, China and Iran Could Target UK via Irish "Backdoor", Thinktank Warns',

Guardian, 4 February 2024, https://www.theguardian.com/politics/2024/feb/04/russia-china-iran-could-target-uk-irish-backdoor-thinktank-warns.

21 See Matt Kennard, 'The Vanishing UK Military Presence in Northern Ireland', Declassified UK, 9 April 2024, https://www.declassifieduk.org/the-vanishing-uk-military-presence-in-northern-ireland/.

22 See Fergal O'Brien, 'Four More Russian Vessels Observed Off Irish Coast', RTE, 7 May 2023, https://www.rte.ie/news/2023/0507/1381249-russian-warships-ireland/.

23 See Alex Wickham, Jennifer Jacobs and Jennifer Duggan, 'Russia Twice Sent Kilo Attack Submarine Toward the Irish Sea', Bloomberg News, 1 July 2024, https://www.bloomberg.com/news/articles/2024-07-01/russia-twice-sent-kilo-attack-submarine-toward-the-irish-sea.

24 Lisa O'Carroll, 'Russian Spy Ship Escorted Away from Area with Critical Cables in Irish Sea', *Guardian*, 16 November 2024, https://www.theguardian.com/world/2024/nov/16/russian-spy-ship-escorted-away-from-internet-cables-in-irish-sea.

25 See Stevenson, 'Does Brexit Threaten Peace in Northern Ireland?'.

26 See Marisa McGlinchey, '"While There's British Interference, There's Going to Be Action": Why a Hardcore of Dissident Irish Republicans Are Not Giving Up', *Guardian*, 22 July 2021, https://www.the-guardian.com/news/2021/jul/22/dissident-irish-republicans-new-ira-continuity-belfast-lyra-mckee.

27 Hendriks and Halem, 'Closing the Back Door', p. 65 (emphasis in original).

28 For a strident but not entirely baseless statement of this position, see Tom Sharpe, 'Putin's Subs Have Exposed Ireland's Shameless Hypocrisy', *Telegraph*, 4 June 2024, https://www.telegraph.co.uk/news/2024/06/04/nato-sea-power-cui-russian-submarines-ireland-eu/.

29 See, for example, Elizabeth Braw, 'Irish Neutrality Is Unsustainable', Engelsberg Ideas, 27 September 2024, https://engelsbergideas.com/notebook/irish-neutrality-is-unsustainable/; and Philip Stephens, 'Europe Is Menaced by Putin. And Ireland Has Outlived Its Neutrality', *Encompass*, June 2023, https://encompass-europe.com/comment/europe-is-menaced-by-putin-and-ireland-has-outlived-its-neutrality.

30 See Niall O'Connor, 'Friends with Benefits? Ireland Moves Closer to NATO as Alliance Looks to Protect Atlantic Flank', *Journal*, 7 September 2024, https://www.thejournal.ie/nato-analysis-brussels-shape-ireland-links-6479931-Sep2024/.

31 See Clea Simon, 'Ukraine War Testing Irish Neutrality', *Harvard Gazette*, 4 May 2022, https://news.harvard.edu/gazette/story/2022/05/ukraine-war-testing-irish-neutrality/.

32 Michael Brennan, 'Poll Shows 46% in Favour of Irish Troops Serving in European Army', *Business Post*, 26 March 2022, https://www.businesspost.ie/politics/poll-shows-46-in-favour-of-irish-troops-serving-in-european-army/.

33 See Shawn Pogatchnik, 'Poll: More Irish Want to Join NATO in Wake of Ukraine Invasion', *Politico*, 27 March 2022, https://www.politico.eu/article/poll-more-irish-want-to-join-nato/.

34 See Simon Carswell, 'Public Divided on Nato Membership, Survey Finds', *Irish Times*, 28 August 2022, https://www.irishtimes.com/ireland/2022/10/18/public-divided-on-nato-membership-survey-finds/.

35 Consultative Forum on International Security Policy, 'Report to an Tánaiste', 10 October 2023, https://www.gov.ie/pdf/?file=https://assets.gov.ie/275081/6cbe12c4-2f01-4fdc-a8e5-98e14c0e1546.pdf.

36 See, for example, Sophie Boulter, 'Will Ireland's Neutrality Survive Putin's Aggression?', Center for European Policy Analysis, 10 November 2020, https://cepa.org/article/will-irelands-neutrality-survive-putins-aggression/. For a decidedly negative assessment of Ireland's prospects for joining NATO coupled with a calibrated alternative, see Andrew Cottey, 'Why Ireland Matters for European Security', Carnegie Endowment for International Peace, 7 November 2023, https://carnegieendowment.org/europe/strategic-europe/2023/11/why-ireland-matters-for-european-security.

37 See, for example, Eoin Daly, 'Neutrality and the Irish Constitution', *Verfassungsblog on Matters Constitutional*, 13 April 2022, https://verfassungsblog.de/neutrality-and-the-irish-constitution/.

38 See, for instance, Edward Luce, 'Irish Neutrality No Longer Adds Up', *Financial Times*, 19 June 2023, https://www.ft.com/content/619652eb-6ae1-428d-ba75-532d3809d32e.

39 A December 2022 Ipsos poll conducted for the *Irish Times* indicated 66% support for a united Ireland in the republic but only 27% support in Northern Ireland. 'Unification – Poll Questions About Support for a United Ireland', CAIN Web Service, University of Ulster, https://cain.ulster.ac.uk/issues/unification/polls.html. Former taoiseach Leo Varadkar has characterised the republic's support as large but shallow and argued that it needed to undertake an aggressive effort to make unionists feel more welcome to make unification feasible. See Keiron Tourish, 'Irish Unity Cannot Just Be an "Aspiration" – Varadkar', BBC News, 26 September 2024, https://www.bbc.com/news/articles/c20m1ejjoovo. Ireland's NATO membership could be cast as part of that effort.

40 See Eoin Drea, 'Ireland Is Europe's Weakest Link', *Foreign Policy*, 8 November 2022, https://foreignpolicy.com/2022/11/08/ireland-military-neutrality-russia-ocean-communication-energy-infrastructure-sabotage/; and Pogatchnik, 'Poll: More Irish Want to Join NATO in Wake of Ukraine Invasion'.

41 See Hendriks and Halem, 'Closing the Back Door', pp. 57–9.

42 See, for example, William Alberque and Benjamin Schreer, 'What Kind of NATO Allies Will Finland and Sweden Be?', *Survival*, vol. 64, no. 6, December 2022–January 2023, pp. 123–36.

43 For these tasks, Hendriks and Halem's analysis could provide some guidance.

44 See Fotios Kotzakioulafis, 'Iceland: Unique Among NATO Allies', Defence Industry Europe, 21 February 2023, https://defence-industry.eu/iceland-unique-among-nato-allies/; Spencer Mah, 'Iceland in NATO: An Unlikely yet Invaluable Partner', NATO Association of Canada, 24 January

2027, https://natoassociation.ca/iceland-in-nato-an-unlikely-yet-invaluable-partner/; and John R. Morgan III, 'No Country an Island: Iceland's Contributions to NATO', master's thesis, US Naval Postgraduate School, Defense Technical Information Center, September 2018, https://apps.dtic.mil/sti/tr/pdf/AD1065455.pdf.

45 For a considered pre-Russo-Ukrainian war view from an Irish scholar based in Iceland, now an Irish diplomat, see Steven Murphy, 'Ireland and NATO: Challenges and Opportunities', SSANSE Project, University of Iceland, 2017, https://ams.overcastcdn.com/documents/Nato-Ireland-paper.pdf.

46 Stevenson, *We Wrecked the Place*, p. 258.

47 Russell, 'Election Report: Westminster General Election, 4 July 2024', p. 3.

48 See especially Patrick Radden Keefe, *Say Nothing: A True Story of Murder and Memory in Northern Ireland* (New York: Doubleday, 2019), and the 2024 FX/Disney+ miniseries *Say Nothing* based on the book.

49 See, for example, Rory Carroll, 'Northern Ireland Republican Dissidents Lurk in the Shadows Hoping to Be Noticed', *Guardian*, 23 February 2023, https://www.theguardian.com/politics/2023/feb/23/republican-dissidents-lurk-in-the-shadows-hoping-to-be-noticed.

Copyright © 2025 The International Institute for Strategic Studies